The Situatedness of Translation Studies

# Approaches to Translation Studies

*Founded by*

James S Holmes

*Developed by*

Ton Naaijkens (*Utrecht University, the Netherlands*)

*Edited by*

Karen Bennett (*Universidade Nova de Lisboa, Portugal*)
Leo Tak-hung Chan (*Lingnan University, Hong Kong*)
Şehnaz Tahir Gürçağlar (*Boğaziçi Üniversitesi*)
Hephzibah Israel (*University of Edinburgh, UK*)
Gabriela Saldanha (*University of Birmingham, UK*)
Tom Toremans (*KU Leuven, Belgium*)
Michaela Wolf (*Universität Graz, Austria*)

VOLUME 48

The titles published in this series are listed at *brill.com/atts*

# The Situatedness of Translation Studies

*Temporal and Geographical Dynamics of Theorization*

*Edited by*

Luc van Doorslaer and Ton Naaijkens

BRILL

RODOPI

LEIDEN | BOSTON

Cover illustration: pixabay.com.

The Library of Congress Cataloging-in-Publication Data is available online at http://catalog.loc.gov
LC record available at http://lccn.loc.gov/2021001668

Typeface for the Latin, Greek, and Cyrillic scripts: "Brill". See and download: brill.com/brill-typeface.

ISSN 0169-0523
ISBN 978-90-04-43779-1 (hardback)
ISBN 978-90-04-43780-7 (e-book)

Copyright 2021 by Koninklijke Brill NV, Leiden, The Netherlands.
Koninklijke Brill NV incorporates the imprints Brill, Brill Hes & De Graaf, Brill Nijhoff, Brill Rodopi, Brill Sense, Hotei Publishing, mentis Verlag, Verlag Ferdinand Schöningh and Wilhelm Fink Verlag.
All rights reserved. No part of this publication may be reproduced, translated, stored in a retrieval system, or transmitted in any form or by any means, electronic, mechanical, photocopying, recording or otherwise, without prior written permission from the publisher. Requests for re-use and/or translations must be addressed to Koninklijke Brill NV via brill.com or copyright.com.

This book is printed on acid-free paper and produced in a sustainable manner.

# Contents

Notes on Contributors  VII

1  Temporal and Geographical Extensions in Translation Studies:
   Explaining the Background  1
   *Luc van Doorslaer and Ton Naaijkens*

**PART 1**
*Theorizing the Concept, the Object and the Discipline*

2  Approaches to a Historiography of Translation Studies  17
   *Yves Gambier*

3  Historiosophy of Translation
   *Reflecting on Ukrainian Translation Conceptualizations—from Ivan
   Franko to Maksym Strikha*  34
   *Iryna Odrekhivska*

4  Translation Seen through the Prism of the Tartu-Moscow School of
   Semiotics  60
   *Elin Sütiste and Silvi Salupere*

5  Heeding the Call for Transfer Theory  87
   *Shaul Levin*

**PART 2**
*Localizing the Concept, the Object and the Discipline*

6  Political Ideology in the Translation of Occidental Modernist
   Literature in China in the 1950s
   *The Case of French Modernist Literature in Shijie Wenxue*  107
   *Feng Cui*

7  The Art and Craft of Translation
   *The Historical and Political Background of the Russian Translation
   Scholarship*  135
   *Natalia Kamovnikova*

# CONTENTS

8 Travelling Theories in Translation Studies
   *Rediscovering Fedorov*   155
      *Anastasia Shakhova*

9 Appropriation of Central Discourses versus Local Tradition
   *Translation Studies in the Greek-Speaking World*   182
      *Georgios Floros and Simos Grammenidis*

10 Total Translation: From Catford to Torop   204
      *Anne Lange*

   Index of Personal Names   229
   Index of Subjects   230

# Notes on Contributors

*Feng Cui*
is a Senior Lecturer and a Ph.D. Supervisor at the Chinese Department at Nanyang Technological University (NTU), Singapore. He is also serving as the Deputy Director of Master of Arts in Translation and Interpretation programme, the Coordinator of Minor in Translation programme, and the Coordinator of Han Suyin Scholarship Fund (in Translation Studies) at Nanyang Technological University (NTU), Singapore. He received his Ph.D. in Translation Studies from NTU in 2012. His research focuses on the history of translation in China, translation theories, 20th-century Chinese literature, and comparative literature. Dr. Cui has published nearly 40 journal papers and book chapters, including papers in SSCI, A&HCI, CSSCI, and THCI journals, such as *Chinese Modern Literature, Comparative Literature in China, Chinese Translator, Shanghai Journal of Translators*, and Babel. His book *Translation, Literature, and Politics: using World Literature as an Example (1953–1966)* was published by Nanjing University Press in 2019.
cuifeng@ntu.edu.sg https://orcid.org/0000-0002-5818-8398

*Georgios Floros*
currently holds a position as Associate Professor of Translation Studies at the University of Cyprus, Department of English Studies. He received a BA in German Studies with a major in Translation from the University of Athens in 1996, and a Ph.D. in Translation Theory from Saarland University, Germany, in 2001. He teaches translation theory and translation methodology, text linguistics and theory of interpreting. His research areas also include translation ethics, pragmatics, translation pedagogy, terminology, translation history and the uses of translation in other disciplines. He was academic coordinator of the MA in Conference Interpreting (2004–2007) and has participated in or led international and locally-funded projects. He is the author of the monograph *Kulturelle Konstellationen in Texten* (Narr, 2002), of several articles and chapters in international refereed journals and handbooks, as well as the co-editor of a volume on *Translation in Language Teaching and Assessment* (Cambridge Scholars Press, 2013).
gfloros@ucy.ac.cy
https://orcid.org/0000-0001-9736-4203

VIII

*Yves Gambier*

is professor emeritus of the University of Turku where he taught translation and interpreting (1973–2014). He is a visiting professor at Immanuel Kant Baltic Federal University in Kaliningrad, Russia (2016–2019), a coordinator of a Research project at the Kaunas Technological University, Lithuania, and a visiting scholar of several Chinese universities. He has published on socio-terminology, translation studies, audio-visual translation, bilingualism in Finland. He has been involved in several European research projects. He was the General Editor (2005–2017) of the Benjamins Translation Library; he is on the editorial board of several Journals in Translation Studies. Among his commitments, he was the Chair of the group of experts in the project EMT/ European Master's in Translation (2007–2010) and member of the EMT Board (2010–2014); he was the Vice-president (1993–1998) then President (1998–2004) of the European Society for Translation Studies/EST.
yves.gambier@utu.fi
https://orcid.org/0000-0002-1858-4281

*Simos Grammenidis*

holds a position as Professor of Translation Studies at the Department of Translation of the School of French, Aristotle University of Thessaloniki, Greece. He received his Ph.D. in Theoretical and Formal Linguistics from University Paris VII—Denis Diderot in 1994, with specialization in Contrastive Linguistics and Translation. Academically, his interest has focused on transla-tion problems from linguistic, cultural and historical perspectives. He is the author of three books, *La deixis dans le passage du grec vers le français*, Ophrys, 2000, Μεταφράζοντας τον κόσμο του Άλλου: Θεωρητικά αδιέξοδα – Λειτουργικές προοπτικές, Diavlos, 2009, Διεπιστημονικές Προσεγγίσεις της μετάφρασης, [https://repository.kallipos.gr/handle/11419/3901] and he has published several scientific articles in Greek, French and English. He has translated several sci-entific books and he is the President of the Hellenic Society for Translation Studies.
simgram@frl.auth.gr
https://orcid.org/0000-0002-3626-8493

*Natalia Kamovnikova*

is Associate Professor at the Department of Linguistics and Translation Studies, St. Petersburg University of Management Technologies and Economics, St. Petersburg, Russian Federation. She lectures in British and American Literature and Translation Studies and teaches practical English and German

NOTES ON CONTRIBUTORS

courses, as well English/Russian consecutive and simultaneous interpreting. Her research focuses on literary translation in the contexts of surveillance, censorship, and threat, as well as on the ways translation activism manifests itself in a closed society. Her first research monograph *Made under Pressure: Literary Translation in the Soviet Union, 1960–1991* was published by the University of Massachusetts Press in February 2019. She is currently working on a new research project devoted to the role of women-translators in the history of translation and in the promotion of controversial works of literature of the twentieth century. Natalia Kamovnikova is also a practicing conference interpreter and translator.
natalie_kamov@yahoo.com
https://orcid.org/0000-0001-7388-2743

### Anne Lange

is Associate Professor of Translation Studies at Tallinn University. Her main research interest is the history of translation against the background of cultural history. She is the author of a monograph on Ants Oras (Tartu: Ilmamaa 2004), a leading Estonian translator and cultural critic in 1930–1960, and *Tõlkimine omas ajas* (Towards a Pragmatic Understanding of Translation in History; Tallinn University Press 2015). She has co-edited *Between Cultures and Texts: Itineraries in Translation History* (Frankfurt: Peter Lang 2011) together with Antoine Chalvin and Daniele Monticelli; and the special issue of *Methis. Studia humaniora Estonia* on the Estonian history of translation together with Daniele Monticelli (2012). Currently she is co-editing with Christopher Rundle and Daniele Monticelli the forthcoming collection *Translation under Communism* and *Routledge Handbook on the History of Translation Studies.*
anne.lange@tlu.ee

### Shaul Levin

holds a PhD in Translation Studies from Tel Aviv University. He is an independent scholar and a literary and academic translator of more than 50 published titles from English into Hebrew. Together with Prof. Nitsa Ben-Ari, he directed the Diploma Studies for Translation and Revision program at The Porter School of Cultural Studies at Tel Aviv University. He teaches translation theory, history and workshops at Tel Aviv University and Oranim College. His main research deals with translation as one possible form of transfer among others in the flow of models in culture, and its relation to a general, interdisciplinary theory of transfer.
saulole@gmail.com

## Ton Naaijkens

is a full Professor of German Literature and Translation Studies at Utrecht University. In his research, he focuses on translation and translation history and more generally on the cultural transfer between the Dutch and German-speaking areas, particularly where intercultural exchange culminates in translation. He is one of the editors of the Dutch-language journal of translation and translation studies *Filter*. From 1997 until 2017 he was co-editor of the series *Approaches to Translation Studies* (Brill Publishers). Relevant publications: *The World of World Poetry: Anthologies of Translated Poetry as a Subject of Study* (2006); *Event or Incident. On the Role of Translations in the Dynamics of Cultural Exchange* (2010); *The PETRA-E Framework of Reference for the Education and Training of Literary Translators* (2016).
a.b.m.naaijkens@uu.nl

## Iryna Odrekhivska

is Associate Professor at the Department of Translation Studies and Contrastive Linguistics at Ivan Franko National University of Lviv. In 2019, she was affiliated as the Wayne Vucinich Fellow at Stanford University. Her teaching and research interests include translation history and historiography, sociology and ideology of translation, community translation, as well as reception of Slavic literatures in the Anglophone world. She has widely published on the development of Translation Studies in East Central Europe. Among the recent contributions are "The Metaturn in Translation Studies, and the Images of Knowledge on Translation" (2019), "Consolidating Anton Popovič's "metacommunicational context of translation" as a conceptual cluster" (2017), "In the Realm of Translation Studies in Ukraine: Re-visiting Viktor Koptilov's Translation Concept" (2017), and "Anti-illusionist Trend in Drama Translation: Re-framing Jiří Levý's Concept" (2016). She is also the co-coordinator of an annual international translation workshop *LitTransformer* within the network of UNESCO Cities of Literature. Aside from her scholarship, Iryna Odrekhivska is a translator of artistic literature and non-fiction.
iryna.odrekhivska@lnu.edu.ua
https://orcid.org/0000-0002-2568-8775

## Silvi Salupere

is a lecturer at the Department of Semiotics, Institute of Philosophy and Semiotics, University of Tartu (Estonia). She works as an editor of *Sign Systems Studies, Tartu Semiotics Library*, and *Acta Semiotica Estica*, and is also a translator. Her articles appeared in *Chinese Semiotic Studies* and *Sign Systems Studies*.

NOTES ON CONTRIBUTORS

She is a co-editor of *Conceptual dictionary of the Tartu-Moscow semiotic school* (in Russian, 1999), and co-editor and author of *Theoretical schools and circles in the twentieth-century humanities: Literary theory, history, philosophy* (2015). Her research interests include history of semiotics (especially French structuralism and Tartu-Moscow School), semiotics of culture, translation studies.
silvi.salupere@ut.ee

*Anastasia Shakhova*
is a PhD student at the Johannes Gutenberg University of Mainz (Germersheim), Germany. After graduating from Saint Petersburg State University, she moved to Germany to continue her studies in the field of translation theory and linguistics. The main focus of her research lies in travelling theories in the discourses of translation studies. Shakhova is particularly interested in the role of translation in the circulation of knowledge within the discourses of humanities. Her key topics are reception and evolution of the German functionalist approach (Hans J. Vermeer) in the discourse of contemporary Russian Translation Studies. She is also known as a contemporary Russian poet, her literary works being published in Russian and European media. She is currently participating in a media project "Living Poets" (Moscow).
ashakhov1988@gmail.com

*Elin Sütiste*
Associate Professor at the Department of Semiotics, Institute of Philosophy and Semiotics, University of Tartu (Estonia), has published foremost on topics of semiotics of translation, including the legacy of Roman Jakobson, and Estonian translation history. Besides semiotics of translation, her research interests include semiotics of culture; intersemiotic, intermedial and transmedial translation; history of translation and culture. Her current research project focuses on transmedial translation history, that is, on interrelations between literary and other kinds of translations (adaptations, reworkings, versions, etc.) in various media and their role and significance in cultural history.
elin.sytiste@ut.ee
https://orcid.org/0000-0001-7899-8227

*Luc van Doorslaer*
is Chair Professor for Translation Studies at the University of Tartu (Estonia), the former President of CETRA (2014–18), the Centre for Translation Studies at KU Leuven (Belgium), and Professor Extraordinary at Stellenbosch University (South Africa). Since 2016 he is Vice President of EST, the European Society

for Translation Studies. He is book series editor of 'Translation, Interpreting & Transfer' at Leuven University Press. Together with Yves Gambier, he is the editor of the online *Translation Studies Bibliography* and the four volumes of the *Handbook of Translation Studies*. Other recent books edited include *Eurocentrism in Translation Studies* (2013), *The Known Unknowns of Translation Studies* (2014), *Interconnecting Translation Studies and Imagology* (2016), *Border Crossings. Translation Studies and other Disciplines* (2016) and *Methods in News Translation*, a special issue of 'Across Languages and Cultures' (2018). His main research interests include journalism and translation, ideology and translation, imagology and translation, institutionalization of translation studies. luc.vandoorslaer@ut.ee or luc.vandoorslaer@kuleuven.be
https://orcid.org/0000-0003-0487-0663

CHAPTER 1

# Temporal and Geographical Extensions in Translation Studies: Explaining the Background

*Luc van Doorslaer and Ton Naaijkens*

## Abstract

This background chapter explains why the present publication sees itself as part of an ongoing critical tendency in the discipline of translation studies, questioning—among other things—its own scope and fields of application. In this sense, the chapter partly relates to older discussions on topics such as translation universals and Eurocentrism. Here, the aim is to focus on both temporal and geographical extensions of theorization and conceptualization. Scholarly ideas and concepts are transported and transferred, both inter- and intralingually. They also originate in very divergent frameworks, affected by societal and institutional circumstances, with varying degrees of (non-) interaction, at different moments, in different places. Simultaneity, diachrony and synchrony in conceptual thinking become relative under these circumstances. The last part briefly presents the chapters and how they contribute in their own right to resituate the (center of the) discipline, both temporally and geographically.

When the notion of 'situatedness' was used in translation studies up to now, it was mostly associated with the practice of translation or the translation products, such as in the situatedness of translatorial work within a particular publishing scene (Tashinskiy 2019), in the cognitive act of translating (Ehrensberger-Dow and Englund Dimitrova 2016; Risku 2010), or in translation students' situated learning (Prieto Velasco and Fuentes Luque 2016). In the title of the present volume, however, the notion refers to situational aspects of the discipline and of different theoretical conceptualizations under varying circumstances. This volume sees itself as part of an ongoing and self-critical tendency in TS to question its sources, its scope, its influences, and fields of application. As in other disciplines, such discussions exemplify the living character of the field, the dynamics expressed in the subtitle of this publication. Illustrations of that disciplinary tendency are manifold, but this book concentrates on examples of different accents in theorization from a temporal and/or geographical point of view.

© KONINKLIJKE BRILL NV, LEIDEN, 2021 | DOI:10.1163/9789004437807_002

## 1 Universals and Eurocentrism

This publication only partially relates to an approach as adopted in Susam-Sarajeva (2005), where the travel and transfer of (literary) theories through translation proper was investigated. The import of schools of thought such as structuralism and semiotics into Turkish or feminism into English, the cases studied by Susam-Sarajeva, shows the impact of translation proper on the transfer and circulation of ideas. Such a transformation inevitably involves conceptual and terminological changes and discussions. The present book, however, does not start from literary or other theories, but from the situatedness of translation conceptualization, translation reflection, and TS. Besides institutional and historical circumstances, particularly temporal and geographical aspects co-determine the development of a line of thinking, a concept or a cluster of concepts. Not only are scholarly concepts and ideas transported and transferred, both inter- and intralingually, they originate in very divergent societal and (non-)academic frameworks, in varying degrees of (non-)interaction, at different moments, in different places.

This viewpoint is related to the continuing discussions in TS on so-called universals, probability laws or—more generally speaking—patterns (for instance in Baker 1993, Toury 2012[1995], Halverson 2003, Mauranen and Kujamäki 2004), as variations in the conceptualization and use of terms and theories obviously affect the degree of homogeneity or heterogeneity. The search for universal or generalized patterns in translation practice cannot be disconnected from the content of terms such as 'translation' or 'transfer'. The latter is an example that illustrates the broad range of possible interpretations depending on the traditions and frameworks. It has been used by many for referring to 'linguistic transfer' only—and has also been largely criticized for that restrictive point of view. Others have used it based on the much larger perspective of cultural transfer. In that case it is a candidate to be an umbrella term covering not only all sorts of text-modifying practices, but also contributing to a conceptual and methodological framework for studying the complexity of intercultural processes. From a chronological perspective, "the notion of transfer in a narrow (linguistic) sense has been opened up toward the sociocultural settings in which translation (as a process that never stands on its own) is performed and translations (as products) function" (Gonne and Meylaerts 2020: 13–14). However, this temporal logic becomes more complex and has to be nuanced when one considers the different usages and developments of the term in varying traditions (see for instance chapter 5 in this book). As such this example illustrates the raison d'être of this volume, showing the dynamic interplay of both temporal and geographical elements in the development of theorization.

Another interesting related suggestion in that regard is to work with cluster concepts, open clusters of related concepts that can be dealt with through an umbrella approach, as suggested in Tymoczko (2006). Such conceptualized clusters could introduce both geographical and temporal variation. However, they would equally be challenged by the pitfalls of comparability, as the "creation of typologies and explanatory schemes that have the ambition of being universal runs many risks and will inevitably be a long-term project with an uncertain outcome" (van Doorslaer 2017a, 227).

The call for this publication focused on "lesser known forms of conceptualization and theorization of translation", in an attempt to widen the scope of 'modern' TS, both geographically and temporally. Although the development of a "full-fledged institutionalized expert system" (Duarte 2012, 30) since the 1970s in several countries and/or language areas has gradually professionalized the discipline, translation reflection has, of course, been conducted centuries, even millennia before. Such reflections might not have met the same scholarly norms and criteria, but many of them incorporated theorizing and conceptualizing elements. These evolutions do not run in parallel with each other, leading to divergent views on the diachrony and synchrony of idea development. The editors intended to attract lesser-known translation knowledge that contributes to broadening this temporal horizon.

The second level of broadening is geographical. Over the past decades, several TS authors have pointed to the fact that a majority of (acknowledged) theorizing in TS has (Western-) European origins. There have been several explicit attempts to extend the scope and include translation reflection from other regions and continents. This publication is one of them. Although it does not cover all parts of the world, the principle of explicit or (often) implicit interaction between lines of thinking is global as such. This volume connects that principle to the idea that such an extension might also resituate the position and conceptualization of TS as a discipline. Different cultural climates and different timespans will inevitably lead to variation and nuances in theorizing and conceptualizing.

> It is obvious that groups of scholars within a particular country or area do sometimes influence each other, so that ideas of a certain kind sometimes merge around particular approaches or major projects. It is well known that much of the literature on functional approaches in TS stems from scholars in German-speaking countries. Brazilian ideas about translation

as cannibalism have nourished both translation and its research especially in that country [...]. In Finland, the quest for translation universals has stimulated many projects [...], and still does.

CHESTERMAN 2014, 84

In the same position paper on "Universalism in translation studies", however, Chesterman also advocates for not including a particular idea or reflection "*because* it comes from the West or the non-West" (ibid., italics in original), but only because it is different—for its intrinsic scholarly added value, that is. This echoes the older Eurocentrism discussion in the discipline (see for instance van Doorslaer and Flynn 2013). On the one hand, it is acknowledged that European sources and data are sometimes excessively present in TS. On the other hand, the discourse on Eurocentrism has also been criticized, in particular the occasionally unsubtle use of a geographically based term for a complex phenomenon. As early as 1995, Cronin deplored the essentialist use of 'European' and 'Europe'. "The signal failure to account for the linguistic and translational complexity of Europe in part stems from the tendency by post-colonial critics to reduce Europe to two languages, English and French and to two countries, England and France" (Cronin 1995, 85–86).

Although in postcolonial thinking "[s]ome redress is in order on ideological grounds" (Tymoczko 2014, 105), attracting studies with new data that illustrate the differences in the situatedness of TS was the clear intention of this publication. The call (again) generated far more response in Europe than outside of the old continent. After the peer-review process, only two contributions dealing with non-European data made it to the final stage. This includes Shaul Levin's chapter on transfer theory with an explicit Israeli component, although it also connects to several lines of thinking mainly developed on the European continent.

At the same time, the remaining chapters also show the intra-European diversity, as indicated in Cronin's quote above. It is interesting to note that a focus on Western-European conceptualizations is underrepresented. Despite the existing research on the relatively central role of translation in Russian literature (for instance Baer 2011 and 2016), earlier publications have shown that there is still a need in the discipline for catching up with theorization and conceptualization in Central and Eastern Europe. 'Western' thinking is often present there as well, but used as a background and sometimes for comparing with similar developments in Russia and countries under the Russian sphere of influence in the Cold War era.

## 2 Simultaneously Originating Ideas with Different Accents

The publication most explicitly thematizing that (lack of) interaction is Schippel and Zwischenberger (2017), symbolically titled *Going East*. With a clear focus on Eastern Europe, the editors have delivered an important contribution to the geographical extension of the discipline. The sometimes slightly confusing synchronic and diachronic relationships between the different ideas are also part of their framework.

> One finds trailblazers, pioneers and precursors, who according to some papers were the very first ones who, even before their counterparts in the West, brought certain Translation studies' ideas and theses onto paper. They remained, however, largely unknown because they were written in languages with a limited range. Research in the humanities, however, does not follow clear lines of demarcation. Ideas do not follow a certain track and halt in front of borders; they circulate, they are in the air, they are linked to other disciplines in the humanities, they are born out of discursive streams in the humanities and they also develop in parallel.
>
> SCHIPPEL AND ZWISCHENBERGER 2017, 10

The *Going East* publication, as well as the preceding symposium in Vienna with the same name (December 2014), exemplify TS's interest in actively discovering lesser-known territories and periods. In 2013, a conference on "Transferring Translation Studies" had already taken place in the Low Countries (Antwerp and Utrecht). It focused on a variety of local and international traditions in TS and the extent to which the distribution and transfer of TS knowledge, including methodological traditions, is influenced by linguistic transfer and power relationships. Some of the authors in the present publication attended that conference and later expanded on topics discussed there. However, as the call was launched more broadly, there are also several contributions not related to that conference.

Despite the worldwide character of the call, this publication also shows that there is a considerable interest from scholars in focusing on the (relatively) unknown theorizing and conceptualizing in Russia and states under Soviet influence in the 20th century. As many of the contributions point to interaction with other traditions, the editors have deliberately chosen not to structure the publication according to national categories. This would be a sign of reducing the perspective and underestimating the complexity of the interactions between researchers and ideas. More determining for classifying and arranging chapters was whether the concept, object and/or discipline were approached from a more theoretical or localizing and applied perspective.

Also, earlier studies have shown that the Iron Curtain might have been dominant in dividing scholarly thinking into several disciplines, nevertheless, contacts existed and were developed. In their contribution on the development of the equivalence concept, for instance, Ayvazyan and Pym (2017) note that the two sides may have functioned as "two separate hubs" (ibid., 221), but transnational borrowing certainly occurred through "more international ideas than is nationalistically acknowledged" (ibid., 241). Another example is the collaboration and extensive contacts between Anton Popovič and James Holmes, as for instance described in Špirk (2009). Despite the parallels in their conceptualizing of translational terms and their extensive collaboration, it has also led to a quite divergent "bibliographical presence" (van Doorslaer (2017b, 17)) of Popovič and Holmes in the discipline, partly due to the languages of publication.

Although the Iron Curtain has been down for more than three decades, many political, economic, but also scholarly categorizations in European presentations are still based on the former dichotomy. Exactly because of the sometimes-hidden connections and influences described above, this publication does not use an East-West framework as a point of departure neither at a European, nor at a global level. This also extends to the view on the discipline and the object of study. TS is not a 'Western' given, but it is interested in all translation-related data and reflection from all over the world. Nor is it a discipline that "chose to distance itself from other traditions and reflections on translation in the humanities which were declared to have pre-scientific status" (Schippel and Zwischenberger 2017, 11). It does distinguish between different approaches based on criteria of institutionalization (Duarte 2012, see above) or scientificity (Gile 2013), yet this should not be confused with a choice to distance itself from other traditions or reflections.

The editors are aware that several of the conceptualizations presented in the chapters can seem contradictory to a certain extent. Some traditions and approaches explore exclusively linguistic perspectives on translation, whereas others extend the object of the discipline far beyond the linguistic scope—a fundamental and still ongoing object discussion within TS (see recent publications such as Gentzler 2017, van Doorslaer 2018, Chesterman 2019, or Zwischenberger 2019). A concept such as "total translation", for instance (chapter 10), shows interesting parallels with aspects of transfer theories as presented elsewhere (chapter 5). However, the differences related to their context of origin are probably even more substantial—not only temporal

TEMPORAL AND GEOGRAPHICAL EXTENSIONS IN TRANSLATION STUDIES

and geographical, but to some extent even epistemological divergences. As this publication does not want to start from conceptual, nor methodological *a prioris*, it is obvious that the editors have allowed, even welcomed oppositional views. Therefore, it is perfectly possible that one author adopts a scientometric approach, whereas another is very critical about the limitations of such a method.

Through the presentation of lesser-known translation knowledge, forms of translation reflection from less central traditions, and new data illustrating the TS differences in approaches and concepts, *The Situatedness of Translation Studies* aims to reflect the diversity and multidimensionality of a subject field. This field has a long history and has matured in several different regions with very different accents. This publication aims at contributing to the growing awareness of the wide range of conceptual thinking and its history—some creative ideas and concepts apparently originated partly simultaneously in a multitude of places. As such, it may also contribute to problematizing, adjusting and to a certain extent recalibrating the (center of the) discipline, both temporally and geographically.

The inclusive approach is also shown in a formal suggestion made to all authors. In an attempt to stress the multilingualism of the discipline and diversity of cultural influences, we asked to use the quotes in the source languages before giving the English translations. This makes the discipline's linguistic and cultural diversity explicitly visible, countering a growing practice in TS where only English translations are presented without problematizing the preceding language transfer. As a result, in several chapters, the reader will be confronted with quotes and titles in Chinese, Estonian, Greek, Russian, and Ukrainian before reading the English translations.

## 3    The Chapters

This discussing and rethinking the discipline from both a theoretical and geo-historical perspective is reflected in the two main parts. The four chapters of Part 1 illustrate how the concept, object, and discipline are subject to theoretical reflection. The five essays of Part 2 reposition their attitude towards translation reflection and TS by applying local perspectives. The presentation in two parts, however, does not mean that theoretical and geo-historical perspectives are to be considered separately. Although the focus and emphasis in the two parts may vary, all of the chapters connect the layers of conceptual reflection and local application through topics such as interdisciplinarity, the traveling of theories, the localization of research trends in scholarly communities or the establishment of translational knowledge.

Is TS a poly-discipline? The movement of theories is inherent to both the history and sociology of scientific disciplines, but applies especially to the case of TS, according to *Yves Gambier*. In this chapter with a metatheoretical impact, he observes a simultaneous struggle for interdisciplinarity and compartmentalization, characterizing TS and its dissemination. When describing the origins, traditions and filiations of what he sees as a poly-discipline, Gambier proposes focusing on the various contrasting conceptualizations of translation to uncover the conditions for their possible coexistence. The postulates and assumptions of theories, models and schools and the methodological choices made by them should be described in respect to languages and geographical zones. The author considers TS concepts as fluent and nomadic; disciplinary borders are not a given, but are historically and geographically flexible and changing. He especially advocates for shedding light on the real impact of media and technology on conceptions of the poly-discipline.

After Gambier's historiographical approach, *Iryna Odrekhivska* revisits the history of the discipline of TS and reframes the thematic analysis of the field by exploring its historiosophy. Drawing inspiration from Ukrainian reflection on translation, translating, and the Ukrainian translation culture, she approaches translation from four perspectives: as a cultural force and social capital, a linguoaesthetic phenomenon, a functional stylistic parallel, and a form of cultural interpretation and re-creation. Odrekhivska reveals a network of working concepts that foster not a unidirectional, but a multisided vision of translation, grounded on local scholarly practice. In the structure of this volume, this chapter builds the perfect transition from the broad historical perspective to the concrete application to a local situation.

Another still relatively unknown approach to TS is that of semiotics as developed by the Tartu-Moscow School, mainly unfolded in the journal *Sign Systems Studies* (since 1964). Starting from the theoretical assumption that all human activity concerned with the processing, exchange and storage of information possesses a certain unity, *Elin Sütiste* and *Silvi Salupere* describe the school's background and its interest in structural linguistics, machine translation and cybernetics to shed more light on the translational reflection in the approaches of the school under discussion. Special attention is paid to the works of Juri Lotman (1922–1993), in which the concept of translation occupies a subtle but crucial place. Lotman considers translation a central mechanism of culture; for him, it becomes an analogue of the act of communication itself, which should not be seen as "a simple transmission of a message which remains adequate to itself from the consciousness of the addresser to the consciousness of the addressee", but literally, "as a translation of a text from the language of my 'I'

TEMPORAL AND GEOGRAPHICAL EXTENSIONS IN TRANSLATION STUDIES 9

to the language of your 'you'". Like the process of communication, translation involves manipulation and deformation, therefore, the text that has been produced and transferred is called "a new one" by Lotman, stemming from an act of translation that in its essence is creative. Sütiste and Salupere draw attention to the fact that several ideas of the Tartu-Moscow School influenced mainstream translation theories as developed by Itamar Even-Zohar and Gideon Toury, which convincingly illustrates one of the central theses in this volume.

In a similar vein, *Shaul Levin* rethinks earlier positions in TS by taking up Itamar Even-Zohar's call for transfer theory as a general framework for dealing with translation. Even-Zohar published this call in 1981 in *Poetics Today*, at the same time his Tel Aviv colleague Gideon Toury published his groundbreaking search for a translation theory. Levin explores the relationship between translation and transfer to come closer to a fruitful formulation of a general theory of transfer. He suggests that transfer in its various forms can be conceptualized in economic, semiotic, epistemological, and functional terms. In his view, two characteristics of transfer processes are especially important for the conceptualization: temporality and continuity. Transfer is actually seen as a fragmented process, consisting of separate segments behaving differently and dealt with differently by the various theories. According to the author, TS could hold a venerable position among the relevant disciplines by investigating the various manifestations of translational transfer and thus contribute to the ongoing development of an umbrella theory.

In the second part of this publication, more locally elaborated visions of TS are analyzed, in particular as situated in China, Russia, Greece, and Estonia. *Feng Cui* focuses on mainland China in the 1950s, a period in which the country was dominated by Maoism and a unifying Marxist ideology. He examines the only official journal of the period, *Shijie Wenxue* (World Literature), which published occidental modernist literature in translation. He takes a temporal and geographical approach and examines translational behavior in the respective cultural climates and timespans, with special attention to the relation between poetics and ideology. The magazine was launched in 1953, and in the first few years showed a selective introduction and intentional selection of Western modernist works. Over the course of time, "aesthetic translation" was also practised, until modernism was defined as reactionary, pessimistic and incorrect, leading to the complete exclusion of occidental modernist literature in the 1960s. In contrast, literature from third-world countries began to gain recognition in the magazine, in that way illustrating not a static but rather a dynamic concept of the canon.

The historical and political background of Russian translational reflection is described by *Natalia Kamovnikova*. Her article is a study of the ways in which the political climate affected the development of TS and translation practice in the Soviet Union until the country's final collapse in 1991. The development of the discipline was actively shaped by censorship, which impeded scholars' access to foreign sources and discouraged practicing translators from applying techniques other than those approved by leading Soviet theorists. 'Free' translation fit perfectly with censorship, which ideologically promoted modification to source texts. Scholarship and practice were deeply rooted in the Socialist Realism movement, propagated by the communist party as the basis for the approval of text domestication. As a consequence, a different tradition was followed within TS; the main approaches are described in the article, with special attention to a historical translation project in the 1940s and the influential introduction in 1953 of Andrey Fedorov's translation theory. The study draws translation into the focus of observation, thorough analysis, statistics and argumentation. Fedorov's progressive linguistic approach was severely criticized by his opponents but turned out to be inextricably bound up with TS in Russia.

We meet Fedorov again in *Anastasia Shakhova*'s chapter, in which she describes Fedorov's book as the first consistent theory of translation based on linguistics in more detail and highlights the trajectory of his theory within global and post-Soviet discourses on TS. The article comments on the assumption of missing Russian translation theories in the global debate and enhances notions of travelling theories (Said, Susam-Sarajeva) and travel concepts in the humanities (Bal), to modify the disciplinary discussions temporally, geographically, and ideologically. Thus, Fedorov's case is perceived through the prism of the supposed ideological incompatibility with Western discourses in the discipline. Fedorov's 1953 introduction to translation theory followed the prevailing scientific approach chosen after the intervention into linguistics of Stalin's 1950 essay on "Marxism and the problem of linguistics". De-Stalinization changed the principles of scientificity, but Fedorov never replaced examples of translation strategies borrowed from the works of Marxist classics. Despite that, the recent discussion of his theory and ideology shows that Fedorov should be seen as a precursor of modern TS. The rediscovery of his missing theory may lead to its reintegration into the historical paradigm of global TS, a discipline that "does apparently need to translate itself to overcome time, space, language, and ideological borders".

The transition to the next chapter shows how differently the discipline of TS came into being and developed depending on local, sometimes national or language-related circumstances. In the Greek-speaking world, the discipline in its own right has only emerged over the past decades. *George Floros* and *Simos Grammenidis* take stock of the directions in which it is developing now. Their contribution aims to explore the local epistemological profile of TS between

# TEMPORAL AND GEOGRAPHICAL EXTENSIONS IN TRANSLATION STUDIES

1990 and 2011. Their analysis offers insights into the processes by which translational knowledge is distributed and diffused and the ways it is positioned within the existing situation. By locating research trends prevalent in the study of the various aspects of translation, they first give an account of the current situation in the Greek-speaking world and next focus on prevalent research trends. They restrict their study to publications in the given period, focusing both on areas of research and on researchers and trends, and offer statistical data. They conclude that most publications by Greek-speaking scholars focus on issues pertaining to descriptive and theoretical TS, being the most significant area of it, according to the authors. Reinterpreted in the Greek debate were not so much the concepts and methodologies imported from international trends and centers, but chiefly their own tradition, in terms of both research focus and conceptualization of the translational object itself.

The multiple conceptualizations of translation and its multiple theories—the main subject of this volume—are a result of exchange between the various localities where research and debate were processed, and, as *Anne Lange* claims, they are also the result of adequate communication within and for a cultural community. Her contribution focuses on Estonia, where translation became a field of academic research in the 1960s, and she concentrates on Peeter Torop's concept of total translation (1995). The concept stems from the Tartu-Moscow School of Semiotics. Torop, once a student of Juri Lotman, conceptualized translation in terms of communication and auto-communication and developed a cultural and semiotic interpretation of one of Catford's types of translation. In Torop's work, translation becomes a metaphor for the universal mechanisms of producing meaning. Lange compares Torop's concept with postcolonial approaches to translation, especially with Tymoczko's concept of cultural translation. In the Estonian case, culture is interpreted as a 'text' functioning in different sign systems that are not isolated but mutually dependent to be of communicative significance: "Culture operates largely through translational activity, since only by the inclusion of new texts into culture can the culture undergo innovation as well as perceive its specificity".

### Acknowledgments

The editors would like to thank Cees Koster and Peter Flynn for their valuable advice in the earlier stages of this book project, as well as Irmak Uğur for her meticulous copy-editing. This work was supported by the University of Tartu Astra Project Per Aspera and grant number PHVLC19917.

## References

Ayvazyan, Nune and Anthony Pym. 2017. "West enters East. A strange case of unequal equivalences in Soviet translation theory." In Schippel and Zwischenberger, 221–245.

Baer, Brian James (ed.). 2011. *Contexts, Subtexts, and Pretexts: Literary Translation in Eastern Europe and Russia*. Amsterdam and Philadelphia: John Benjamins.

Baer, Brian James. 2016. *Translation and the Making of Modern Russian Literature*. New York and London: Bloomsbury.

Baker, Mona. 1993. "Corpus linguistics and translation studies: Implications and applications." In *Text and technology: In honour of John Sinclair*, edited by Mona Baker, Gill Francis, and Elena Tognini-Bonelli, 233–250. Amsterdam and Philadelphia: John Benjamins.

Chesterman, Andrew. 2014. "Universalism in translation studies." *Translation Studies* 7 (1): 82–90.

Chesterman, Andrew. 2019. "Consilience or fragmentation in Translation Studies today?" *Slovo: Baltic accent* 10 (1): 9–20.

Cronin, Michael. 1995. "Altered states. Translation and minority languages." TTR 8 (1): 85–103.

Duarte, José Ferreira. 2012. "Trusting translation." *Anglo Saxonica* 3 (3): 17–36.

Ehrensberger-Dow, Maureen, and Birgitta Englund Dimitrova (eds). 2016. *Cognitive space: exploring the situational interface*. Special issue of *Translation Spaces* 5 (1).

Gentzler, Edwin. 2017. *Translation and rewriting in the age of post-translation studies*. Abingdon: Routledge.

Gile, Daniel. 2013. "Scientificity and theory in translation studies." In *Handbook of translation studies*, vol. 4, edited by Yves Gambier and Luc van Doorslaer, 148–155. Amsterdam and Philadelphia: John Benjamins.

Gonne, Maud, and Reine Meylaerts. 2020. "Introduction." In *Transfer thinking in translation studies: playing with the black box of cultural transfer*, edited by Maud Gonne, Klaartje Merrigan, Reine Meylaerts and Heleen van Gerwen, 9–31. Leuven: Leuven University Press.

Halverson, Sandra. 2003. "The cognitive basis of translation universals." *Target* 15 (2): 197–241.

Mauranen, Anna, and Pekka Kujamäki, eds. 2004. *Translation Universals: Do They Exist?* Amsterdam and Philadelphia: John Benjamins.

Prieto Velasco, Juan Antonio, and Adrián Fuentes Luque. 2016. "A collaborative multimodal working environment for the development of instrumental and professional competences of student translators: an innovative teaching experience." *The Interpreter and Translator Trainer* 10 (1): 76–91.

Risku, Hanna. 2010. "A cognitive scientific view on technical communication and translation: do embodiment and situatedness really make a difference?" *Target* 22 (1): 94–111.

Schippel, Larisa and Cornelia Zwischenberger, eds. 2017. *Going East. Discovering New and Alternative Traditions in Translation Studies*. Berlin: Frank & Timme.

Špirk, Jaroslav. 2009. "Anton Popovič's contribution to translation studies." *Target* 21 (1): 3–29.

Susam-Sarajeva, Şebnem. 2005. *Theories on the move: translation's role in the travels of literary theories*. Amsterdam and New York: Rodopi.

Tashinskiy, Aleksey. 2019. "Wessen Übersetzung? Möglichkeiten und Grenzen des Begriffs 'übersetzerisches Œuvre' am Beispiel der Klagenfurter Übersetzerin Hertha Lorenz (1916–1989)." *Chronotopos* 1 (1): 40–64.

Toury, Gideon. 2012 [1995]. *Descriptive translation studies—and beyond*. Amsterdam and Philadelphia: John Benjamins.

Tymoczko, Maria. 2006. "Reconceptualizing Western translation theory: Integrating non-Western Thought about translation." In *Translating others, vol. 1*, edited by Theo Hermans, 16–32. Manchester: St Jerome.

Tymoczko, Maria. 2014. "Response." *Translation Studies* 7 (1): 104–107.

van Doorslaer, Luc. 2017a. "The relative need for comparative translation studies." *Translation and Interpreting Studies* 12 (2): 213–230.

van Doorslaer, Luc. 2017b. "Holmes and Popovič in the 21st century. An empirical-bibliographical exercise." *World Literature Studies* 9 (2): 12–21.

van Doorslaer, Luc. 2018. "Bound to Expand. The Paradigm of Change in Translation Studies." In *Moving Boundaries in Translation Studies*, edited by Helle V. Dam, Matilde Nisbeth Brøgger, and Karen Korning Zethsen, 220–230. Abingdon: Routledge.

van Doorslaer, Luc, and Peter Flynn (eds.). 2013. *Eurocentrism in translation studies*. Amsterdam and Philadelphia: John Benjamins.

Zwischenberger, Cornelia. 2019. "From inward to outward: the need for translation studies to become outward-going." *The Translator* 25 (3): 256–268.

# PART 1

## *Theorizing the Concept, the Object and the Discipline*

∵

CHAPTER 2

# Approaches to a Historiography of Translation Studies

*Yves Gambier*

## Abstract

The movement of theories belongs both to the history and the sociology of disciplines, especially to their institutionalization. Epistemology should also be added here, though sometimes disguised as the History of Ideas, sometimes labelled as the Philosophy of Science. One of the major paradoxes, or even contradictions, in translation studies (TS) seems to be the double bind of opening borders and establishing limits—hence the simultaneous struggle for interdisciplinarity and for hyper-specialized compartmentalization. The field has yet to acknowledge the fragmented nature of its origins, traditions and filiations. To date, the dissemination of TS, along with its different paradigms and approaches, has become visible through certain concepts such as "age, turn, meme, and model" among other ways. This paper examines certain conditions underlying the development of a historiography of TS. In particular, it insists on the relevance of a media history of translation.

Despite the questions and suggestions by Lambert (1993) and the questioning by D'hulst (2010), the historiography, or how to tell the history of translation,[1] does not seem to have strong foundations, although a certain number of recent publications deal with methods in such a history (Bastin and Bandia 2006; O'Sullivan 2012; D'hulst and Gambier 2018). Nevertheless, sources, genealogies, filiations, influences, cross-fertilization and borrowings in translation studies (TS) remain poorly accounted for, whatever the perspective—linear and factual, or long-term (*longue durée*), or global (taking into account the different discourse and theories on translation, in different parts of the world).

In this exploratory paper, we do not pretend to tell how to write a historiography of TS. We aim first at defining different types of discourse and models

---

1  "History of translation" encompasses here the history of translated texts (from the decision to translate them to their reception), the history of translators (their profile, their practice), and the history of translation studies.

© KONINKLIJKE BRILL NV, LEIDEN, 2021 | DOI:10.1163/9789004437807_003

in the history of TS. Secondly, we advocate for a media history of translation. Some scholars have dealt with the classic seven key questions, focusing on translation history: Who? What? Where? With whom? Why? In what way or how? When? (D'hulst 2010). But also, other questions can be asked, such as, for instance: what are the effects of a given way of theorizing (when the history of translation is also understood as a history of TS)? What is the impact of the means of production and dissemination of translations?

## 1    A Polymorphous Object for a Poly-Discipline

How does one write a history of a polysemous object (translation) in TS as a poly-discipline (Morin 1986)? What would be the basis of such a history given that TS defies disciplinary borders (Gambier and van Doorslaer 2016)?

Perceptions and conceptualizations of translation go hand in hand—our way of understanding affects our descriptions and vice-versa. To support the concept of transfer, the binary oppositions (written/oral codes, source/target texts, original/translation, literal/free translation, author/translator, content/ form) (Blumczynski and Hassani 2019) imply the neglect of some characteristics of translations—their process as their position in cultural spaces and socio-symbolic exchanges. In the same vein, our concepts of translation should not forget the writing systems, the place of writing in our society, nor the material and technical factors which are part of the translation event and act.

Today, we are facing a set of labels that denominate translation (adaptation, localization, transediting, versioning, transcreation, co-writing, mediation, self-translation, etc.) and *a posteriori* we are facing the ambiguity of the concept. Giving a name to translation contributes to working out the object, to developing it as an independent object of inquiry and to considering the changes of the relationship between all forms of language production. Our discourse can then be homogenizing, gathering or differentiating, hybridizing: either the concept of translation is defined with clear-cut borders and covers different practices, or we have a continuum from intralingual translation, interlingual translation, adaptation, co-writing, etc. The diversity of modalities in naming, defining and categorizing translation is based on our beliefs, values, assumptions and experience. This article is neither the place to lay out the full evolution of translation nor to provide an overview of its different definitions, with their descriptivist, feminist or deconstructionist premises (Halverson 2010). From an Aristotelian conceptualization to a prototypical definition, the history of the concepts of translation over time (mimesis, appropriation, imitation) and in various cultures (reversal, transmigration, substitution, metamorphosis, etc.) is to be written (Gambier and Stecconi 2019). Over a few decades, TS has developed to cope with this plurality—from translation understood as a 'simple' transfer between languages, reproducing the same text, to translation as an interpretation,[2] as a mixed space and locus of power (and therefore of conflicts), and the recent rediscovery of multimodal communication (see section 3), through translating advertisements, audiovisual programs, software, websites and video games.

An infinitely variable object opens up to a poly-disciplinary TS (Morin 1986), especially if one tackles all the aspects (context, practice, process, agents, product and effects). Again, as for translation, the ways to consider TS as a way of knowing, an empirical science, a hermeneutics, an applied science (Chesterman 2000) direct the objectives, research methods and theorizing. Its diversity is to acknowledge the multiplicity of linguistic, historical, cultural, social factors regarding translation and TS. However, the trend towards greater empiricism, linked to the possible wealth of data to be collected, increasingly moves TS away from epistemology, whereas law, political sciences, hard sciences and education possess such meta-approach (Basalamah 2012; Ladmiral 2012).

For the time being, TS is unable to avoid a certain hyper-specialization, nor a certain rejection of theorizing. Does interdisciplinarity (possible with disciplines such as linguistics, comparative literature, psycholinguistics, anthropology, sociology, etc.) really exceed the limits of the different bibliographies, the methodological commitments to reach theoretical discussion? One must admit that it is not easy to learn to talk to each other, with hidden assumptions about your own disciplines and other disciplines, with different terminologies, with different expectations regarding the definition of problems, the selection of variables and models, the interpretation of data. In addition, gaining recognition, securing research grants, publishing might differ between disciplines. To date, only very few disciplines (such as organization studies and sociology[3]) have entered into dialogue with TS, even though translation as a metaphor goes beyond TS (Gambier and van Doorslaer 2016). Is TS ready to open up when "cultural translation" (Bhabha 1994) is excluded by Trivedi (2007) and Pym (2009)? The polarization (sometimes caricatural) between empirical and conceptual approaches (Gile 2005) has given birth to many case studies based

---

2   However, plurality is not to be reduced to a binary logic as, for instance, in Venuti's bivalent opposition between the instrumental model and the hermeneutic model (Venuti 2018, 2019).

3   In Gambier and van Doorslaer (2016, 120), Buzelin and Baraldi claim that there is still "a persisting lack of sociological research on translation" but what about all the studies carried out by Sapiro and her team, by Heilbron, in the last 20 years?

on observations and experiments, thus today the feeling of repetition, if not of an epistemological stagnation in TS: could it be that most of the scholars start from the same sources, the same paradigms, with the same methodological consensus? What has happened to the so-called convergence between cultural/textual approaches and empirical ones (Chesterman and Arrojo 2000)?

## 2 Towards a Socio-Historiography of TS?

Today, theories travel through conferences, publications and online websites. They are pulled by phenomenological epistemology (which studies agents in interaction with structures of realities) rather than by positivist epistemology. Below, we refer to four perspectives based on a certain key concept.

How does TS picture its own progress, beyond 'theorems' (Ladmiral 1979) and below a 'theology' (Ladmiral 1989)? Ladmiral (1987) talks about four ages of TS or methodological approaches:

- prescriptive (or normative): "before yesterday" TS
- descriptive (mainly linguistic): 'yesterday' TS
- productive (practice-oriented): 'today' TS
- inductive (or scientific), under the influence of cognitive psychology: 'tomorrow' TS.

This typology has not been invalidated by his latest proposal (Ladmiral 2009) on the law of three stages, inspired by August Comte (in *The Course of Positive Philosophy*, written in French between 1830 and 1842) for hard sciences and of larger impact than the four ages because they have been illustrated by other social sciences and reach back to ancient times:

- the metaphysical or cultural stage where human sciences, including TS, are still indistinct from other types of knowledge
- the polemical stage where there is an increase in the number of schools which confront or do not know each other, such as, for instance, the dispute over literalism between 'sourciers' (in favor of foreignization) and 'ciblistes' (in favor of domestication), or the dispute over 'deverbalization'
- the pragmatic stage[4] which focuses on the diversity of research, provided that they follow reflexivity and responsibility, leading to an epistemological metatheory able to problematize the status of discourse in TS.

Another type of historiography is based on the concept of the turn (Snell-Hornby 2006)—such as the linguistic, textual/ pragmatic (reinforced by

---

4 Ladmiral speaks here of an ecumenical turn, maybe because the diversity of research is subsumed under the single "pragmatic stage".

electronic corpus-based studies), philosophical (with Quine, Benjamin), educational (since Vinay and Darbelnet), cultural, sociological, fictional, ideological, postcolonial, ethical and technological turns. The high quantity of turns makes you dizzy and compels you to question them: are they new directions deriving from the internal dynamics of TS or alternatives suggested by interdisciplinary contacts? Are they crossroads which change our perspectives or curves which hardly modify the course, nevertheless with a sufficient element of fashion that a given turn sparks off a plethora of publications in a short period of time? Such turns and re-turns are a certain angle, a reductionist view to investigate translation as a complex reality, a way of splitting up our knowledge, a risk also of fragmentation of our field. Nevertheless, one can seek to place the history in order by classifying precursors, pioneers, masters and disciples (Snell-Hornby, 2006, chapter 1): it is a way to add a personal touch to the poly-discipline without necessarily apprehending its assumptions, and postulates and *a priori*.

Another approach is based on the concept of meme or units of cultural transfer, spread by imitation, as if pieces of ideas or discourse could replicate themselves like genes do. We do not wish to discuss here the complex relation between genes and cultures, between biological universals and cultural achievements (Vermeer 1997; Chesterman 2005a). In TS, supermemes are, for instance, source-target, equivalence, untranslatability, free-vs-literal, and all-writing-is-translating, while meme-complexes are the word with its lexical and semantic features, the word of God (a constraining textual source), rhetoric (underlying the importance of reception), logos, the contrastive study of languages, the concept of communication and target, and cognition (Chesterman 2016[1997], 3–48). Supermemes and memes have allowed researchers no doubt to set up a research program, to list factors and variables to take into account in the study of translation but certainly not to think about a history of TS, partly because memetics sees evolution as copying, overlapping, cumulative and ahistorical stages ("representing primarily clusters of ideas rather than historical periods", id.: 18). Today, the meme perspective cannot unify the different approaches in TS.

Chesterman has proposed another angle in 2012 with his three basic models of translation—the comparative, process and causal models, models being defined as a "kind of empirical theory", reflecting again his tension between the justified need for a so called hypothetico-deductive theory (a Popperian-type theory) (Chesterman 2016[1997]) and the current pressure for an inductive empiricism in TS. Can we believe that the acknowledgment of this tension brought him to advocate for 'consilience'—unifying the poly-discipline with concepts connecting the textual, cultural, social and cognitive perspectives

(2005b; 2007)? Chesterman would then concur with Ladmiral and his 'ecumenism' (2009). Would those calls against the obsession of fragmentation and this dizziness of turns lead to something other than an epistemological eclecticism or to a discontinuity of discourse and theoretical stances?

The history of TS, still to be written, covers a rather short period of time (about 50–70 years[5]). It will be unable either to forget or to ignore its sociological dimension as a field, with networks and legitimizing authorities (journals, book series, conferences, associations, training programs, mailing lists and anthologies, etc.) (Gambier 2007). The TS scholars' habitus is not foreign to the way they form their own history (D'hulst 1995). In this perspective, scientometric studies do not help in measuring the past and current dynamics of TS; they rather make the poly-discipline blind about itself, unable to understand the conditions of its own practice, namely the pressure of competition, the commodification of knowledge, the confusion between quantified correlation and causality and the increase in the number of turns as a sign of fragmentation (Delabastita 2013). In addition, scientometric counting cannot explain the theoretical moves, their dissemination, their internationalization, nor their national roots. Why has Newmark remained so dominant in the British tradition and for a while in China (with Nida) while Ladmiral dominated the French stage and for a while in Kazakhstan, just because the French Embassy there wished to disseminate French theory about translation, as if diplomatic agreement and financial support of cultural exchanges were enough to promote Ladmiral. In any case, the geo-linguistic origin of the references, cited in books on TS (for example, in North American books), indicate how monolingualism is maintained, and how a greater diversity of sources and channels of distribution is resisted. It is out of our scope here to discuss Englishization and Eurocentrism in TS (Delabastita 2011; van Doorslaer 2011, 2012). Here is a paradox: while TS is becoming more global, both in its territorial and scholarly spread, its intellectual horizon seems to be shrinking. The promotion, if not the domination, of the empirical trend is sometimes justified by its Anglo-Saxon philosophical and cultural base (with Bacon, Locke, Hume) and English as a *lingua franca*—the Globish which make people come and go as goods, in a kind of equivalence in the capitalist world. No scholar can escape these ethnocentric marks (Eurocentrism, Sinocentrism, etc.), including the author of this chapter.

---

5   This is not the place to argue about the sources of TS. However, the relation between linguistics, language management and translation indicates that the sources are not limited to Western Europe (Gambier 2020).

# APPROACHES TO A HISTORIOGRAPHY OF TRANSLATION STUDIES

## 3 Plea in Favor of a Media History of Translation

The set of epistemic and socio-institutional elements of any discipline cannot neglect the impact of the material forms on the production and circulation of discourse and knowledge. In this section 3, we will advocate the need of a media history of translation: after a connection between the digital technology and some practices of the past, we will remind how translating was done before the print culture and then how the move from books to the Web is changing rapidly our concepts of text and reading.

### 3.1 *How the Present Meets the Past*

When one refers to collaborative translation (crowdsourcing) by a group of amateurs (with or without a formal training in translation), two remarks come up:

- collaborative translations challenge a certain ideology which claims that a translation is always an individual act, focused on a written text, and considers the translator as a substitute for the author
- collaborative translations recall the type of work done translating in pairs in the 12th century (one working from Arabic to spoken Romance, the other one from Romance to Latin). This way has not disappeared with, for instance, the new translation of the Bible into French (2001), made by specialists in exegesis and writers, or with the new translation of Joyce's *Ulysses* (2004) by a group of eight translators, or any project of localization in which agents are either in face-to-face contact or are so in cyberspace (Pym 2004a, 171–172).

The tension between the individualistic approach and the collaborative approach is not new: the former has been dominant in Western Europe from the Renaissance, that is, the mid-14th–mid-16th centuries (Bistué 2013), with a peak in the Romantic period (19th century), to the end of the 20th century. The latter seems to be spreading today through the use of translation memory systems, cloud translation, fansubbing and the use of different types of communities on the Web.

Why do we need a media history of translation, related to the channels of production, distribution, circulation and reception of translations? Practices of writing and reading have changed according to the material forms (wood, stone, human body, tablet, roll, codex, book and computer) available at a given time for the storage and retrieval of data and information. The physical supports (voice, clay, wax, silk, papyrus, parchment, paper and screen) make a difference to our practices of writing, reading—and translating. We know how Luther (mid-16th century) combined printing and translation and how Google uses the power of computer memory and calculation to develop machine translation.

Cultural history has easily traced the influence of technical tools, for instance in the evolution of printing, but our attention has not yet been drawn to this influence in translation (Cronin 2003; Littau 2011). Book historians have opened up the way when describing oral, printed and digital cultures. Today, as in the past, several types of culture in relation to media co-exist: paper and screen, one being, temporarily, in a dominant position in certain spheres of activities (journalism, administration) until a balance between the two is found or paper is completely replaced by computer—just as individualistic and collaborative approaches overlap to a certain degree in different types of translation.

So called 'mediology' can here be a source of inspiration (Debray 1991, 1994, 2004): this media philosophy refuses to separate culture from technology. In studying methods used to store, transmit, pass down and disseminate cultural knowledge, mediology sets out to demonstrate how media do not only serve to conserve data, information and knowledge, but are also constitutive: they shape our mind-set, our beliefs, our social organization. Let us take some examples. Because of the lack of space and the lack of systematic knowledge of media history of translation in China, in the Arabic world, etc., I limit the presentation to Europe, admittedly in a too linear way—the goal here being only to emphasize the importance of the materiality of translation in the historiography of TS.

### 3.2 *From Cicero to the Print Culture*

Cicero is often quoted in TS as the father of the dilemma regarding translating sense-for-sense as opposed to word-for-word. We tend to forget that interventions (labelled today as political, literary, legal and philosophical) were public and oral, bodily expressed (there was no microphone to amplify the voice). The oral competences and the oratorical style were put to advantage, and not only by the great orators and the lawyers. Cicero translated speeches into textual forms as a speaker—eloquence taking precedence over fidelity (Weissbrot and Eysteinsson 2006, 21; McElduff 2013, chapter 4). It is also more likely that he would have composed orally, dictating his translations to a slave or his secretary who wrote it down on a roll (the two wooden cylindrical sticks held in two hands by somebody else). A roll is not without analogy to a computer or tactile tablet where you scroll up and down the document you want to read. In other words, in the 1st c. BC, a translation was transmitted by means of a certain written code while the text itself was mediated by two forms of oral delivery (the performance of the speaker and reading aloud for an audience). Another fact is that, when translating, Cicero was not necessarily using a text on a roll but his memory. Working with the human voice and the memory is far from our graphocentric perspective—including digital, in which memorizing is a part of the technology, and no longer plays a major role in learning and reading.

What about the European Middle Ages—a culture largely based on a handwritten codex when translations were made under the patronage of the king, the church or a prince? Codices appeared in the Byzantine Empire, in particular in the 8–9th c., giving rise to what has been called "Byzantine Iconoclasm". Codices were made by scribes and illustrators and produced for a particular patron, usually its future owner, with a specific audience in mind. This is quite different from book production aiming at a large market but rather similar to an iPad with a lot of pictures. Each codex is a unique artefact; it was a localized undertaking, involving personal relations and collaborative work.

When a codex was lost or only available as copies (often textually corrupted over time), the translator had to reconstruct the text by using a variety of sources: surviving fragments held in different locations (codices were travelling and copied), translated parts in different languages or dialects, quotations embedded in other works, etc. The translation could not and cannot be compared to the fragmented, misrepresented, manipulated 'original'; it could be a 'source' text as a point of departure for the translation but not a standard against which to evaluate the new version (Ellis 2000).

Codices are both derived from the oral tradition (promoting adaptation and free translation) and introduce textual features found in a print culture (promoting a more literal translation strategy) (Tymoczko 2010, 219 and 228; Hermans 1992, 1997). The literal approach was justified in a monastic scriptorial context where assumed faithfulness to the Word of God demanded a word-for-word rendition. Between the variations in the production and circulation of codices and the insistence on remaining as close as possible to the sacred text, we can appreciate the complexity of translating in the Middle Ages. That could explain the diversity of labels for translation: *compilatio, ordinatio,* and *imitatio*. In the handwritten tradition, various forms of writing had arisen; composing, annotating, glossing, translating, and copying, with omissions, additions and comments—to the extent that the receiver had a central position in interpreting texts. Besides, when parchments became more common than papyrus and therefore the codex less fragile and more capacious than the roll, readers could have easier access to any part of the text—pagination, internal division of the text and a table of contents transformed the codex little by little. Several texts could be then gathered in the same codex and a codex could be held with one hand—enabling the reader to make notes with the other hand (Cavallo 1999). The monastic habit of reading aloud gave way to new scholastic habits (reading silently and annotating).

What happens with a print culture? The invention of moveable type printing technology in the mid-15th century in Europe led to new changes in the production, consumption and transmission of texts. From now on, presses could produce multiple identical copies, admittedly with unintentional variations in spelling, textual modifications because of the printing process and also pirated and counterfeited editions. However, and more importantly, there was an increasing demand for reading material (RED 1996). The vernacular languages became languages to be learned. In translations, the layout of the originals in Latin shaped the translation strategy. Translation is then not only an inter-lingual process but also an inter-medial transfer, as today with tourist brochures, illustrated books and advertisements, etc. for which many scholars speak of adaptation (and not translation, too much considered as a word-for-word substitution).

In parallel to these changes, a literate bourgeoisie and a national language emerged. Translations served a new readership (Jouhaud and Viala 2002) and a certain ideology. Berman (2012) talked about the twofold origin of the institutionalization of translation in France, between the 14th century (with Oresme, tutor of the king Charles V and designer of the learned French within the transfer of knowledge from Latin) and the 16th century (with Amyot, in favor of free adaptation, creating a certain type of prose). Between the Renaissance and the mid-20th century, since the source text can be identified and replicated as such, a new concept of translation and a comparative approach between the source and target texts became established, supporting the concept of equivalence, the translation as a secondary text and the illusion of equal languages (Pym 2004a, 173–174; 2004b). In the following centuries, the circulation of texts accelerated. The business and trade of books encouraged the development of secular literature, journals and newspapers. The expansion of book production was then boosted again with popular and pulp literature (around 1860) and the launch of pocketbooks (around 1950), while legal protection (copyrights) of foreign works did not then exist. "Active retranslations" (Pym 1998, 82–83) became relatively frequent in markets which are more competitive. We are now far from rolls with tied words and no punctuation and from codices with illuminated pages.

From then on, the need to be able to read fast and silently was satisfied since printers and typesetters had systematized, though not yet standardized, both layout and spelling. Another reason for this twofold demand in reading could also be, at least in certain societies, that translators had opted for fluency as the dominant strategy in order to suit (Venuti 2018[1995]).

### 3.3 *From the Print Culture to the Digital Culture*

In our digital culture today, fluency aiming at optimal readability according to linguistic, rhetoric and stylistic criteria, is being replaced by accessibility and usability; the focus is then less on the text than on the receivers (readers, viewers and users)—changes anticipated in a way by the Skopos theory—moving away from a contrastive approach towards a target approach. Today, an online text (but not necessarily a book in an electronic format which retains its forms derived from the print culture) can have a new configuration thanks to its users: they are invited to add their own words and images to co-construct the meaning.

A hypertext, materially and semantically open, takes over the print text, limited in its materiality but open semantically. The traditional division of labor between the production of a text, a film, a piece of music and their distribution is blurred with the Information and Communication Technology (ICT) easily accessible today. The collaboration in translating also changes the process. In some twenty to thirty years, ICT has transformed the concepts of text and book and our experience of reading, writing and translating. The translation act is now visible on the computer screen: readers (including other translators) can partake in the process and have the possibility to compare multiple translated versions, rather than just compare the source and target texts.

From Cicero to today, translations have always been marked by the technical environment, even though we have paid little attention to it in the past. Their existence is inseparable from the material medium which embodies them. However, there is no clear-cut correspondence between a medium and a given period of time: different media co-exist in a culture at a certain moment. The linear presentation of some examples should not fool anyone: time and space are not monolithic. The same caution applies to interpreting: seen as exclusively an oral performance for a long time, interpreting has been under pressure from technology for at least the last 40 years (not to mention the birth of the simultaneous mode)—from telephone to speech recognition systems, from the tools available online to virtual reality (Berber 2010). At the moment, the changes are so complex and rapid, and sometimes controversial, that it is difficult to follow and understand what is happening. Nonetheless, the transition from printing to digitization explains (to a considerable degree?) the ambiguities or even the contradictions of TS: indeed, the concept of text, the relationship between oral and written codes, and our hesitation to use the word 'translation' combine to force us to rethink our technical approaches and our conceptualizations inherited from the technical paradigm of the printed book.

## 4     A Forgotten Concept: Language?

There is another aspect to be taken into account in parallel with the technology: how languages are categorized. As soon as there is language planning, language management, language standardization and language technology, borders are set up. Here again, reflections are limited to Europe.

Early in the Middle Ages, intercultural communications were regulated within a certain hierarchical system of languages, with languages supposed to be close to the word of God, namely Aramaic, Hebrew, Greek and Latin, at the top, followed by vernaculars based on Latin and then by dialects/patois, as shown by the polyglot Bible preserved in Salamanca and Antwerp. Today, the hierarchy still remains but also inspired by technologies, and not by God: there is a *lingua franca* for the internationalization of business and goods, then languages which justify a full localization, languages which imply a partial localization and, at the bottom, languages which could require localization but, because of a lack of means, do not localize at all.

The Renaissance was the age of vernaculars, equal in principle. However, at around the same time, the concept of the nation-state began to emerge, with a language as one of its attributes. Translators as mediators begin to be placed into a kind of double bind; their linguistic loyalty contradicts the national borders they are trying to overcome. Their identification is two-way. The association of state, nation, territory, language and culture rejects the continuum between languages and leads to typologies of languages, as if languages could be isolated, counted as apples, separated and without contacts (Sakai 2009; Mezzadra and Sakai 2014). Dialects, patois and standard forms became connoted, anchored in a certain political and linguistic ideology, like 'purism' which excludes any forms of 'contamination' or hybridization—thus discrete categories are created, such as, to give only a few examples, Serbo-Croatian, Serbian, Croatian (Hlavac 2015), or the Belgian French, Québécois French, trendy French—variations of the same 'language' or different 'languages'. From the 13th c., with Dante Alighieri (*De Vulgari Eloquentia*), who divided languages between Si, Oc and Oil languages, up to the 18–19th c. with that period's genetic categorizations (William Jones, Franz Bopp) and the different typologies, for instance those by the brothers Von Schlegel, languages are defined in order to be adapted to political agendas. Antoine Meillet (1928) has identified two types of languages: on the one hand, dominant, written, national languages, and on the other hand the spoken languages, dialects, popular languages and local languages. In his list, there is a clear hierarchical system between the so-called prestigious languages (Greek, Latin and "civilized languages") and the stigmatized ones, with national languages in an in-between position.

TS remains dependent upon such categorizations. The postcolonial approach calls them into question as it also does the heterolingualism of certain literary and filmic works.

## 5 By Way of Conclusion

The historiography of TS should be based on an epistemology of the poly-discipline that is able to shed light on:
- the different conceptualizations of translation and the conditions for their possible co-existence
- the postulates and assumptions of theories (such as the polysystem theory, the interpretive theory, and the Skopos theory), of models and schools, and their methodological choices, in particular the tendency to give priority to empirical studies
- and the real impact of media (or technical support) in our conceptions.

This triple light would not be limited to a geographical zone (Eurocentric or not). Besides, the concepts are nomadic and defy disciplinary borders. These borders which exclude (beyond) and include (on this side) are also lines which emancipate and liberate when they are crossed and broken. An epistemology of complexity (Delabastita 2005; Marais 2015; Marais and Meylaerts 2019) rejects monological, self-assertive attitudes, binary thinking and tries to go beyond partial knowledge of reality: the need of such an epistemology can help us to rethink the relationships between structure and agency, between cause and effect, between local and global, between habitus and evolution.

### References

Basalamah, Salah. 2012. "En deçà des méthodes et des théories, l'horizon d'une philosophie." TTR 25(1): 13–49.

Bastin, Georges and Paul Bandia, eds. 2006. *Charting the future of translation history*. Ottawa: University of Ottawa Press.

Berber, Diana. 2010. *Information and communication technologies in conference interpreting. A survey of their usage in professional and educational settings*. Saarbrücken: LAP Lambert Academic Publishing.

Berman, Antoine. 2012. *Jacques Amyot, traducteur français. Essai sur les origines de la traduction en France*. Paris: Belin.

Bhabha, Homi. 1994. *The location of culture*. London: Routledge.

Bistué, Belén. 2013. *Collaborative translation and multi-version texts in early modern Europe*. London and New York: Routledge.

Blumczynski, Piotr and Ghodrat Hassani. 2019. "Towards a meta-theoretical model for translation." *Target* 31 (3): 328–351.

Cavallo, Guglielmo. 1999. "Between volumen and codex: Reading in the Roman world." In *A history of reading in the West*, edited by Guglielmo Cavallo and Roger Chartier, translated from Spanish by Lydia G. Cochrane, 64–89. Cambridge: Polity Press.

Chesterman, Andrew and Rosemary Arrojo. 2000. "Shared ground in translation studies." *Target* 12 (1): 333–50. Forum followed by responses: 2000, 12 (2): 333–362; 2001, 13 (1): 149–168; 13 (2): 333–350; 2002, 14 (1): 137–148.

Chesterman, Andrew. 2000. "What constitutes progress in translation studies?" In *Översättning och tolkning. Rapport från ASLA hösy symposium, Stockholm 5–6.11.1998*, edited by Birgitta Englund Dimitrova, 33–49. Accessed November 23, 2013. http://helsinki.fi/~chesterman/2000cProgress.html.

Chesterman, Andrew. 2005a. "The mimetics of knowledge." In *Knowledge systems and translation*, edited by Helle Vronning Dam, Jan Engberg, Heidrun Gerzymisch-Arbogast, 17–30. Berlin: Mouton.

Chesterman, Andrew. 2005b. "Towards consilience." In *New tendencies in translation studies*, edited by Karin Ajimer and Cecilia Alystad, 19–27. Göteborg: Göteborg University.

Chesterman, Andrew. 2007. "Bridge concepts in translation sociology." In *Constructing a sociology of translation*, edited by Michaela Wolf and Alexandra Fukari, 171–183. Amsterdam and Philadelphia: John Benjamins.

Chesterman, Andrew. 2012. "Models in translation." In *Handbook of translation studies: Volume 3*, edited by Yves Gambier and Luc van Doorslaer, 108–114. Amsterdam: John Benjamins.

Chesterman, Andrew. 2016[1997]. *Memes of translation. The spread of ideas in Translation Theory*. Amsterdam and Philadelphia: John Benjamins.

Cronin, Michael. 2003. "The Empire talks back. Orality, heteronomy and the cultural turn in interpreting studies." In *Translation and Power*, edited by Maria Tymoczko and Edwin Gentzler, 45–62. Amherst, MA: University of Massachusetts Press.

D'hulst, Lieven and Yves Gambier, eds. 2018. *A history of modern translation knowledge*. Amsterdam and Philadelphia: John Benjamins.

APPROACHES TO A HISTORIOGRAPHY OF TRANSLATION STUDIES 31

D'hulst, Lieven. 1995. "Pour une historiographie des theories de la traduction." TTR 8 (1): 13–33.

D'hulst, Lieven. 2010. "Translation history." In *Handbook of translation studies: Volume 1*, edited by Yves Gambier and Luc van Doorslaer, 397–405.

Debray, Régis. 1991. *Cours de médiologie*. Paris: Gallimard.

Debray, Régis. 1994. *Manifeste de médiologie*. Paris: Gallimard.

Debray, Régis. 2004. *Transmitting cultures*, translated from French by Eric Rauth [Original version *Transmettre* 2000/1997]. New York: University of Columbia Press.

Delabastita, Dirk. 2005. "Research in Translation between Paralysis and Pretence." *Revista Canaria de Estudios Ingleses* 51 (November): 33–49.

Delabastita, Dirk. 2011. "Continentalism and the invention of traditions in translation studies." *Translation and Interpreting Studies* 6 (2): 142–156.

Delabastita, Dirk. 2013. "B2B in translation studies". *The Translator* 19 (1): 1–23.

Ellis, Roger. 2000. "The middle ages." In *The Oxford guide to literature in English translation*, edited by Peter France, 39–45. Oxford: Oxford University Press.

Gambier, Yves and Luc van Doorslaer, eds. 2016. *Border crossings. Translation studies and other disciplines*. Amsterdam and Philadelphia: John Benjamins.

Gambier, Yves and Ubaldo Stecconi, eds. 2019. *A World Atlas of Translation*. Amsterdam and Philadelphia: John Benjamins.

Gambier, Yves. 2007. "Y a-t-il une place pour une socio-traductologie?" In *Constructing a sociology of translation*, edited by Michaela Wolf and Alexandra Fukari, 205–217. Amsterdam and Philadelphia: John Benjamins.

Gambier, Yves. 2020. "Historique de la relation entre linguistique, traduction et traductologie." In *Les sciences du langage et traductologie*, edited by Yusuf Polat, 13–40. Paris: L'Harmatan.

Gile, Daniel. 2005. "The liberal arts paradigm and the empirical science paradigm." http://est-translationstudies.org/2005/the-liberal-arts-paradigm-and-the-empirical-science-paradigm/.

Halverson, Sandra. 2010. "Translation." In *Handbook of translation studies: Volume 1*, edited by Yves Gambier and Luc van Doorslaer, 378–84. Amsterdam and Philadelphia: John Benjamins.

Hermans, Theo. 1997. "The task of the translator in the European Renaissance. Explorations in a discursive field." In *Translating Literature*, edited by Susan Bassnett, 14–40. Cambridge: D.S. Brewer.

Hlavac, Jim. 2015. "Pre- and post- conflict language designations and language policies." *Target* 27 (2): 238–272.

Jouhaud, Christian and Alain Viala, eds. 2002. *De la publication. Entre Renaissance et Lumières*. Paris: Fayard.

Ladmiral, Jean-René. 1979. *Traduire. Théorèmes pour la traduction*. Paris: Payot.

Ladmiral, Jean-René. 1989. "Principes philosophiques de la traduction." In *Encyclopédie philosophique universelle, Volume 4*, 977–998. Paris: PUF.

Ladmiral, Jean-René. 2009. "Le statut théorique du discours traductologique." In *La traduction sous tous ses aspects au centre de gravité du dialogue international*, edited by Hasan Anamur, Alev Bulut, and Arsun Uras-Yilmaz, 5–17. Istanbul: Baski Edition.

Ladmiral, Jean-René. 2012. "Une anthropologie interdisciplinaire de la traduction." Interview by Jane Elisabeth Wilhelm. *Meta* 57 (3): 546–563.

Lambert, José. 1993. "History, historiography and the discipline. A programme." In *Translation and knowledge. SSOTT IV: Scandinavian symposium on translation theory*, edited by Yves Gambier and Jorma Tommola, 3–25. Turku: University of Turku.

Littau, Karin. 2011. "First steps towards a media history of translation." *Translation Studies* 4 (3): 261–281.

Marais, Kobus and Reine Meylaerts, eds. 2019. *Complexity thinking in translation studies. Methodological considerations*. London: Routledge.

Marais, Kobus. 2015. *Translation theory and development studies: A complexity theory approach*. London: Routledge.

McElduff, Siobhán. 2012. *Roman theories of translation. Surpassing the source*. London and New York: Routledge.

Meillet, Antoine. 1928[1918]. *Les langues dans l'Europe nouvelle*. Paris: Payot.

Mezzadra, Sandro and Naomi Sakai, eds. 2014. Special issue on politics. *Translation Journal* 4.

Morin, Edgar. 1986. *La méthode. Volume 3, La connaissance de la connaissance*. Paris: Le Seuil.

O'Sullivan, Carol, ed. 2012. "Rethinking methods in translation history." Special issue. *Translation Studies* 5 (2).

Pym, Anthony. 1998. *Method in translation history*. Manchester: St. Jerome.

Pym, Anthony. 2004a. *The moving text. Localization, translation, and distribution*. Amsterdam and Philadelphia: John Benjamins.

Pym, Anthony. 2004b. "The medieval postmodern in translation studies." www.tinet.cat/~apym/on-line/translation/2004_medieval.doc.

Pym, Anthony. 2009. "On empiricism and bad philosophy." http://usuaris.tinet.cat/apym/on-line/research_methods/2009_lille.pdf.

RED. The Reading Experience Data Base 1450–1945. Launched in 1996 at the UK Open University. http://www.open.ac.uk/Arts/RED/index.html.

Sakai, Naoki. 2009. "How do we count a language? Translation and discontinuity." *Translation Studies* 2(1): 71–88.

Snell-Hornby, Mary. 2006. *The turns in translation studies*. Amsterdam and Philadelphia: John Benjamins.

Trivedi, Harish. 2007. "Translating culture vs. cultural translation." In *In Translation—Reflections, refractions, transformations*, edited by Paul St-Pierre and Prafulla C. Kar, 277–87. Amsterdam and Philadelphia: John Benjamins.

Tymoczko, Maria. 2010. "Ideology and position of the translator: In what sense is a translator in-between?" In *Critical readings in translation studies*, edited by Mona Baker, 213–228. London: Routledge.

van Doorslaer, Luc and Peter Flynn, eds. 2011. "Eurocentrism in translation studies.", special issue of TIS (*Translation and Interpreting Studies*) 6 (2).

van Doorslaer, Luc. 2010. "Eurocentrism." In *Handbook of translation studies: Volume 1*, edited by Yves Gambier and Luc van Doorslaer, 397–405. Amsterdam and Philadelphia: John Benjamins.

Venuti, Lawrence. 2018. [3rd edition, earlier editions 1995 and 2008]. *The translators' invisibility*. London and New York: Routledge.

Venuti, Lawrence. 2019. *Contra Instrumentalism. A translation polemic*. Lincoln: University of Nebraska Press.

Vermeer, Hans. 1997. "Translation and the meme." *Target* 9 (1): 155–166.

Weissbort, Daniel and Astradur Eysteinsson, eds. 2006. *Translation—Theory and practice. A historical reader*. Oxford: Oxford University Press.

Wolf, Michaela and Alexandra Fukari, eds. 2007. *Constructing a sociology of translation*. Amsterdam and Philadelphia: John Benjamins.

CHAPTER 3

# Historiosophy of Translation

*Reflecting on Ukrainian Translation Conceptualizations—from Ivan Franko to Maksym Strikha*

*Iryna Odrekhivska*

## Abstract

Any research in translation historiography presents a methodological problem: in studying or re-considering theoretical concepts of the past, the scholar inevitably 'translates' them from the present perspective (i.e., from the premises of one's current scholarship), an approach that postulates a "double historicity". On the one hand, the present context of increased institutionalization and social organization of TS stimulates and justifies meta-reflection on different traditions of translation theorization as systematic constructs, framed in their 'chronotope'. On the other hand, extensive accentuation of national or geographical inquiries in translation historiography without adequately linking them to global debate marginalizes and even simplifies conceptual problematization and research programs developed therein. This chapter aims to foreground the historiosophy of translation, by focusing on complex, relational interpretation of reasoning and change in translation theorization and the ontological, epistemological and methodological premises of a certain disciplinary tradition. Thematic analysis of science with its key notion of 'themata', advocated by Gerald Holton, appears to be quite applicable to historiosophical redux of translation, as evident in the analysis of the historiosophy of Ukrainian reflection on translation and Ukrainian translation culture—a culture, if to extrapolate Henri Meschonnic's words, "born of translation and in translation".

## 1 Introduction

Contemporary translation studies has entered a new phase of self-reflexivity engendered by the dialogic interpretation of translation conceptualizations currently emanating from different scholarly practices. Disciplinary progress now lies not only in accumulating, 'superstructing' new knowledge, but also

# HISTORIOSOPHY OF TRANSLATION

in reorienting existing knowledge about the discipline (its logic, its definition) towards its development and growth. Metaphorically speaking, James Holmes' call-to-arms "Let the meta-discussion begin" (1988, 80), is presently taking a new meta-turn, namely towards construing a 'new' self-concept for translation studies that would further enhance its explanatory capacities and frame the institutionalization process.

In the new phase, translation studies scholars attempt at reaching discourse 'cohesiveness' (Gile 2012, 74) by re-visiting the history of the field while at the same time considering the manifold theoretical traditions fieldwise. Illuminating examples include collective monographs (see Schippel and Zwischenberger 2017; Ceccherelli, Costantino and Diddi 2015), themed conferences (*Some Holmes and Popovič in all of us? The Low Countries and the Nitra Schools in the 21st century* (2015); *Going East: Discovering New and Alternative Traditions of Translation Studies* (2014); *Translation Theories in the Slavic Countries* (2014)), English translations with critical introductions of 'bypassed' seminal texts in translation studies (see Levý 2011). In such instances, translation theory is considered from various geographical and historical perspectives. More importantly, this tendency is mutual, figuratively "West enters East" (Pym and Ayvazyan 2017, 221) and "East meets West" (Jettmarová 2005, 95), resisting area-restricted isolationism.

Yet any research of this scope presents a methodological problem: studying or re-considering the 'events' of the past—i.e., concepts, theories, research programs—the scholar inevitably 'translates' them from the present perspective, that is, from the premises of one's current scholarship, which implicitly becomes a certain point of reference, a measure against which the 'events' are re-defined. Arising thus is a "double historicity", which accounts for the historicity of the translation concept being researched and the historical context of the interpretational position of its researcher. On the one hand, the present context of increased institutionalization and social organization of translation studies stimulates and justifies meta-reflection on different traditions of translation theorization as systematic constructs, substantiated by translation concepts framed in their 'chronotope'. On the other hand, extensive accentuation of national or geographical enquiries in translation historiography (beyond doubt, translation studies cartography is essential) without due attention to linking them to global debate marginalizes and even simplifies thematic problematization and research programs developed therein.

Taking both stances into account, the paper argues that the insights into particular, differential national disciplinary 'profiles', determined substantially by historical underpinnings and adaptation to research environments, can still be the way to 'perfect' and/or solidify the claims and explanatory capacities of current translation theories, yet the matter lies in the approach.

The present paper foregrounds a "historiosophy of translation" by re-framing Gerald Holton's concept of "thematic analysis of science" and emphasizing its productivity for translation studies. Taking Holton's concept as a yardstick in our study, this contribution aims at exploring the historiosophy of Ukrainian reflection on translation and Ukrainian translation culture—a culture, to extrapolate Henri Meschonnic's words "born of translation and in translation". The materials investigated include mainly theories of literary translation and span from the articles written in the 1900s by Ivan Franko, the initiator of translation research in Ukraine, to contemporary 'manifestos', notably by Maksym Strikha. The central insights of the paper would elicit the views on translation as a "cultural force and social capital" (Ivan Franko), "linguoaesthetic phenomenon" (Oleksandr Finkel, Mykola Zerov), 'stylization' (Volodymyr Derzhavyn), "functional stylistic parallel" (Maksym Rylskyi, Hryhoriy Kochur, Victor Koptilov), "cultural interpretation and re-creation" (Maryna Novykova), "identitarian act" (Maksym Strikha) employed in Ukrainian meta-reflection, but not restricted to Ukraine only. The ultimate objective is not to focus on the metaphorical plane of these conceptualizations but to re-visit them in analytical terms.

## 2 Why and How to 'Translate' Translation Studies

Alluding to a renowned assertion by Theo Hermans (2014, vii) that "Translation Studies need translation, in more than one sense", one of the strands in this complex understanding of translation is the meta-theoretical reflection on conceptual constructs, elaborated in lesser known disciplinary traditions. It would hence open the door for greater synthesis, reaching invariance in variance and reinforcing "theory in translation theory" (Chesterman 1993, 69). In this regard, Peeter Torop and Bruno Osimo (2010, 392) quite reasonably advocate the concept of "historical identity of translation", a notion that "may function as a bridge connecting the history and the general theory of translation" and that bolsters an intra-disciplinary dialogue within translation studies, in other words, makes translation studies dialogic, considering theoretical concepts not as closed—discrete in time and place—entities, but as open texts that actuate new interpretations. From such meta-perspective, histories of thinking on translation may also guide and form an "epistemological laboratory" (Dijksterhuis 1959, 165) so as to enable re-envisioning and identify opportunities for advancing translation research.

In the background chapter of the collective volume *Border Crossings: Translation Studies and other disciplines*, the editors clearly state that "the history of Translation Studies is still largely lacking—either external, elaborated retrospectively, or internal, as understood today by scholars themselves" (Gambier and van Doorslaer 2016, 5). This statement aptly points, first of all, to the problem of 'historiology', i.e., the methodology of writing history of translation studies, and, secondly, to the existence of external ("public science") and internal ("private science") modes of viewing any history of any discipline. Concerning the latter, any re-contextualization or re-consideration of a given translation concept is held against certain 'internalized' theoretical and epistemological dispositions on the part of its researcher and accords with his/her horizon and interests.

As for historiology, today we may witness the proliferation of nationally framed translation historiographies. Judith Woodsworth (2001, 101) once rightly asked: "Can one history paint an objective picture of changing ideas about translation?", Her question simultaneously brings about other questions: "Can a given theory exist and operate outside of history? Does scholarship function outside of culture?" (Lambert 2006, 81). Every translation scholar is profoundly affected by the way his/her culture "denotes, delineates and constructs translation" (Hermans 2002, 10); however, the concepts whose potency is entirely relative to a specific 'constellation'—whether real-world, spatio-temporal or theoretical—do not provide an adequate ground for scientific generalizations.

Andrew Chesterman, for instance, does not object to the claim that it is worth taking a given context of discovery into consideration when examining a hypothesis, since it is known that all thinking is affected by our culture, and conceptualization of translation is, in fact, socioculturally determined (Chesterman 2014). However, one cannot merely assess an idea or theory in accordance with its origin, in Chesterman's words (2014, 83), "because they arise there is a bad argument". Anthony Pym noted: "There are a hundred petty nationalisms operative in translation theory: every tradition invented its most valuable concepts first; every nation deserves better international recognition of its contribution" (Pym and Ayvazyan 2017, 240).

Underscoring the importance of not falling into the trap of "committing theory to cultural activism" (Simeoni 2008, 329), national translation historiographies are relevant for validating traditions in light of recent developments, since the institutionalization process is known to be anchored and heavily dependent on the disciplinary tradition in each culture which, for instance, 'moulds' the approaches to education in the area of translation at universities. As José Lambert states: "To the extent that universities still heavily represent national traditions, especially in matters of language and culture, it would be amazing if the field like Translation Studies did not reflect particular traditions" (Lambert and Brunelière 2016, 24).

In such a vein, historical reconstructions of different theoretical landscapes do increase our meta-awareness of translation studies and clarify the process of forming its entity. In addition, they also safeguard translation studies from "exaggerated claims of novelty, originality, breakthrough, and revolution in our (re)discoveries and, hence, lead to a less polemic discourse, to moderation in translation theory" (Kalnychenko 2017, 312). Novel conceptualizations are to stand the tests of fit and approbation to case studies so as to sustain their 'selection' for further effective integration into a discipline.

What is more, in many cases one tradition has directed the focus to issues which simply have not been considered by another school, so it is of definite value to gain the current of other orthodoxies without rejection of any principles of one's own and/or to learn about past theories in order to see why they were 'wrong' (Sampson 1980, 9). So critical re-reading of scholarly texts implies assessing the strength of their conceptual structures, their contribution and relevance, but not "judging them for failure to achieve objectives which were not on their authors' agenda" (Gile 2002, 150).

Undoubtedly, some theories are accepted more widely simply because they were not written in languages of lesser dissemination and, in fact, had an "increased chance of reception" (Schäffner 2017, 406). Today, a telling illustration of such academic obscurity of Central and Eastern European translation scholarship might be the legacy of Jiří Levý and Anton Popovič, Viktor Koptilov, Efim Etkind or Andrei Fedorov (see Špirk 2009; Pym and Ayvazyan 2014; Odrekhivska 2017b). Luc van Doorslaer (2017, 12–13) gave an interesting comparative study of Holmes' and Popovič's positions in translation studies bibliography, pointing to the fact that although they belonged to a similar research tradition and represented the same period, there is a significant quantitative difference in their presence in the world discourse of translation studies. Given this scenario, those who "wrote in their own languages and in their home countries are bound to be heard only by their local audience, however important and useful their work might have been for the rest of the world" (Susam-Sarajeva 2002, 202). Accepting the limitations within which translation theoreticians do work, the interpretive enterprise within translation studies—from translating as communicating 'unheard' theories in global languages, predominantly English, towards translating as re-thinking and re-conceptualizing them in new perspectives has been in progress (see Odrekhivska 2016; Odrekhivska 2017a). Taking into account its long-range promise is also a pursuit of the present study.

## 3 Historiosophy of Translation as a Direction

Almost three decades ago, during the 1991 Belgrade-based FIT Congress quite a visionary perspective was presented by Lieven D'hulst, later summarized by Judith Woodsworth: "Much work remains to be done in order to formulate adequate models [for writing history]. Other disciplines, such as the *philosophy of science*, can provide guidance" (2001, 101, my clarification and emphasis—I.O.). Philosophy of science, i.e., "a science of science", which reflects on the epistemology, causality, structure, and dynamics of science, still holds considerable relevance for contemporary translation historiography and generally translation studies. It is especially pertinent in the attempts of the latter to arrive one day at some platform of consolidation—shared ground—that would bring together differential conceptualizations. Having assembled extensive data in translation historiography, after "broadening the Translation Studies database" (Tymoczko 2014, 105), philosophy of science provides indispensable footing to hold a further insightful analysis into the "inner connection" of ideas and elaborate a conceptual unity which could link a number of theories across cultures and histories, forming so-called "nets of theories" (Elkana 1981, 14).

Certain foundational conceptions in the history and philosophy of science provide useful lens through which to view the scientific knowledge production in a discipline. Among the vogue and quite productive are Karl Popper's 'falsificationism' and "third world", or Thomas Kuhn's "paradigm shifts", and both have been operationalized in translation studies, notably by Andrew Chesterman and Mary Snell-Hornby. They were of great intellectual fit for marking the turns in the discipline of translation studies, for highlighting certain patterns in the elaboration of translation theories, and for abstracting the consensus on certain theoretical problems. More recent undertakings attempted at applying Luhmann's social system modeling to translation studies (see Tyulenev 2012) or relating Pierre Bourdieu's key concept of 'habitus' into translation metadiscussions (see Hanna 2016).

The historiosophy of translation generally departs from translation historiography and, by drawing heavily on the philosophy of science, is targeted at complex, relational interpretation of reasoning and change in translation conceptualization by considering the ontological, epistemological and methodological premises of a certain disciplinary tradition in a wider context. Therefore, the principle of relativity becomes the cornerstone of designing historiosophy of translation.

If translation historiography mainly concerns itself with discussing the development of conceptual networks in one tradition of thinking on translation, translation historiosophy is primed on setting the "network of conceptual networks", eliciting competing research programs in a diachronic perspective and manifesting how theories are developed, questioned, disputed, refuted and contemplated, how they are subjected to historically defined standards. My proposition to turn to the historiosophy of translation is a stimulus to start an "open-ended" discussion that would only benefit from multiplying points of view, stemming from various philosophical, historical and meta-theoretical perspectives. The general claim is to rely in principle on the lines of reasoning in the philosophy of science so as to put forward carefully grounded visions.

Hence, the vantage point selected for the present study—thematic analysis of science with its key notion of 'themata', was advocated by Gerald Holton, the Harvard physicist, philosopher and historian of science. Holton's conceptual nexus, elaborated in a series of book publications *Thematic Origins of Scientific Thought* (1973), *The Scientific Imagination* (1978), *Einstein and History and Other Passions* (1995), is the dimension of 'themata' that is considered to play a crucial role in the initiation and acceptance or rejection of certain key scientific insights. The scholar clearly stresses that themata have a profound impact on underwriting scientific explanations:

> It is the interdisciplinary spread or sharing of such fundamental themata that has produced something like a scientific imagination shared by all scientists, forming one of the bonds among them, and making possible the interdisciplinary approach that characterizes so many of the new developments.
>
> HOLTON 1988, 16

Furthermore, the philosopher underlines the productivity of themata in defining the character and substance of the discipline even in cases when it does not share a common theory: "The persistence in time [...] of these relatively few themata may be what endows science, despite all its growth and change, with what constant identity it has" (Holton 1975, 331).

Arguing for a thematic dimension in science, Holton distinguished between science in a sense of the "personal struggle" ($S_1$) and an institutional science ($S_2$), where the latter—public science, science of textbooks and of well-worked

# HISTORIOSOPHY OF TRANSLATION

clear concepts—is indifferent to the creativity of the scientist. Consequently, a new theory or scientific work is a tension-filled event, emanating from criss-crossing matrices of ideas, visions and motivations (between $S_1$ and $S_2$). Holton places much attention on the role of creativity in scientific endeavors ($S_1$), asking what leads the scientist to pose certain questions and interpret data in accordance with specific patterns.

From this standpoint, if we want to understand how concepts and scientific ideas evolve, it is necessary to define a three-dimensional x-y-z space (not merely x-y contingent plane) within which a more complete analysis of scientific statements and processes should proceed (Holton 1988, 14). To outline, x-dimension is determined by the internal logic and structure of the science in a definite period, y-dimension stands for the external socio-cultural conditions in the development of science in the period, while z-axis, perpendicular to the x- and y-axes of the contingent plane, is thematic, i.e., preferences to certain kinds of concepts, methods, forms of solution etc. (Holton 1988, 13). To proceed, the thematic structure of the scientific work emerges from the study of the options that were in principle open to a scientist and culminates in understanding the "thematic commitment of a scholar" (Holton 1975, 333).

Furthermore, Holton (1988:16–17) admitted that for every thematically informed theory in any science there is invariably a theory using the opposite thema, i.e., antithema. Apparently, the changes do take place on the level of thematic orientation of researchers. It is possible to outline such scenarios that would elucidate the mechanisms how themata change: previous themes may become only schemes that gain new content; old themes are changed with alternative ones, or substituted with the opposite; the changes in the structure of the themata may result in maintaining a part of the previous theme and the substitution of another part with a new one, and new themes may appear. In addition, Holton's theory manifests that one of the forces or stimuli to enhance the science is the 'competition' of themata. Through thematic analysis, controversies in science may be viewed from an alternative perspective: "For example, the awareness of themata which are sometimes held with obstinate loyalty helps to explain the character of the discussion between antagonists far better than do scientific and social content alone" (Holton 1975, 331).

Re-reading diverse studies, recurrent themata and thematic couples can be delineated that ground the preconceptions of scholars, namely: complementarity, constancy, hierarchy, infinity, planum, symmetry, unity, discontinuity – continuum, evolution – devolution, reductionism – holism, simplicity – complexity, etc. Thematic analysis lies not in adopting "a label" or "taking a side," but in understanding the process of 'innovation' in the actual work of scholars. According to Holton (1975, 333), the "search for answers in the history of science is itself imbued with themata" which leads to posing a question why some themata are disregarded, some rise from oblivion, while others have only appeared in the discipline very recently. Interestingly, the philosopher—with a pertinent reference to chaos—enlists complexity as a new but neglected theme in the scholarly discourse (see Holton 1988), which is presently sketching its place in the theory of translation (see Marais 2014).

Viability of 'thematics' in the framework of translation historiosophy lies in the identification of 'vertical' overarching themata in a certain tradition of translation theorization that may as well predict its course of development and further 'events'. Thereon—despite the differences in nationally-framed translation historiographies—themata might become a "common denominator" to relate, connect and compare translation conceptualizations in one interpretational space. In other words, by linking themata profiles it would be possible to elaborate a network of translation conceptualizations in a global spectrum. To note, productive attempts at thematizing the comparability of translation conceptualizations have been initiated by the research group under the lead of Sergey Tyulenev at the Centre for Intercultural Mediation at the University of Durham, who also spearheaded the publication of the special 2017 issue "Toward Comparative Translation and Interpreting Studies" of the journal *Translation and Interpreting Studies* (see Tyulenev and Zheng, 2017).

## 4 From Historiography to Historiosophy of Translation in Ukraine

A shift of emphasis towards foregrounding translation historiography as a research area took place in the Ukrainian studies on translation in the post-independence period, i.e., since 1990s. Translation historiographers turned to re-narration by dethroning the dominant Soviet epoch-framed narrative ($S_2$) that lacked thematic understanding of the local Ukrainian tradition, imposed methodological limitations and "forcefully silenced the Ukrainian advances in translation theory" (Pym 2016).

Beyond any doubts, a dialogue between "internal central players" in the former Soviet space (on the basis of all-Soviet symposia and on the platform of Moscow-based periodicals *Masterstvo perevoda* [Art of Translation] and *Tetradi perevodchika* [Translator's Notes] or Kyiv-published one *Teoriya i praktyka perekladu* [Theory and Practice of Translation]) played quite an influential role in translation theory development, however it is a rather simplistic premise to talk about a 'general' monolithic Soviet theory of translation.

# HISTORIOSOPHY OF TRANSLATION                                      43

Translation studies scholars manifest that one may only infer a set of principles (undoubtedly, with ideological tonality) that define the scholarly discourse on translation for all researchers working within the former Soviet institutional translation studies (see Komissarov 1976; Levý 1970). Specifically, three key stances were of paradigmatic 'mainstream' mandate: possible translatibility of every work; the need to reproduce a "formed content" of the source text; and dialectics of the unit and the whole of the literary work to be transposed in translation.

A return to itself in the Ukrainian science sets out the process of enquiry into the foundations and development of research on translation in Ukraine. It has become apparent that translation studies in the Ukrainian domain constitutes a complex, dynamic and non-linear system of translation conceptualizations, since translation scholars aimed not to merely theorize, but to problematize and model the translation practice in the Ukrainian culture so as to expose a broader scope of the phenomenon of translation. Apart from 'institutional' research on translation, represented by university professors and academicians (Maxym Rylskyi, Mykola Bazhan, Viktor Koptilov, Maryna Novykova et al.), one cannot but mention visionary texts on translation authored by 20th-century exile translators and scholars-dissidents who remained 'informal' prophets (Mykola Zerov, Hryhoriy Kochur, Mykola Lukash).

Given this, the research in translation historiography in the Ukrainian context processed through the following three phases: (1) re-discovery in archives and anthologization of theoretical and critical works on translation authored by one scholar; (2) compilation of tempo-specific Ukrainian readers of seminal texts in translation theory with extensive introductory notes; (3) elaboration of historiographic accounts and bibliographies. To be precise, the research resulted in the re-publication of all major—heretofore unavailable to a wider readership—texts in the history of Ukrainian translation scholarship: 2003 collected edition of Mykola Zerov's *Ukrayinske pysmenstvo* [Ukrainian Literature] (see Zerov 2003) which comprised, among others, his 1928 paper *U spravi virshovanoho perekladu* [On the Problems of Verse Translation], 2007 republication of Oleksandr Finkel's 1929 monograph *Teoriya i praktyka perekladu* [Theory and Practice of Translation] jointly with Finkel's papers on translation history, self-translation and re-translation (see Finkel 2007), 2008 two-volume edition *Literatura i pereklad* [Literature and Translation] of Hryhoriy Kochur's works in translation theory, criticism and history (see Kochur 2008), 2015 collection of papers by Volodymyr Derzhavyn (see Derzhavyn 2015) etc.

The first attempt at providing a systematic account of Ukrainian translation historiography with a detailed account of its key periods and problematics is the 2009 monograph *Istoriya ukrayinskoho perekladoznavstva XX storichchia* [History of Translation Studies in the 20th-century Ukraine] by the Lviv-based scholar Taras Shmiher (see Shmiher 2009). Worth mentioning is the joint initiative of the Department of Translation Studies and Contrastive Linguistics at Ivan Franko National University of Lviv to compile the bibliographical guide *Translation Studies in the 20th-century Ukraine*, published under the lead of Taras Shmiher in 2013 (see Shmiher 2013).

Taking advantage of such rigorous consolidations of the 'past' and straying from the assertion that every epoch has its understanding of the concept 'translation' (Rylskyi 1975, 69), it proves valid to identify implicit themes of the Ukrainian discourse on translation and to highlight conceptual threads that run through the theories elaborated herein, pinpointing how historical past is related or has led to the historical present.

## 5    Translation as a Cultural Force and Social Capital

In the Ukrainian scholarship, translation has invariably been conceptualized as a cultural act since the meta-discussions initiated in early 20th century by Ivan Franko, a Ukrainian intellectual and poet-translator-scholar, who lived during the Austro-Hungarian Empire. As in the Russian Empire (present-day Ukraine was then split between two empires) Ukrainian language was officially banned in public use since 1863, it was the Western part of the country, known as Eastern Halychyna (Galicia) under the far more liberal Habsburg Empire, that was able to accommodate the Ukrainian press, academia and schools. Deeply committed to the Ukrainian cause, Franko claimed that translation could become a force for empowering the oppressed and inferior Ukrainian culture.

In 1880, his Ukrainian translation of an excerpt from *Faust* by Johann Wolfgang Goethe was published in Lviv-based journal *Pravda*, to which Franko had prepared a brilliantly polemical preface under the title *U nas nema literatury!* [We do not have literature!]. Due to its debatable and uncompromising character the foreword was barred from print. Made public only in 1941, the preface crystallizes Franko's strategic views on translation as an indispensable element in the "entire cultural organism" that fosters the resistance to the assimilative work of dominant cultures and constructs instead the identity of Ukrainians. The same message runs across Franko's review of Stanisław Przybyszewski's selected poetry in the Ukrainian translation where the critic articulated, among other things, the criteria of social relevance in consolidating translation repertoire: "What could the translator fancy in this collection and wanted to introduce to our society?" (Franko 1981, 32—Translated by I.O.). In addition, he openly undermined then-running translation projects of decadent literature, claiming their irrelevance for the Ukrainian culture of that period. Ancient literature, Dante and Shakespeare, Byron and Shelley, Goethe and Schiller were the pillars of his translatorship. Franko believed that Ukrainian translations of world classics would become the cultural capital of the nation and hence boost the degree of its prestige and recognition. In a continuous critical dialogue on translations, he underlined:

> Embarking on evaluating the literary work, I consider it to be a fact of "spiritual" history of the society in question as well as a fact of the individual history of a certain writer. So I attempt at treating it by way of historical and psychological methods. When examining the genesis, worth and scope of the literary piece, I try to position it through the lens of our contemporary societal aspirations and cultural needs, and ask myself what is valuable, educational and beneficial in it for us, in other words— whether and to what extent the writer and his/her work has value for us to presently read, study, engage and reconsider.
>
> FRANKO 1980, 311—Translated by I.O.

In this regard, the scholar was quite resolute about choosing those works for translation that align with and promote social, political and cultural beliefs of Ukrainians, thus refraining from translating foreign writings which would not present the anticipated cultural or symbolic profit. Apart from treating translation as a deliberate act of socially conditioned selection, Franko consistently stressed the importance of paratexts (prefaces, footnotes, commentaries etc.) that enabled common people to perceive the literary piece. It follows that the critic consistently epitomized both—the social function of translation and a translator as a constructing subject in the society, considering translation to be a social capital of a cultural nation. To note, Franko translated into Ukrainian the 24th chapter of the first volume of *Das Kapital* by Karl Marx, and was the first Ukrainian translator and scholar who dealt with his theory. Intrigued by Marxian general propositions on capital, Franko implicitly transplanted some ideas on translation.

Franko's particular choice of focus concerning translation conceptualization was conditioned by "culture-centrism" of his general scholarly practice (or scientific Weltanschauung), the socio-political circumstances of Ukrainian scholarship (y-dimension) as well as his awareness of German philosophy and

Marxism which in fact shaped his thematic commitment (z-axis) to treat translation in 'unity' with the culture and to view it as part of societal 'dynamics.' What is more, with time it led to his inauguration of social institutionalization of research on literary translation within the Ukrainian context (x-dimension), integrating translation problematics into the content of then-leading journal *Literaturno-naukovyi visnyk*.

In 1911, Franko—already with a detachment of a scholar—presented the first insightful study on translation in the Ukrainian scholarship *Kameniari. Ukrainskyi text i polskyi pereklad. Deshcho pro shtuku perekladannia* [The Stone Crashers. Ukrainian Text and Polish Translation. On Some Aspects of the Art of Translation], in which he put forward the holistic vision of translation as "historical literary" fact and an "aesthetic phenomenon". Ivan Franko claims that translation as a 'literary' fact forms a vital part in the emanation of cultural reality and literature in the target medium: "Successful translations of important and influential works in every cultured nation, starting from Romans, belonged to the foundations of their own literature. The translations of ancient Greek and Roman texts did play a beneficial role for Western European literatures" (Franko 1983, 7—Translated by I.O.).

Dependent on the artistic continuum of the target culture, translation is simultaneously an aesthetic whole, an entity constituted by the level of translator's 'grasp' of the source text—"whether the faithful and insightful or superficial one" (Franko 1983, 9). Franko discussed the aesthetics of translation in stylistic terms, drawing crucial attention to the range and depth of changes in the target version. Reproduction of key "units of meaning" (rhythm, metaphors, 'vertical' images, allusions etc.) and of the overall interrelation of *minutae* and the whole of the source text are regarded by Franko as core maxims for a translator, since any translation that overuses poetic license subverts the single, general *impressio* of the original, provoking its unfaithful psychological and stylistic picture (Franko 1983, 10). This stance is definitely not novel and alludes to German Romanticist translation hermeneutics, yet it launched discussions on translation quality in the Ukrainian context.

Having defended in 1893 his doctoral thesis in Vienna, Franko was generally well-read in German philosophy and cultural psychology. Under the influence of Wilhelm Wundt's theories, the scholar put an emphasis on psychological, individual facets of the translation act, accentuating translator's associative power to give analogies and transplant the phenomenal character and ideational structure of the source text into the target version.

The development of Franko's views on translation marks a balance between a socially centered and culture-participative conceptualization of translation pointing towards an aesthetically-focused elaboration of translation culture in

HISTORIOSOPHY OF TRANSLATION  47

his later years. It underscores his adherence to the themes of 'unity' and 'dynamism' in his logic of studies on translation.

## 6    Translation as a Linguoaesthetic Phenomenon

Oleksandr Finkel, a Kharkiv-based translation theoretician and the author of the first systematic book on translation in the entire USSR (see Finkel 2007), was familiar with critical works on translation by Ivan Franko and developed further his stance that translation should be viewed through its cultural and social function in aesthetic manifestation. Despite the fact that the scholarly setting (y-dimension) was already different, as Russian Formalism gained prominence, Ukrainian modernism in literature was flourishing, and the discussion of Humboldt and Potebnia's conceptualities were lively in academia, Franko's premises did provide the structure for Oleksandr Finkel's theorization (x-axis).

Finkel's famous assertion that "the problem of translation starts when the problem of the word is finished" (Finkel 2007, 56) clearly exhibits his optics on viewing translation as a complex aesthetic system within a system of culture. When Finkel turned his focus on Fiodor Batiushkov's essay in now legendary 1920 Russian collection, *Printsypy khudozhestvennoho perevoda* [The Principles of Literary Translation], he entered a hot debate at the time that prompted the discussion of different approaches to translation presented by Kornei Chukovskiy, Nikolai Humiliov and Batiushkov himself. In Finkel's critique, Batiushkov's paper obtained a different valence in the Ukrainian theoretical discourse since the Russian translation historiography had foregrounded his postulate on possible translatability of any text. Finkel (2007, 60) principally reflected on Batiushkov's elaboration of translation tendencies that derive from cultural and social premises, as in the following scenarios: (1) when the translator belongs to a nation which regards itself culturally superior, he/she is predisposed to produce an unfaithful translation; (2) the opposite condition tends towards a 'slavish' dependence on the source language; and (3) when working between cultures that perceive each other as equals, the translator aspires to achieve thematic and stylistic adequacy (Batiushkov 1920). This approach alludes today to the renowned postulates of Itamar Even-Zohar's model.

For Finkel (2007, 61–62) this delineation might show validity in some cases but it sketches the tendencies without presenting insight into the stylistic essence of translations. A scrupulous analysis may reveal that some translations exhibit simultaneously all three tendencies at once: in some parts—copying the source text structures, in others—correcting, yet in others—adequately reproducing the style. Finkel argues that aside from the cultural context, the stylistic character of translations is heavily conditioned by aesthetic views of the epoch which influence translation method. The stylistics of translation is precisely its linguoaesthetics that makes it possible to treat the literary work as a symbolic manifestation of a certain worldview.

In Finkel's language, if the lingual aesthetics of the translated text lies in its stylistics, then the stylistic choices of the translator are dependent, first of all, on his/her understanding of the relations between the parts of the source text, and, secondly, their role in uncovering the deep meaning as well as authorial poetics (Finkel 2007). The value of any translation is hence determined by its degree of proximity to the entirety of sense actualized in the reproduction of lexis, semantics, imagery and emotional tone, in preserving rhythmical, intonation specificities and sound patterning.

Finkel's ideas accorded with those of his Ukrainian peer Mykola Zerov, who introduced the typology of translation genres (from travesty to translation), based on linguoaesthetic desiderata, that later found fuller elaboration in Ilko Korunets' matrices of translation (see Korunets 2008). A matrix product, translation is a result of the transposition of external and internal matrices of the source text. While the external matrix embraces dominant formal peculiarities, including rhythm, intonation, sound patterning and lexical choices, the internal matrix is built on imagery, semantic loading, ideational structure and allusions (all have an inextricable link to the source culture).

Considering translation as a hierarchical system, Finkel also prioritizes the role of "the dominant": "Every literary piece has its central, the most important element, and this aesthetic, historical and cultural dominant can be found in different dimensions of the work" (Finkel 1929, 166). The dominant, according to the scholar, depicts the artistry of the literary piece and cannot be neglected in the process of translation so as not to lose the symbolism of the work in question.

Following thus Franko's theme of 'unity', Finkel centered his translation concept on the theme of 'hierarchy': translation is a hierarchical aesthetic system; the re-creation of the literary dominant is the critical point in every translation act.

## 7 Translation as Stylization

In the 1920s, Oleksandr Finkel, Mykola Zerov and the Russian theoretician Andrei Fedorov entered an interesting debate with Volodymyr Derzhavyn,

# HISTORIOSOPHY OF TRANSLATION

who was an exponent of "homological translation" (Derzhavyn 2015, 192). Derzhavyn launched a theory of translation-stylization in his 1927 paper *Problemy virshovanoho perekladu* [The Problems of Poetry Translation], stressing that the widespread statement about the "stylistic correspondence to the source text" lacks specificity. Member of the Kharkiv circle of translation scholars and collaborating with the colleagues from Kyiv, thus working along the same the x-y axis, Derzhavyn adopted a different thematic commitment, presumably the anti-thema.

Derzhavyn draws a distinction between analogical translation (in present terms, domestication) and homological translation (foreignization, correspondingly), and operates on the assumption that the translator should, in principle, not adhere to the normative structures of the target language, but attempt at such combination of target-language patterns (even while violating them) that could be convergent with the aesthetics of the literary language used in the source text (Derzhavyn 2015, 53). Having a "fantastic erudition backed up with a sophisticated literary taste" (Kachurovskyi 1991, 113), he argued for a more foreignizing approach:

> First and foremost, we need to admit that literary translation is to be—when possible—literal, which lies not in rendering separately each word of the source text, but in the fact that the artistic (literary) value of any sentence, word, grammatical or phonetic structure should find its reproduction in the style of the target text. For many, this translation would seem too exotic and even close to parody; let it be so—the stylistic tact of the translator always determines whether to preserve a line between a stylization and a parody or not ...
>
> DERZHAVYN 2015, 57—Translated by I.O.

For the scholar, the artistry of translation indeed rests on its virtuosic correspondence to the artistry of the source text, even if Derzhavyn's call for stylistic accuracy, for "intellectually challenging" so-called "textual literalism", is to be differentiated from understanding literalism as a mere transfer of dictionary meanings of the source text elements. Translation-stylization demands a high level of literary and linguistic sophistication on the part of the target reader as well as open-mindedness towards exoticisms (Derzhavyn 2015, 58).

Be that as it may, Finkel dedicated his 1929 monograph *Theory and Practice of Translation* to Derzhavyn, still refuting his definition of translation as stylization:

> Stylization is possible within one language: the Ukrainian language of the 20th century can be stylized into the language of the 17th century, or the poetic means of one literary trend can be altered with the devices of the other. Yet the Ukrainian language cannot be stylized into Chinese or any other ....
>
> FINKEL 2007, 73—Translated by I.O.

Furthermore, for Finkel (2007, 73) the weakness of Derzhavyn's proposition resides in its neglect of social and cultural substance of the stylistic elements of a given literary piece which therefore has an impact on their rendition. Finkel asserts that the concrete sense of the metaphor might totally depend on sociocultural conditions, thus "translation is not the reproduction of pure ideal stylistics, but the perception of the foreign culture" (Finkel 2007, 74). Later in his article on Oleksandr Finkel as a theoretician, Iaremiya Aizenshtok (1970, 105) would call Derzhavyn's conception to be the extreme embodiment of translation formalism.

To sum up, Derzhavyn's ground-breaking ideas (as for early 20th century Ukraine) echo Schleiermacher's line of thinking on foreignizing translation. In our view, it displays Ukrainian scholar's guiding conceptual theme of aesthetic 'symmetry' of the target version to its proto- or source text.

## 8    Translation as a Functional Stylistic Parallel

In the 1950–1970s, Ukrainian translation scholarship, represented chiefly by Maksym Rylskyi, Hryhoriy Kochur and Viktor Koptilov, set out to frame the culture of translation in Ukraine, advocating for a 'balanced' approach to translation. It was targeted at bringing to equilibrium a source-oriented, 'reproductive' norm of translation and aesthetically-driven view of translation as a target-language production, as a fact of the Ukrainian literary field (in this case).

In this new frame, translation is a creative act, and the translator a co-creator of the literary work (Rylskyi 1975, 79). Nicolai Gogol's maxim, "sometimes the translator needs to take a step back in order to get closer to the source text," was often quoted (see Rylskyi 1975, 67) alongside the prioritized conventions about "internal affinity" and empathy to authorial style, the "ability to enter" the world of the author and to reproduce faithfully his/her tonality" (Rylskyi 1975, 80).

"Translator-centered" discussion of creativity is aptly illustrated with Maksym Rylskyi's quotation (1975, 60) when Alexander Tvardovky comments

# HISTORIOSOPHY OF TRANSLATION

on Samuil Marshak's translation of Burns' poetry, "He made him Russian, leaving him to be Scottish", and Rylskyi's addition—"He made him Marshak, leaving him to be Burns". In the same vein, Hryhoriy Kochur, in his papers on translatorship of prominent Ukrainian writers, observes that the features of a translator's poetics become quite noticeable when viewing various translations by one translator, even though the same features may remain invisible in separate texts. For Kochur, every translation is provisional, having the imprint of the translator's worldview, hence the historically situated function of the translated text. The same reasoning valorizes retranslations because it foregrounds translation multiplicity: every new translation "opens news facets of the source text and helps to cognize it deeper, but the process of cognition is limitless" (Koptilov 1972, 115—Translated by I.O.).

The theoretical underpinning of the 1970s' translation conceptualizations was based on functional structuralism, since Koptilov drew considerably from Jiří Levý, Zenon Klemensiewicz and Olgierd Wojtasiewicz; yet the discourse of the period also brought about an "enhanced" conceptualization of translation as a 'parallel' production. In more specific terms, translation was positioned to "preserve an ideational and imagery structure of the source text and become its semantic-stylistic parallel in the target culture" (Koptilov 1971, 52—Translated by I.O.). The expression "semantic-stylistic parallel" was chosen to indicate the 'creative' (as opposed to 'copying' or literalist) nature of translation (see Odrekhivska 2017b). Nonetheless, the notion of translation as a parallel text— by preserving the ideational and imagery structure of the original—limited the "creative freedom" of the translator by establishing certain boundaries (Koptilov 1971, 54).

Koptilov further argued that the translator's consciousness builds the "intermediate instance" between the source and target texts which is the result of the first and simultaneously the working sketching for the construction of the second. This abstract sketch anchors the crucial points—artistic dominants— of the source text, signifies the functionality of the target text and delineates 'translatemes', which are defined as follows:

> In the realistic drama or comedy the translateme might involve the speech act exchange between the characters, in lyrical poetry it could be approximated to a metaphor or simile, while in the text of the novel or short story it might extend from a sentence to a whole paragraph. In each instance, translateme stands as a certain "atom of the content" that cannot be subdivided without ruining this content.
>
> KOPTILOV 2003, 13—Translated by I.O.

Translateme is of relational nature and construed in each and every case. If the translator takes on a diametrically opposing orientation in his production—by not drawing the semantic-stylistic parallel with the preservation of ideational and imagery structure—and views instead a source text as a 'raw' material for his/her experimentation, Koptilov calls this derivative literary work a 'pseudotranslation' which, incidentally, assumes a different meaning in the Ukrainian tradition from the one accepted in the Western discourse.

With this in mind, we may postulate that the Ukrainian scholarship of this period theorized translation along the thematic concept of 'balance'.

## 9 Translation as Cultural Interpretation and Re-creation

Elaborating a culture-interpretational approach to translation in the mid-1980s, Maryna Novykova (1986, 4) agreed with the assertion that every translation is interpretation, and every interpretation is, in principle, multiple, personal and personalized. In her framework, translational interpretation is dependent on the interpretational setting of a translator as well as on interpretational resources of a source text. Interpretational setting of a translator supports a dynamic, systematic and individual approach to viewing the text, which functions like a filter, passing the information it is set on and transforming or leaving the rest of it (Novykova 1986, 85). Filtering involves a text's content and style and embraces not only the source text but the whole literature, culture and history (ibid.). Interpretational resources of the text comprise all internal meaningful and formative links, and cohesive devices which the translator views in a unified system (Novykova 1986, 138). The introduction of the target text—as the product of translational interpretation—into the target culture is a complex dialogic re-creation of the text and the—broader—the context. For Novykova (1986, 136), the translated text is a new system, never identical to the authorial one, or to the other translations of the same original.

Every translation has its context, built on the interplay of the translator's context and the text's unique linguistic and historical, social and aesthetic contexts particular to its epoch. The novelty of Novykova's contribution to the Ukrainian discourse is evident in her shift of emphasis from the source-text context towards the "translational contexts", defined as "complex multi-layer interrelations between the target text and the target culture" (Novykova 1986, 169). Arguing that the translation draws its value, function and overall meaning from translational contexts, the scholar expounded key dimensions of their interrelation as follows:

# HISTORIOSOPHY OF TRANSLATION

(1) the context of "translation cycle", when translations are selected according to unifying features and grouped to create a new dialogue, i.e., translator's anthologies, selected poetry collections in translation etc.;

(2) the context of the entire "translator's oeuvre";

(3) the context of the "stylistic tradition and poetics" in the target language;

(4) the context of the "national culture", which relates to the norms, conventions and preferences developed in a certain epoch;

(5) the 'international' context, which allows to cross the boundaries of one culture and to observe the trends in the inter-cultural spectrum, for instance, the culture of translation in the Eastern European countries (Novykova 1986, 169–210).

Consequently, Novykova states that multiple translations allow us to understand the text better, since it is through these translations the text discloses how dynamic it is, how inextricably it is linked with the system of contexts—authorial, translational—creating together not a sum but a dialogue, thus showing the objective interpretational resources of the literary work in question (Novykova 1986, 101).

Considering the abovementioned, one can encapsulate that Novykova's conceptualization of translation as cultural interpretation and contextual recreation fits within the thematic frame of 'holism' that attempts at drawing an encompassing image of the phenomenon of translation with zoom-in and zoom-out options.

## 10 Translation as an Identity-Forming Act

In 1995, the Kyiv-based publishing house *Dnipro* under the editorship of Mykhailo Moskalenko published a grand-anthology *A Thousand Years. Poetry Translation in Ukraine-Rus'*, where all outstanding, inaccessible and even some legendary translated texts as well as plethora of proscribed translations were finally printed for the Ukrainian readership. Aside from this, the launch of research on Bible translation into Ukrainian, the publication of several translators' anthologies and the critical studies of translations published in diaspora explicitly demonstrated the crucial role of translation in forming Ukrainian cultural identity through the 20th century. These developments found their theoretical treatment in Maksym Strikha's 2006 book *Ukrainian Literary Translation: between Literature and Nation-Building*.

Taking into account that translation is a purpose-driven activity, Strikha (2006, 8) initiated a discussion about the intended audience of translations into Ukrainian in the early decades of the 19th century when Ukraine was under the colonial rule. Since all literate Ukrainians of that epoch could read translations into either Polish or Russian, and even some were competent enough to read the texts in French or Latin, Ukrainian translations of Virgil, Horace, Mickiewicz and Pushkin were undoubtedly not targeted at bringing these texts to a "new audience," rather they were aimed at 'returning' the educated Ukrainians and intellectuals to the Ukrainian language, giving them pleasure to read world classics in their native language and showing the potential of its further development. Therefore, in the Ukrainian domain translation played a nation-making function. Translation into Ukrainian showed the possibility of direct—without any mediators—'communication' of Ukrainian culture with foreign literatures and refuted a stereotyped vision of the Ukrainian language as a "home dialect of peasantry" (Strikha 2006, 10). In this regard, the language of translations always played an identitarian function in the Ukrainian milieu. Due to the absence of higher strata of Ukrainian-language society, it was through translations that the Ukrainian lexis was formed in the spheres, namely army, church, administration and science, where it could not be coined otherwise (Strikha 2006, 11–12). Likewise, the choice of works for translation was deliberate and relied on a well-thought cultural and political program, which is reminiscent of Franko's statements in the early 20th century.

In his reasoning, Strikha (2006, 12) puts forward the idea that translation in Ukraine is to be conceptualized as a very complex self-organized entity, which formed a particular "nation-making" relationship among literate Ukrainians in the 19th century. Analogies on such role of translations can be drawn only in 'small' nations, the neighboring Russian or Polish literatures never treated translation in such profile (Strikha 2006, 13). Given this, translation in the local vein is treated as an identity-forming act, constituted by language and text choices, ideological and historical factors etc., simultaneously playing an immense role in the emergence of the present-day cultural reality of Ukraine. Translation has been and still is a force for knowledge enhancement and integration, creating a dialogue inside the culture and society, which even dominated the dialogue outside the culture.

To conclude, the thematic concept of 'synergy' fully designates the orientation in translation research, adopted—yet not explicitly—by Maksym Strikha. By adopting key translation theorizations in Ukraine (x-axis), as well as focusing on the socio-historical calls in the studies on translation in the 21st-century Ukraine, Strikha took a novel approach in treating translation as a conceptual prism (z-axis) that promoted the self-organization of the Ukrainian culture and literary field.

# HISTORIOSOPHY OF TRANSLATION

## 11     Instead of Conclusions: Themata of the Ukrainian Tradition in Translation Studies

Contemporary translation studies in Ukraine are based more on reflections articulated within the national borders, however they do not deliberately 'exclude' interest in other translation conceptualizations elsewhere. The principal point is to surpass the borders and enable a synthetic representation of the histories of translation conceptualizations in various veins with due regard to their "vertical themata". To this end, embarking on a wide-ranging interpretative enterprise of differential translation theories that would lead to their productive 'afterlife', in Walter Benjamin's terms, it is essential to trace their core premises in the three-dimensional spectrum (x-y-z space) which conditioned the scholar either to solicit the institutional (perhaps, 'local') discourse ($S_2$), or to take a personal scholarly initiative of challenging it ($S_1$). Holton's framework seems very effective in terms of taking a bird's-eye view on the development of translation theories and ingraining new ideas into the existing concepts.

The central insights of this paper—most prominent 20th-century Ukrainian translation conceptualizations—form a network of working concepts that foster not a unidirectional, but a multisided vision of translation—as a cultural act, as a social capital, as a *linguoaesthetic* phenomenon, as a target-language stylization, and as a cultural re-creation and identity-forming action. The existence of this set of translation concepts is grounded on the local scholarly practice and is confined to the three-dimensional x-y-z space which determined the scientific imagination and thematic commitments of key actors. To sum up, vertical 'themata' of Ukrainian theoretical tradition encompass the trajectory of such thematic concepts in developing the thoughts on translation: unity → dynamism → hierarchy → symmetry → balance → holism → synergy. In the historiosophical redux, the mentioned themata mark the meaning of studies on translation as a whole in this tradition, as well as the common ground with other traditions that must be at work.

### References

Aizenshtok, Ieremiya. 1970. "A.M. Finkel—teoretyk khudozhestvennoho perevoda." [A.M. Finkel—Literary Translation Theoritician]. *Masterstvo perevoda* 7: 91–118.

Batiushkov, Fiodor. 1920. "Zadachi khudozhestvennogo perevoda" [Problems of Literary Translation]. In *Printsypy khudozhestvennogo perevoda [The Principles of*

*Literary Translation*], edited by Fiodor Batiushkov, Nikolai Gumiliov, and Kornei Chukovski, 7–15. Petersburg: Vsemirnaya literatura. Gosudarstvennoie izdatelstvo.

Ceccherelli, Andrea, Lorenzo Constantino, and Cristiano Diddi, eds. 2015. *Translation Theories in the Slavic Countries*. Salerno: Università di Salerno.

Chesterman, Andrew. 1993. "Theory in translation theory." *The New Courant* 1: 69–79.

Chesterman, Andrew. 2014. "Universalism in translation studies." *Translation Studies* 7 (1): 82–90.

Derzhavyn, Volodymyr. 2015. *Pro Mystetstvo Perekladu. Statti i retsenzii 1927–1931 rokiv* [*On the Art of Translation. Articles and Reviews 1927–1931*], edited by Oleksandr Kalnychenko, and Yuliya Poliakova. Vinnytsia: Nova Knyha.

Dijksterhuis, Eduard. 1959. "The origins of classical mechanics." In *Critical Problems in the History of Science*, edited by Marshall Clagett, 163–184. Madison: University Wisconsin Press.

Elkana, Yehuda. 1981. "A programmatic attempt at an anthropology of knowledge." *Sciences and Cultures. Sociology of the Sciences*, 5: 1–76.

Finkel, Oleksandr. 2007. *Oleksandr Finkel—zabutyi teoretyk ukrayinskoho perekladoznavstva: zbirka vybranykh prats* [*Oleksandr Finkel—The Forgotten Theoritician of Translation Studies in Ukraine: Selected Works*], edited by Leonid Chernovatyi et al. Vinnytsia: Nova Knyha.

Franko, Ivan. 1980. "Vidpovid krytykovi Perebendi." [The Response to the Critic of Perebendia]. In *Zibrannia tvoriv u 50 tomakh. Tom 27. Literaturno-krytychni pratsi (1886–1889)*, edited by Stepan Shchurat, 308–311. Kyiv: Naukova dumka.

Franko, Ivan. 1981. "Stanisław Przhybyszewski z tsyklu Wigilii, pereklav Antin Krushelnytskyi: retsenziya." [Stanisław Przhybyszewski from the cycle Wigilii, translated by Antin Krushelnytskyi: review]. In *Zibrannia tvoriv u 50 tomakh. Tom 32. Literaturno-krytychni pratsi (1899–1901)*, edited by Yevhen Kyryliuk, 32–33. Kyiv: Naukova dumka.

Franko, Ivan. 1983. "Kameniari. Ukrayinskyi tekst i polskyi pereklad: deshcho pro shtuku perekladannia" [Kameniari. Ukrainian Text and Polish Translation: On Some Aspects of the Art of Translation]. In *Zibrannia tvoriv u 50 tomakh. Tom 39. Literaturno-krytychni pratsi (1911–1914)*, edited by Volodymyr Krekoten, 7–20. Kyiv: Naukova dumka.

Gambier, Yves, and Luc van Doorslaer, eds. 2016. *Border Crossings: Translation Studies and Other Disciplines*. Amsterdam: John Benjamins.

Gile, Daniel. 2002. "Being constructive about Shared Ground: A response to Andrew Chesterman and Rosemary Arrojo's forum statement." *Target* 13 (1): 149–153.

Gile, Daniel. 2012. "Institutionalization of translation studies." In *Handbook of Translation Studies, vol. 3*, edited by Yves Gambier and Luc van Doorslaer, 73–80. Amsterdam: John Benjamins.

Hanna, Sameh. 2016. *Bourdieu in translation studies: The socio-cultural dynamics of Shakespeare translation in Egypt*. New York: Routledge.

Hermans, Theo. 2002. "Paradoxes and aporias in translation and translation studies." In *Translation Studies: Perspectives on an Emerging Discipline*, edited by Alessandra Riccardi, 10–23. Cambridge University Press.

Hermans, Theo. 2014. *Translation in systems: Descriptive and system-oriented approaches explained*. London and New York: Routledge.

Holmes, James. 1988. "The name and nature of translation studies." In *Translated! Papers on Literary Translation and Translation Studies*, edited by James S. Holmes, 67–80. Amsterdam: Rodopi.

Holton, Gerald. 1975. "On the role of themata in scientific thought." *Science, New Series*, 188 (4186): 328–334.

Holton, Gerald. 1988. *Thematic origins of scientific thought: from Kepler to Einstein*. Cambridge and London: Harvard University Press.

Jettmarová, Zuzana. 2005. "East Meets West: On social agency in translation studies paradigms." In *New Trends in Translation Studies. In Honour of Kinga Klaudy*, edited by Krisztina Karoly, Agota Foris, et al., 95–105. Budapest: Akadémiai Kiadó.

Kachurovskyi, Ihor. 1991. "Perekladachi ukrainskoyi diaspory" [Translators in the Ukrainian Diaspora]. *Vsesvit*, 11: 109–113.

Kalnychenko, Oleksandr. 2017. "History of Ukrainian thinking on translation (from the 1920s to the 1950s)." In *Going East: discovering new and alternative traditions in translation studies*, edited by Larisa Schippel, and Cornelia Zwischenberger, 309–338. Berlin: Frank & Timme.

Kochur, Hryhoriy. 2008. *Literatura ta pereklad: Doslidzennia. Retsenzii. Literaturni portrety. Interviu* [*Literature and Translation: Research. Reviews. Literary Portraits. Interviews*], edited by Andriy Kochur and Maria Kochur. Kyiv: Smoloskyp.

Komissarov, Vilen. 1976. "Teoriya perevoda na sovremennom etape." [The Current State of Theory of Translation]. *Tetradi perevodchika*, 13: 3–12.

Koptilov, Viktor. 1971. *Aktualni pytannia ukrainskoho khudozhnoho perekladu* [*Topical Problems of Ukrainian Literary Translation*]. Kyiv: Kyiv University Publishing.

Koptilov, Viktor. 1972. *Pershotvir i pereklad: Rozdumy i sposterezhennia* [*Original and Translation: Reflections and Observations*]. Kyiv: Dnipro.

Koptilov, Viktor. 2003. *Teoriya i praktyka perekladu* [*Theory and Practice of Translation*]. Kyiv: Universe.

Korunets, Ilko. 2008. *Vstup do perekladoznavstva* [*Introduction to Translation Studies*]. Vinnytsia: Nova Knyha.

Lambert, José, and Jean-François Brunelière. 2016. "From translation to organization to international business: An academic no man's land." *Cad. Trad. Florianópolis*, 36 (2): 15–45.

Lambert, José. 2006. "Shifts, oppositions and goals in translation studies: Towards a genealogy of concepts." In *Functional Approaches to Culture and Translation: Selected Papers by José Lambert*, edited by Dirk Delabastita, Lieven D'hulst, and Reine Meylaerts, 75–86. Amsterdam: John Benjamins.

Levý, Jiří. 1970. "Sostoyaniye teoreticheskoy mysli v oblasti perevoda." [The state of theoretical thought in the sphere of translation]. *Masterstvo perevoda*, 6: 406–31.

Levý, Jiří. 2011. *The art of translation*. Translated by Patrick Corness. Amsterdam and Philadelphia: John Benjamins.

Marais, Kobus. 2014. *Translation theory and development studies: A complexity theory approach*. Abingdon and New York: Routledge.

Novykova, Marina. 1986. *Prekrasen Nash Soiuz: Literatura—Perevodchik—Zhyzn* [*Our Wonderful Union: Literature—Translator—Life*]. Kyiv: Radianskyi pysmennyk.

Novykova, Marina. 2005. *Mify ta Misiya* [*Myths and Mission*]. Kyiv: Dukh i Litera.

Odrekhivska, Iryna. 2016. "Anti-illusionist trend in drama translation: Re-framing Jiří Levý's concept." *Mutatis Mutandis* 9 (2): 247–266.

Odrekhivska, Iryna. 2017a. "Consolidating Anton Popovič's metacommunicational context of translation as a conceptual cluster." *World Literature Studies* 9 (2): 62–72.

Odrekhivska, Iryna. 2017b. "In the realm of translation studies in Ukraine: Re-visiting Viktor Koptilov's translation concept." In *Going East: discovering new and alternative traditions in translation studies*, edited by Larisa Schippel, and Cornelia Zwischenberger, 513–535. Berlin: Frank & Timme.

Pym, Anthony and Nune Ayvazyan. 2014. "The case of the missing Russian translation theories." *Translation Studies*, 7 (3): 1–21.

Pym, Anthony and Nune Ayvazyan. 2017. "West enters East: A strange case of unequal equivalence in Soviet translation theory." In *Going East: Discovering New and Alternative Traditions in Translation Studies*, edited by Larisa Schippel, and Cornelia Zwischenberger, 221–46. Berlin: Frank & Timme.

Pym, Anthony. 2016. *Translation solutions for many languages: Histories of a flawed dream*. Bloomsbury Academic.

Rylskyi, Maksym. 1975. *Mystetstvo perekladu: statti, vystupy, notatky* [*The Art of Translation: articles, reports, comments*], edited by Hryhoriy Kolesnyk. Kyiv: Radianskyi pysmennyk.

Sampson, Geoffrey. 1980. *Schools of linguistics*. Stanford University Press (Language Arts & Disciplines).

Schäffner, Christina. 2017. "Socialist translation studies—Theoretical justification and implications for training." In *Going East: Discovering new and alternative traditions in translation studies*, edited by Larisa Schippel, and Cornelia Zwischenberger, 405–428. Berlin: Frank & Timme.

Schippel, Larisa, and Cornelia Zwischenberger, eds. 2017. *Going East: Discovering new and alternative traditions in translation studies*. Berlin: Frank & Timme.

Shmiher, Taras, ed. 2013. *Ukrayinske perekladoznavstvo XX storichchia: bibliografia* [*Translation Studies in the 20th-century Ukraine: bibliography*]. Lviv: NTSH, Ivan Franko National University.

Shmiher, Taras. 2009. *Istoriya ukrainskoho perekladoznavstva* [*History of Translation Studies in Ukraine*]. Kyiv: Smoloskyp.

Simeoni, Daniel. 2008. "Norms and the state: The geopolitics of translation theory." In *Beyond descriptive translation studies: Investigations in homage to Gideon Toury*, edited by Anthony Pym, Miriam Shlesinger, and Daniel Simeoni, 329–342. Amsterdam: John Benjamins.

Špirk, Jaroslav. 2009. "Anton Popovič's contribution to translation studies." *Target* 21 (1): 3–29.

Strikha, Maksym. 2006. *Ukrayinskyi Khudozhniy Pereklad: mizh Literaturoiu i Natsiyetvorenniam* [*Ukrainian Literary Translation: between Literature and Nation-Building*]. Kyiv: Fact.

Susam-Sarajeva, Sebnem. 2002. "A 'multilingual' and 'international' translation studies?" In *Crosscultural transgressions: Research models in translation studies II: Historical and ideological issues*, edited by Theo Hermans, 193–207. Manchester: St. Jerome.

Torop, Peeter and Bruno Osimo. 2010. "Historical identity of translation: From describability to translatibility of time." TRAMES 14 (4): 383–393.

Tymoczko, Maria. 2014. "The "response" in translation studies forum: Universalism in translation studies." *Translation Studies* 7 (1): 104–107.

Tyulenev, Sergey and Binghan Zheng, eds. 2017. "Toward comparative translation and interpreting studies." *Translation and Interpreting Studies* 12: 2.

Tyulenev, Sergey. 2012. *Applying Luhmann to translation studies: Translation in society*. London and New York: Routledge.

van Doorslaer, Luc. 2017. "Holmes and Popovič in the 21st century: an empirical-bibliographical exercise." *World Literature Studies* 9 (2): 12–20.

Woodsworth, Judith. 1998. "History of translation." In *Routledge Encyclopedia of Translation Studies*, edited by Mona Baker, 100–105. London: Routledge.

Zerov, Mykola. 2003. *Ukrayinske pysmenstvo* [*The Ukrainian Literature*], edited by Mykola Sulyma. Kyiv: Osnovy.

CHAPTER 4

# Translation Seen through the Prism of the Tartu-Moscow School of Semiotics

*Elin Sütiste and Silvi Salupere*

## Abstract

While the legacy of the Tartu-Moscow School of Semiotics (TMS) has been discussed in numerous publications, the role of the phenomenon of translation in TMS has so far received little attention. The present article attempts to fill this gap aiming to show how the concept of translation has been approached by TMS members Vyacheslav Ivanov, Isaak Revzin, Vladimir Toporov, and Juri Lotman. It is shown that despite the apparent scarcity of explicit discussion on translation in TMS, the topic of translation has in fact been theorized fairly extensively in the works of TMS leaders. Translation, especially artistic translation is seen as the perfect laboratory for investigating the operation of complex sign systems. The issue of translation is intimately linked with meaning, and TMS members discern between different types of meaning as well as different kinds of translation. Furthermore, the concept of translation is used as a suitable means for explaining the workings of various semiotic phenomena from human consciousness to culture as a whole.

## 1 Introduction

The views and legacy of the Tartu-Moscow School of Semiotics (TMS) have been discussed in a large number of books and articles. Yet until very recently, none focused on the legacy of TMS specifically with regards to the topic of translation. Evangelos Kourdis does exactly that in his 2017 article "The semiotic school of Tartu-Moscow: The cultural 'circuit' of translation". According to Kourdis, "the most important contribution of the Tartu-Moscow School is the correlation of the concept of culture with the concept of translation" (Kourdis 2017, 149). The present paper offers a complementary perspective to that of Kourdis: while there are certainly overlaps in identifying some central concepts of TMS that have a bearing on the issue of translation, there are also significant differences; for instance, in the extent of attention paid to TMS's contemporary scholarly context and in the focus on particular scholars' contributions.

© KONINKLIJKE BRILL NV, LEIDEN, 2021 | DOI:10.1163/9789004437807_005

# THE TARTU-MOSCOW SCHOOL OF SEMIOTICS

In order to explicate how translation has been conceptualized and theorized in TMS, the present paper gives a brief overview of TMS with a focus on how and to what extent the concept of translation appears in the works of TMS members, and where and who have been the sources of inspiration for their conceptualization of translation. Finally, this paper will also discuss the main characteristics of the concept of translation in TMS, as well as the role it plays in TMS semiotic theories.

While many members of TMS were very versatile and published their research widely, TMS as a school is significantly represented by its journal, *Труды по знаковым системам* [Works on Sign Systems], which in 1998 changed its title to *Sign Systems Studies*. The journal was established at the initiative of Juri Lotman in Tartu in 1964, making it the world's oldest semiotic periodical, which continues to be published today.[1] When we take a look at the contents of the first 25 volumes of *Sign Systems Studies*,[2] it becomes quickly evident that translation is not an often-occurring or central topic: between 1964 and 1992, the word 'translation' appears only in two paper titles (Pasternak 1979; Torop 1982); two additional paper titles (Grabak 1967; Toporov 1969) hint that their contents may concern translation in some way. Upon closer inspection, however, it becomes apparent that in one way or another, translation is discussed much more widely, though not always explicitly. In these inexplicit treatments of translation, we can discern the difference between papers in which the word translation is used in a non-terminological and rather general sense (e.g., pointing to a translation of a text etc.) and papers in which translation is present in a much more conceptual and sometimes even foundational role. The present paper will focus foremost on the writings of some of the leading TMS members (published both in *Труды по знаковым системам* and elsewhere) in which translation is not necessarily foregrounded as a central topic (e.g., on the level of the paper titles), but appears nevertheless as a significant and influential concept.[3]

---

1   See http://www.sss.ut.ee/index.php/sss. Published in Russian, *Труды по знаковым системам* formed a subseries of the University of Tartu's scholarly series of publications (*Ученые записки Тартуского университета*). In 1998, together with the change of the title, the publishing language changed into English.

2   In the present paper, volumes 1–25 of the series published in the years 1964–1992 are taken into account. In 1993, with the death of the school's leader Juri Lotman, an era in the history of TMS was finished. Also, there was a pause in the publishing of *Sign Systems Studies*: the publication of the series was resumed in 1998 with the publication of volume 26.

3   It needs to be emphasized that since the 1990s, translation has become one of the most theorized concepts in the 'new' Tartu semiotics, especially thanks to Peeter Torop's 1995 work *Тотальный перевод* [Total Translation] and his later elaborations of the concept. However, in this paper we are focusing on the first generation of TMS and therefore Torop's

## 2 TMS Background

In order to build some necessary ground for the following discussion, we will give a brief overview of TMS before continuing, pointing out the school's most central ideas and important connections to past and contemporary academic developments.

In broad terms, TMS concentrated on culture as a mechanism of information creation, storage, and transmission. The 'manifesto' of TMS, *Theses on the Semiotic Study of Cultures* (1973), begins with a thesis elucidating the school's principal defining view towards culture:

> 1.0.0. In the study of culture the initial premise is that all human activity concerned with the processing, exchange, and storage of information possesses a certain unity. Individual sign systems, though they presuppose immanently organized structures, function only in unity, supported by one another. None of the sign systems possesses a mechanism which would enable it to function in isolation. Hence it follows that, together with an approach which permits us to construct a series of relatively autonomous sciences of the semiotic cycle, we shall also admit another approach, according to which all of them examine particular aspects of the *semiotics of culture*, of the study of the functional correlation of different sign systems.
>
> LOTMAN *et al.* 2013, 53[4]

The above thesis foregrounds the view that culture is regarded as a unity consisting of a vast array of different sign systems, which all stand in relation to each other as well as to the unity of culture. Additionally, it also implies the interrelations and exchange, i.e., translation between the different systems. TMS's interest in culture was manifested in studies of various cultural subsystems, from poetry to jokes to medieval art—"those peculiar meaning-generating devices whose function was to increase the complexity and richness of information, beyond a limited practical purpose" (Grishakova and Salupere

---

contribution will not be discussed separately. Moreover, the concept of 'Total Translation' is the topic of Anne Lange's chapter in this volume.

4  See Lotman and Uspensky: "We understand culture as the *nonhereditary memory of the community*, a memory expressing itself in a system of constraints and prescriptions" (Lotman and Uspensky 1978, 213); "Culture [is] a mechanism for organizing and preserving information in the consciousness of the community" (Lotman and Uspensky 1978, 214); "[we] consider culture as a mechanism creating an aggregate of texts and texts as the realization of culture" (Lotman and Uspensky 1978, 218) [translated by George Mihaychuk].

# THE TARTU-MOSCOW SCHOOL OF SEMIOTICS

2015, 173). In the words of Grishakova and Salupere (2015, 172), "semiotics was a natural extension of the TMS interest in modes and strategies of *making meaning across various systems, media, and cultures* [our emphasis—E.S., S.S.] and the awareness that no artefact, medium or cultural system stands alone".

While it has been argued that "what is currently termed a 'school' was a virtual community rather than a monolithic whole" (Grishakova and Salupere 2015, 174), with the circle of participants in gatherings and publications subject to constant flux, the core group of TMS is generally agreed to have consisted of Juri Lotman, Vyacheslav Ivanov, Vladimir Toporov, Aleksandr Pyatigorsky, Isaak Revzin, and Boris Uspensky.[5] In addition to this core group, the more active participants in the summer schools of semiotics and the first decades of *Sign Systems Studies* included ca. 40–50 more scholars.

In his account of the genesis of TMS, Boris Uspensky notes the strong links between TMS and the preceding philological traditions of Russian Formalism: the literature-focused OPOYAZ in St. Petersburg, and the Moscow Linguistic Circle. However, Uspensky adds:

> Необходимо подчеркнуть в этой связи, что речь идет не только об истоках той или иной культурной традиции, но о непосредственной преемственности. Так, Ю. М. Лотман учился у Гуковского, Жирмунского, Проппа. Вместе с тем, мы непосредственно общались с Р. О. Якобсоном, П. Г. Богатыревым, М. М. Бахтиным. П. Г. Богатырев до самой своей смерти был непременным участником наших конференций и занятий. Р. О. Якобсон принимал участие в одной из тартуских летних школ (в 1966 г. – мы справляли его 70-летие) и пристально следил за нашими занятиями. М. М. Бахтин не мог принимать участия в наших встречах (у него не было ноги, и он был практически немобилен), но живо интересовался нашими работами.
>
> USPENSKY 1987, 20–21

> [It is necessary to emphasize that we are not talking only about sources of a cultural tradition, but about a direct continuity. Thus, J. Lotman studied under Gukovsky, Zhirmunski, Propp [during his student years in Leningrad]. Besides that, we were in direct contact with R.O. Jakobson, P.G. Bogatyrev, and M.M. Bakhtin. Until his death, P.G. Bogatyrev was an ever-present participant in our conferences and activities. R.O. Jakobson

---

5  *Theses on the Semiotic Study of Cultures* (1973) was also authored by this group of scholars, with the exception of Revzin.

took part in one of Tartu summer schools (in 1966—we celebrated his 70th birthday) and kept a keen eye on our activities. M.M. Bakhtin could not participate in our meetings (one leg was amputated and he was essentially immobile), but he took avid interest in our works.]

Translated by E.S., S.S.

The dual nature of Russian Formalism (Petersburgian focus on literature vs. Moscovian focus on linguistics) also finds a parallel TMS, which is already reflected in the name of the school (Tartu-Moscow) as well as in the members' disposition towards either literary studies or linguistics. In addition, TMS scholars also took interest in oriental studies, ethnology, folklore studies, history, cybernetics, etc.

## 3 Structural Linguistics, Machine Translation and Cybernetics

The actual beginnings of TMS can be traced back to the late 1950s–early 1960s. By the end of the 1950s, in Tartu, Lotman had become interested in the structural studies of literature. He prepared and read a course in structural poetics at the University of Tartu in the beginning of the 1960s, which was later published in 1964 as *Лекции по структуральной поэтике* [Lectures on Structural Poetics], constituting the first volume of *Sign Systems Studies* (then, *Труды по знаковым системам*).

In 1956, in Moscow, Vyacheslav Ivanov and Vladimir Uspensky, together with Petr Kuznetsov initiated a series of seminars in computational linguistics at Moscow University. The seminar soon attracted many other outstanding scholars such as Viktor Rosenzweig, Isaak Revzin, Igor Mel'čuk, Sebastian Shaumyan (see V. Uspensky 1992), several of whom were also active in machine translation research. In the USSR, structural linguistics, "shunned by the Soviet linguistics establishment, found a place under the institutional umbrella of cybernetics in the field of machine translation" (Gerovich 2002, 232). And thus, in the second half of the 1950s,[6] research into machine translation progressed significantly in the USSR. Several groups studying machine translation were established, foremost in Moscow but also elsewhere (see Bar-Hillel 2003[1960],

---

6 Mel'čuk writes about the general academic climate of the USSR at the time: "This period between 1956 and 1966 was very favorable to science; the Stalinist terror had ended, Khrushchev had made his famous speech at the 20th Communist Congress, 1957 was the year of the sputnik, the space and arms races against America had begun, science and technology became almost untouchable, so that [Viktor] Rozencvejg [= Rosenzweig] could build upon this esteem and obtain support for MT [= machine translation]." (Mel'čuk 2000, 209).

# THE TARTU-MOSCOW SCHOOL OF SEMIOTICS

65

67). Mathematical methods were introduced into the study of linguistics, translation, poetics, etc.; this intensive work was evidenced by a number of symposia and conferences on related topics, such as in 1958 the First All-Union Conference on Machine Translation in Moscow (among the participants were also Toporov, Ivanov, Revzin), and in 1961 a conference in Gorki on the application of mathematical methods to the study of the language of literary works (participants included, inter alia, Ivanov, Revzin, Zholkovski).

In 1962, during a milestone symposium on the structural studies of sign systems held in Moscow, presentations were held on the topics of semiotics of language, logical semiotics, machine translation, semiotics of art, mythology, and etc. (B. Uspensky 1987, 22). Participants of the symposium included Bogatyrev, Ivanov, Toporov, Revzin, Rosenzweig, Pyatigorsky, B. Uspensky, Zholkovsky, and many others. Having learned about the Moscow symposium, Lotman contacted scholars in Moscow and developed a plan to organize summer schools in Kääriku, near Tartu. The first took place already very soon, in 1964.[7] Many of the presentations made at these summer schools were later elaborated into articles and published in the journal *Sign Systems Studies* (then *Труды по знаковым системам*), which would become the central voice of TMS.

## 4 The Topic of Translation in the Approaches of TMS Members

Returning to the issue of how translation has been conceptualized in the writings of TMS members, we will next turn our attention to some of their most explicit pronouncements of translation-related ideas.

### 4.1 *Vyacheslav Ivanov (1929–2017)*

An erudite scholar and prolific member of TMS, Vyacheslav Ivanov studied and published in a wide variety of subjects, from the Hittite language, mythology, and the analysis of poetry, to the theoretical issues of semiotics, film analysis and visual art, etc. Ivanov was one of the scholars to refer to translation in his writings, which are at first sight not related to translation at all. For example, in his 1976 book *Чет и нечет* [Odd and Even] the workings of human brain, or more precisely the interaction between the right hemisphere (producing constant flow of visual images) and the left hemisphere (responsible for verbal utterances) is described in terms of translation (Ivanov 1978, 33–34). In

---

7 The Tartu summer schools on secondary modelling systems took place in 1964 (I), 1966 (II), 1968 (III), 1970 (IV), 1974 (V).

the same book, translation also appears as a fundamental practical issue for cybernetics in the analysis of the interrelations between natural and artificial language (Ivanov 1978, 117ff).

Ivanov's understanding of translation is similar to that of Roman Jakobson (and Isaak Revzin, whom we will discuss in the following section). According to Jakobson, everything in language is in principle translatable: "the cognitive level of language not only admits but requires recoding interpretation, i.e., translation" (Jakobson 1966[1959], 236). Additionally, as is well known, Jakobson distinguishes between three kinds of translation: intralingual, interlingual, and intersemiotic (Jakobson 1966[1959], 233). In his book *Очерки по истории семиотики в* CCCP [*Outline of the History of Semiotics in the USSR*] Ivanov makes a passing reference to the same trichotomy of translation in his proposed explanation of the formation of a verbal sign as such:

> Не будет преувеличением утверждение, что для формирования слова как знака с двумя вычленяемыми сторонами – означаемой и означающей – соотнесение акустических и оптических систем сигнализации могло сыграть основную роль: значение как особая сторона знака и могло вычлениться только при возможности его передачи некоторым другим знаком (либо в том же языке при синонимии, либо при переводе с языка на другой язык или на другую систему знаков).
>
> IVANOV 1976, chap. 1

> [It is not an exaggeration to assert that in forming the word as a sign with two articulate sides—the signified and the signifier—the correlation of acoustic and optic systems of signification could have played a principal role: meaning as a distinct side of the sign could only become articulated via the possibility of its transfer with some other sign (either in the same language as in the case of synonymy, or in the translation from one language to another language or to another sign system).]
>
> Translated by E.S., S.S.

Besides affirming the general translatability of signs, Jakobson famously makes an exception in cases of puns, jest, dreams, and above all poetry, which "by definition is untranslatable" (Jakobson 1966[1959], 238). In this case, only creative transposition is possible—whether intralingual, interlingual, or intersemiotic (Jakobson 1966[1959], 238). In his book *Outline of the History of Semiotics in the USSR*, Ivanov addresses the issue of translatability in artistic texts in the following passage, among others:

# THE TARTU-MOSCOW SCHOOL OF SEMIOTICS

Для художественного произведения с четко выраженными концептами допустим перевод на другие языки (в случае словесного искусства) или транспонирование их средствами другого искусства. Так, здесь возможно создание музыкального эквивалента стихотворному тексту, например, в 13-й и 14-й симфониях Шостаковича, или тексту прозаическому в операх « Катерина Измайлова » и « Нос » того же композитора [...]. Такой перевод или транспозиция невозможны в тех произведениях искусства, где на первый план выдвигаются собственно эстетические задачи, формулируемые прежде всего в терминах соотношений между разными уровнями знаковой структуры или соотношений внутри одного уровня.

> IVANOV 1976, chap. 3

[An artistic work with clearly expressed concepts [~meanings] allows translation into other languages (in case of verbal art), or their transposition by means of another art. Thus, it is possible to create a musical equivalent to a text of poetry; for example, in Shostakovich's symphonies nos. 13 and 14, or to a prose text as in the same composer's operas *Katerina Izmailova* and *The Nose*[8] [...]. Such translation or transposition is impossible in artistic works that specifically foreground esthetic tasks, defined foremost in terms of relations between different levels of the sign structure or relations within one level.]

> Translated by E.S., S.S.

Ivanov has also written specifically on questions of translation (among others, also e.g. Ivanov 1968), and particularly thought-provoking is his article "Лингвистические вопросы стихотворного перевода" [Linguistic issues of poetry translation] published in 1961. Ivanov writes that the main problem of translation theory (including machine translation) involves the invariant that is preserved in the process of a text's transformation (Ivanov 2004[1961], 570). He further explicates the additional specificity of poetry translation in comparison with translation of other kinds of texts. Ivanov proposes to distinguish between a text of poetry [стихотворный текст] and its poetic model [поэтическая модель стихотворного текста]. The poetic model is to be understood as the text's poetic meaning [поэтическое значение], which cannot be

---

8 The literary source texts of the above-mentioned compositions of Shostakovich: poems by Yevgeni Yevtushenko (the Symphony No. 13), poems on the theme of death (the Symphony No. 14); Nikolai Leskov's novel *Lady Macbeth of the Mtsensk District* (the opera *Katerina Izmailova*); Gogol's story *The Nose* (the opera *The Nose*).

reduced to the meaning of the text's interlinear translation, since the poetic model involves not only the poem's immediate content that can to some extent be retold in prose, but also the model of the poem's structure (Ivanov 2004[1961], 570).

Ivanov explains the nature of a text of poetry that provides grounds for defining the poetic model:

> Стихотворный текст можно рассматривать как обычный языковый текст, преображенный в соответствии с поэтической моделью. [...] Особый – преображенный – характер стихотворного текста можно определить статистически. [...] Количество информации, содержащейся в поэтическом тексте, может быть определено мерой отклонения этого текста от статистических норм обычного языка и от статистических норм поэтического языка данного времени. Нарушение статистических норм обычного языка может стать нормой поэтического языка, что приводит к уменьшению количества информации, содержащегося в поэтических текстах. [...] Точный стихотворный перевод предполагает передачу статистической характеристики языкового текста применительно к языку, на котором делается перевод. Соответствующие статистические работы могут быть в большой степени автоматизированы.
>
> IVANOV 2004[1961], 572–573

> [A text of poetry can be regarded as a usual verbal text that has been transformed in accordance with the poetic model. [...] The special—transformed—character of a text of poetry can be defined statistically. [...] The amount of information contained in a poetic text can be defined as a measure of deviance of this text from the statistical norm of the ordinary language, and from the statistical norm of the poetic language of a given period. The violation of the statistical norm of the ordinary language can become a norm for poetic language that leads to the diminishment of the amount of information contained in poetic texts. [...] Exact poetic translation presumes the transfer of the statistical characteristics of the verbal text as applied to the language of translation. The corresponding statistical operations can to a large extent be automatized.]
>
> Translated by E.S., S.S.

Jakobson's and Ivanov's ideas on the translation of artistic texts are further elaborated in the works of Isaak Revzin.

## 4.2 Isaak Revzin (1923–1974)

Isaak Revzin, a key representative of Soviet structural linguistics, was among the pioneers of semiotics in the USSR. He was one of the founding members of TMS and a leading proponent of introducing rigorous mathematical methods into linguistics, an endeavor closely connected to questions of machine translation. In the introduction to his posthumously published work *Современная структурная лингвистика* [Contemporary Structural Linguistics] (1977), Revzin outlined the main tasks of linguistics of the time:

> В 50-е годы перед [...] языковедами [...] встали совершенно новые задачи, связанные с громадным увеличением потока информации [...] Поскольку большая часть информации записывается при помощи естественных языков, то возникает проблема автоматического решения задач, связанных с языком. С этого времени начинается интенсивное обсуждение следующих задач:
>
> а)  создание машин, автоматически анализирующих тексты на естественных языках;
>
> б)  создание информационно-логических устройств, в компактной форме запоминающих информацию и быстро выдающих ее по первому требованию;
>
> в)  совершенствование способов передачи речи по каналам телефонной, телеграфной, радио связи;
>
> г)  создание устройств, воспринимающих устную речь и воспроизводящих ее в письменной форме («автоматические машинистки»);
>
> д)  машинный перевод с одного языка на другой.
>
> REVZIN 1977, 9–10

[In the 1950s, [...] linguists [...] became faced with totally new tasks, due to the enormous increase in amounts of information [...] Since the majority of information is recorded with the help of natural languages, there emerges the problem of automatically solving problems related to language. From this time, an intensive discussion of the following tasks begins:

a)  creating machines that would automatically analyze texts in natural languages;

b)  creating logico-informational devices that would compactly memorize information and deliver information rapidly on request;

c)  improving the means of speech transference along the channels of telephone, telegraph, radio communication;

d) creating devices that would receive oral speech and reproduce it in written form ("automatic typists");
e) machine translation from one language into another.]
Translated by E.S., S.S.

The above list displays the multidisciplinary (linguistics, information theory, cybernetics, translation theory) context in which Revzin and his colleagues regarded the topic of machine translation.

Revzin elaborated Ivanov's distinction between the poetic text and its poetic model with the help of more explicit terminology, juxtaposing "periphrastic meaning" and "categorical meaning". "Periphrastic meaning" is to be understood as "that which can be retold by other means" (Revzin 1977, 202). Revzin argues that in the translation of a literary work, one criterion of translation adequacy is the transfer of the poetic model of the original, which can also be formulated as the "categorical meaning" of the work as a whole, i.e., the interrelations of the signified [or periphrastic meaning—E.S., S.S.] with the specific organization of the signifier (Revzin 1977, 243–244).

In 1964, Revzin, together with Juri Rosenzweig, published the influential book *Основы общего и машинного перевода* [Fundamentals of General and Machine Translation]. While Revzin and Rosenzweig criticize previous theorists' ultimately subjective viewpoint on translation, they stress that theirs is an attempt to provide a rigorous theoretical account of translation. They write: "Science striving to describe translation as process should not be normative, but theoretical. It should not describe what should be, but what is inherent in the very nature of the phenomenon" (Revzin, Rosenzweig 1964, 21). That is, the authors emphasize the need for a theoretical, rather than normative science of translation, thus anticipating the position of descriptive translation studies by about a decade. On the same page, they also postulate that the object of the theory of translation should not be the result of translation, but rather the process, which can be described in semiotic terms. According to their conviction, language is becoming increasingly understood in a semiotic framework, and the linguists' interest in the theory of translation is related to the issue of meaning (Revzin, Rosenzweig 1964, 27–28). The latter is defined by recourse to Roman Jakobson's formulation: "the meaning of any linguistic sign is its translation into some further, alternative sign" (Jakobson 1966[1959], 232). In principle, they also agree with Jakobson's semiotically-grounded distinction of three kinds (intralingual, interlingual, and intersemiotic) of translation (Jakobson 1959, 233). Elaborating their theory along the same lines, Revzin and Rosenzweig claim that the "types of realization of translation process [...] are common to all kinds of text" (Revzin, Rosenzweig 1964, 173).

# THE TARTU-MOSCOW SCHOOL OF SEMIOTICS

While focusing on machine translation in the context of a general theory of translation, Revzin and Rosenzweig emphasize: "it is necessary to realize that the problems of translation manifest most prominently in the study of translations of literary works" (Revzin, Rosenzweig 1964, 20). Thus they foreground the paramount significance of the study of poetic translation also in view of machine translation, a view that had been expressed earlier already by Ivanov: "Already at the 1958 conference on machine translation Vyach[eslav] Vs[evolodovich] Ivanov underlined that for solving the principal linguistic problems it is extremely fruitful to turn to the facts of poetry translation" (Revzin 1977, 227). Revzin himself explicates the significance that literary translation holds for semiotics—not only for linguistics or the theory of (machine) translation—as follows:

> Проблема перевода воистину стала центральной проблемой семиотики не только в практическом, но и в теоретическом плане. И разумеется, интерес исследователей сосредоточился не на тривиальном перекодировании (при взаимно-однозначном соответствии между знаками двух систем, то есть грубо говоря, при дословном переводе), а на изучении тонких (многозначных) соответствий между знаками двух или более систем. [...]
>
> Из сказанного должна быть очевидна точка зрения автора этих строк на теорию художественного перевода: [...] речь идет о желании понять некоторые общие принципы оперирования со сложными знаковыми системами, для того чтобы усовершенствовать семиотическую теорию применительно к области гуманитарных наук, используя данные, накопленные практикой лучших переводчиков и литературной критикой в области перевода.
>
> Перевод здесь интересен как механизм, обнажающий художественную модель произведения, которую [...] следует искать не в тексте, а в том, что сохраняется в переводе, то есть в том общем, что объединяет текст оригинального произведения и перевода [...] или, еще лучше, разные хорошие переводы данного произведения (в современной науке эту сущность, остающуюся неизменной при разных преобразованиях, принято называть инвариантом).
>
> REVZIN 1968, 426–427

[The problem of translation has indeed become the central problem of semiotics, not only in the practical aspect, but also in the theoretical aspect. And of course, the researchers' interest has not focused on trivial recoding (where there is a mutually unequivocal correspondence between signs of two systems, that is, roughly speaking, in the case of word-for-word translation), but on the study of subtle (ambiguous) correspondences between the signs of two or more systems. [...]

The present author's viewpoint on the theory of literary translation should become obvious from the above-said: [...] it is a matter of desire to understand some general principles of operating with complex sign systems in order to improve the semiotic theory with respect to the sphere of humanities, using data accumulated by the practice of the best translators and literary criticism in the sphere of translation.

Translation is here interesting as a mechanism that reveals the artistic model of the work, which [...] should not be sought for in the text, but in what is preserved in translation, that is, in what is common to the text of the original work and its translation [...] or, even better, in what connects different good translations of the work (in contemporary science, this essence, which remains unchanged under different transformations, is usually called an *invariant*).

Translated by E.S., S.S.

The above quote is from Revzin's 1968 "Семиотический комментарий к чешской книге о переводе" ["Semiotic commentary to a Czech book on translation"]—a review of Jiří Levý's 1963[9] book *Uměni překladu* [The Art of Translation], in which Revzin explains the importance of Levý's work for semiotic theory. TMS scholars were well-aware of works related to their spheres of interest published both in the Soviet Union and abroad. Jiří Levý was recognized as an important author not only in translation theory, but also as a literary scholar, which is evidenced also by his obituary in *Sign Systems Studies* (Grabak 1967). A few years later, the work of the Slovak scholar Anton Popovič would be introduced to Tartu semioticians. In 1974 Popovič's monograph *Teória metatextov* [Theory of Metatexts] appeared in Slovak, and Peeter Torop, then Lotman's student and currently a leading representative of cultural semiotics, introduced it in Tartu that very same year at a seminar in the department of Russian Literature (Peeter Torop, personal communication, October 2015).[10] The TMS members' interest in their Czech and Slovak colleagues' work may be explained at least in part with their shared background tradition, which included Russian Formalism and Prague Structuralism, as well as strong Bakhtinian influences. Roman Jakobson was one of the unifying figures for

---

9  The full Russian translation of Levý's *Uměni překladu* (1963) was published in 1974 under the title *Искусство перевода* [The Art of Translation].

10  See also Torop 1999[1981].

# THE TARTU-MOSCOW SCHOOL OF SEMIOTICS 73

Russian formalism, Prague structuralism and TMS semiotics, having close contacts with and strong influence over members of TMS. Jakobson did much to help information travel between scholars of various countries, including those on different sides of the Iron Curtain.

## 4.3 *Vladimir Toporov (1928–2005)*

Although other members of TMS paid more marginal attention to issues of translation, they also provided some informative examples of a systematic approach to translation. For instance, *Sign Systems Studies* no. 4 (1969) contains a paper by Vladimir Toporov, in which he analyses Konstantin Batyshkov's verse translation of Evariste Parny's "Le torrent, idylle persane" (written in prose). Toporov describes Konstantin Batyushkov's task in translating this poem in the following manner:

> Переводя « Le Torrent », Батюшков должен был решить [...] две задачи – при сохранении данного содержания (а отчасти и формальных требований [...]) построить такой метрически организованный *стиховой* текст (T), соотносимый с оптимальной для данных целей поэтической системой (S) который соответствовал бы *прозаическому* тексту подлинника, точнее, – системе, породившей этот текст [...], т. е. $S_{проз.} \rightarrow S_{стих.}$; построить русский текст, который соответствовал бы французскому в заданном отношении и удовлетворял бы условиям вхождения в круг « поэтических » текстов, т. е. Tфранц. → Tрусск. (и, следовательно, Sфранц. → Sрусск.). Выполнение этих задач осложнялось практическим принципом, выработавшимся у Батюшкова при переводе Парни и заключавшимся в ослаблении, условно говоря, « эротической » ноты Парни за счет усиления « элегической » и « философической » ноты.

> TOPOROV 1969, 312

[In translating "Le torrent", Batyushkov needed to solve [...] two tasks: in retaining the given content (but partly also formal requirements [...]), to construct such metrically organized *verse* text (T) (relatable to a poetical system (S) that would appear optimal with regard to the given aims), which would correspond to the original *prose* text, more precisely, to the *system* that had generated this text [...], i.e., $S_{prose} \rightarrow S_{verse}$; to construct a Russian text that would both correspond to the French one in specified regard and satisfy the conditions of entering the circle of 'poetic' texts, i.e., $T_{French} \rightarrow T_{Russian}$ (and, accordingly, $S_{French} \rightarrow S_{Russian}$). The accomplishing of these tasks was complicated by a practical principle that Batyshkov elaborated while translating Parny, which consisted of weakening the "erotic" tone in Parny at the expense of strengthening the 'elegiac' and 'philosophical' tone.]

Translated by E.S., S.S.

Here we see how Toporov makes use of terms like 'text' and 'system'. He gives an account of the two poetic systems whose differences need to be taken into consideration in translation, with transformations that occur during the translation process appearing natural and expectable. Toporov succeeds in bringing together the terminology and scientific outlook adopted from information theory/cybernetics with his more traditional erudition in poetics and philology.[11]

### 4.4 *Juri Lotman (1922–1993)*

The relevance of translation in TMS leader Juri Lotman's work is already better known (see especially Salupere 2008; Monticelli 2017). Although we cannot find any works by Lotman specifically dedicated to translation, the concept occupies an important place in his research (for a study on a similar situation with Roman Jakobson, see Sütiste (forthcoming)). The dynamics of the word 'translation' (*перевод*) and related terms show two dominants in Lotman's works. The first is related to Lotman's interest in structuralist poetics, and with the publication of his 'trilogy', consisting of *Лекции по структуральной поэтике* [Lectures on Structural Poetics] (Lotman 1994[1964]), *Структура художественного текста* [Structure of the Artistic Text] (Lotman 1970) and *Анализ поэтического текста: Структура стиха* [Analysis of Poetic Text: Structure of Verse] (Lotman 1972). Regarding these as a trilogy is justified by the fact that the second monograph, aimed foremost at specialists, is an elaborated and supplemented version of the first, while the third book on the same topic is aimed at students and instructors.

The second dominant is associated with Lotman's discussions on the phenomenon of culture and its typological characteristics. While in the 'trilogy' the word 'translation' appears in its so-to-say classical meaning, in the texts of the other, cultural-typological group, 'translation' appears in a more general sense. As the texts from both groups appear parallel in time, their different uses

---

11    Toporov has also authored an article "Translation: sub specie culture" (1992), in which translation is described as "a key principle of culture itself, its solid foundation" (Toporov 1992, 29). Discussing concrete "encounters in cultural space", the article is more historical than theoretical in nature, or rather, presents cultural semiotic theory as intermingled with translation history.

THE TARTU-MOSCOW SCHOOL OF SEMIOTICS 75

of the word 'translation' cannot be attributed to chronological differentiation. Furthermore, Lotman repeats his main ideas in different variations throughout a number of his works; the concept of translation is certainly among his recurrent themes. It is important to note that in both text groups, Lotman uses the concept of translation to clarify his main positions, and due to varying contexts, the concept acquires different contents. Thus, 'translation' can appear alongside 'recoding' (*перекодировка*); "exact translation" (*точный перевод*) is contrasted with "adequate translation" (*адекватный перевод*), and translation is also referred to as the principal mechanism of culture.

Within the frames of the 'trilogy', it makes sense to view the term 'translation' alongside 'recoding', since in the *Lectures on Structural Poetics* only 'translation' is used, while in *The Structure of the Artistic Text* 'recoding' prevails. Neither term is used extensively in Lotman's *Analysis of Poetic Text*, since this work focuses on concrete analysis, making it less theoretical than *Lectures on Structural Poetics* and *The Structure of the Artistic Text*. As poetry is his research object in the 'trilogy', Lotman is specifically referring to the translation of poetry when speaking of 'translation' in these monographs. Nevertheless, many of Lotman's theoretical premises are certainly relevant and also applicable to other forms of artistic texts.

The terms "content structure" and "expression structure" are essential components of Lotman's structural poetics; these terms are closely related to Lotman's reasoning about exact and adequate translation. The phonological structure of language predominates the expression structure. Lotman states that in poetic speech, the expression structure becomes the content structure, due to the lexico-semantic significance of phonemes and morphemes being much greater than in non-poetic speech (Lotman 1994[1964], 144).

Lotman devotes more attention to translation-related issues in his *Structure of the Artistic Text*, in which we can also observe a change in his metalanguage. Next to the term 'translation', Lotman also introduces and explicates the term 'recoding'. This shift can be explained by the fact that the Saussurian foundational dichotomy language-speech is replaced by code-message in many structuralist works under the influence of information theory. The same shift can be observed in Lotman's works (see, e.g., 1977, 13).

In *The Structure of the Artistic Text*, Lotman now prevailingly uses terms "plane/system of expression" and "plane/system of content" in place of "expression structure" and "content structure" (since Lotman references Hjelmslev, this shift may have been made due to his influence). 'Recoding' (like 'translation' in *Lectures on Structural Poetics*) involves both the system of expression and the system of content and is directly related to the issue of meaning (see, e.g., Lotman 1977, 35).

Lotman also differentiates between "internal recoding" and "external recoding" (and even further with "plural internal recoding", "paired external recoding" and "plural external recoding"). Internal recoding involves semiotic systems "in which meaning is formed, not by the convergence of two chains of structures, but immanently, within one system. One example of this sort of recoding is the simple algebraic formula: a=b+c" (Lotman 1977, 35). In addition to mathematical expressions, absolute music is another example of a system characterized by internal recoding (Lotman 1977, 36). However, external recoding is more common, as it is present in natural languages. In external recoding, "equivalence is established between two chain-structures of different types, and between their individual elements. Equivalent elements form pairs which combine in signs. We should stress that structures of different types prove to be equivalent" (Lotman 1977, 36). While Lotman's distinction between internal and external recoding may at first sight seem to coincide with Jakobson's intralingual and interlingual forms of translation, the examples Lotman uses to illustrate his two kinds of recoding give a different view. Lotman's distinction is more reminiscent of Hjelmslev than of Jakobson, and even their examples coincide. Nevertheless, Lotman and Jakobson share the view that different types of translation stem in effect from a similar mechanism. To this, Lotman adds his often-repeated claim that it is the differences of the systems between which translation takes place that generate richness in the resulting transfer:

> Although it is difficult to establish the fundamental difference between such types of recoding as the deciphering of content and the translation of a phonic form into a graphic form or translation from one language into another, it is still obvious that the greater the distance between structures made equivalent to each other in the process of recoding, the greater the disparity in their nature, the richer will be the content of the very act of switching from one system to the other.
>
> LOTMAN 1977, 36—Translated by GAIL LENHOFF and RONALD VROON

In his work, Lotman is known to differentiate between exact and adequate translation. He makes this distinction for the first time in *Lectures on Structural Poetics*:

> [...] самый точный перевод поэтического текста воспроизводит лишь структуру содержания в той её части, которая обща у поэтической и непоэтической речи. Те же семантические связи и противопоставления содержания, которые возникают в результате семантизации структуры выражения, заменяются иными. Они непереводимы, как

непереводимы идиомы в структуре содержания. Поэтому применительно к поэтическому тексту правильнее говорить не о точном переводе, а о стремлении к функциональной адекватности.

LOTMAN 1994[1964], 144

[the most exact translation of a poetic text renders only that part of the content structure which is common to poetic and non-poetic speech. These semantic relations and oppositions of the content that arise as a result of semantization of expression structure, are replaced with others. They are untranslatable, as are untranslatable idioms in content structure. Therefore, with regard to poetic text it is more justified to talk not about exact translation, but about striving towards functional adequacy.]

Translated by E.S., S.S.

While the precise meaning of "exact translation" is not explicated here, much attention to the issue of exact translation has been drawn in one of Lotman's programmatic articles, "Феномен культуры" [The Phenomenon of Culture] (1978). In the usage of the terms "plane of content" and "plane of expression", juxtaposition of exact and adequate translation, we can observe a parallel with *Lectures on Structural Poetics*:

Представим себе два языка, $L_1$ и $L_2$, устроенные принципиально столь различным образом, что точный перевод с одного на другой представляется невозможным. Предположим, что один из них будет языком с дискретными знаковыми единицами, имеющими стабильные значения, и с линейной последовательностью синтагматической организации текста, а другой будет характеризоваться недискретностью и пространственной (континуальной) организацией элементов. Соответственно и планы содержания этих языков будут построены принципиально различным образом. В случае, если нам потребуется передать текст на языке $L_1$ средствами языка $L_2$, ни о каком точном переводе не может идти речи. В лучшем случае возникает текст, который в отношении к некоторому культурному контексту может рассматриваться как адекватный первому.

LOTMAN 1992a[1978], 35

[Let us imagine two languages, $L_1$ and $L_2$, built so differently that exact translation from one into another is impossible. Let us assume that one of the languages will contain discrete sign units with stable meanings and linear sequencing in the syntagmatic organization of the text; the other one will be characterized by non-discreteness and spatial (continuous) organization of elements. Hence also the planes of content of these languages will be constructed in principally different manner. In the case we need to transmit a text in language $L_1$ by the means of the language $L_2$, we cannot speak of any kind of exact translation. In the best case we will observe the generation of a text which, with regard to a certain cultural context, will be regarded as an adequate translation.

Translated by E.S., S.S.

Here we should note that Lotman no longer limits himself to speaking solely about natural language. While the description of $L_1$ still corresponds to that of a natural language, $L_2$ can be e.g., a visual or musical language in which it is difficult to articulate discrete elements. Another way to interpret this passage is to say that only in the translation from one discrete language into another discrete language it is possible to speak about "exact translation", since in such a case, translation is conducted on the level of discrete signs. But when we are faced with a non-discrete language in which text as a whole dominates over its separate elements, and which foregrounds the content structure in which everything is semanticized, we can speak of translation only on the level of the whole text. This is a functional approach, the result of which will be adequate translation.

Such considerations lead to the definition of translation as a central mechanism of culture. Lotman's efforts in elaborating a semiotic theory of culture began in his works dating from the late 1960s to the mid-1970s and became consolidated in *Universe of the Mind* (Lotman 1990). With these works, translation acquires an important role in Lotman's model of culture, becoming, among other things, an analogue of the act of communication:

> It follows that the act of communication (in any sufficiently complex, and consequently culturally valuable, instance) should be seen not as a simple transmission of a message which remains adequate to itself from the consciousness of the addresser to the consciousness of the addressee, but as a *translation* of a text from the language of my 'I' to the language of your 'you'.
>
> LOTMAN 1979, 91—Translated by ANN SHUKMAN

Lotman emphasizes that like translation, the process of communication necessarily involves deformation, which turns out to be its asset:

# THE TARTU-MOSCOW SCHOOL OF SEMIOTICS

The very possibility of such a translation is determined by the fact that the codes of both participants in the communication, although not identical, form intersecting sets. But since, in the given act of translation, a certain part of the message is always cut off, and 'I' am submitted to a transformation in the course of translation into language 'you', what is lost is just the individuality of the addressee, that is, what, from the point of view of the whole, is the most valuable thing in the message.

LOTMAN 1979, 91—Translated by ANN SHUKMAN

When discussing the phenomenon of culture, Lotman explains that it is namely the "structure of conditionally adequate translations [that] can perform as one of simplified models of creative intellectual process" (Lotman 1992a[1978], 36). The concept of "conditionally adequate translation" is closely associated with the notion of "thinking device" (*мыслящее устройство*), which "cannot be monostructural and monolingual: it must necessarily include multilingual and mutually untranslatable semiotic formations" (Lotman 1992a[1978], 36).

The above-mentioned 'untranslatability' is characterized by the absence of univocal correspondences between structural units of different languages. When 'untranslatability' correlates with 'translatability', the result is "conditionally adequate translation". It is of utmost importance that the "mechanism of non-adequate, conditionally equivalent translation serves to generate new texts, that is, appears as the *mechanism of creative thinking*" (Lotman 1992b[1983], 115). Here it is worth mentioning that 'adequacy' and 'equivalence' appear as synonyms.

The creative nature of translation is emphasized again in *Universe of the Mind*. A simple example is the possibility of one poem translated many ways by different translators, testifying that instead of a precise correspondence to the source text, translation allows for a space of possible interpretations (Lotman 1990, 14). This asymmetry inherent to the translation process is also characteristic of the semiosphere, the central concept in Lotman's cultural semiotics. Semiosphere depends heavily on translation: the structure of the semiosphere is heterogeneous and asymmetrical, and asymmetry is expressed in the internal translations permeating throughout the semiosphere (Lotman 1990, 127).

In Lotman's later works, translation is regarded as a central component in human mental activity, and also as an instrument of semiotic research. In his final book *Culture and Explosion*, translation again appears as a foundational concept:

A situation in which the minimal meaning-generating unit is not one language, but two, creates a whole chain of consequences. First of all, even the nature of the intellectual act could be described in terms of being a translation, a definition of meaning as a translation from one language to another, whereas extra-lingual reality may be regarded as yet another type of language.

LOTMAN 2009[1992], 6—Translated by WILMA CLARK

An interesting and novel aspect here is the appearance of the term "extra-lingual reality", which may be regarded "as yet another type of language". Nevertheless, this "extra-lingual reality" can also be brought about in moments of explosion; again we can speak of a kind of 'translation': "But the relationships between the translatable and the untranslatable are so complex that possibilities for a breakthrough into the space beyond the limits are created. This function is also fulfilled by moments of explosion, which can create a kind of window in the semiotic layer." (Lotman 2009[1992], 24).

To conclude, for Lotman, the concept of translation gradually acquires the central role in understanding human communication and thought processes in general:

> We have already mentioned that the elementary act of thinking is translation. Now we can go further and say that the elementary mechanism of translating is dialogue. Dialogue presupposes asymmetry, and asymmetry is to be seen first, in the difference between the semiotic structures (languages) which the participants in the dialogue use; and second, in the alternating directions of the message-flow. This last point means that the participants in a dialogue alternately change from a position of 'transmission' to a position of 'reception' [...].
>
> LOTMAN 1990, 143—Translated by ANN SHUKMAN

Lotman's emphasis that a semiotic mechanism must consist of minimally two languages entails that translation is an indispensable feature of semiotic space (i.e., semiosphere). As made evident in the above discussion, one characteristic of both translation and the workings of any semiotic mechanism is asymmetry, which inevitably also entails untranslatability. However, it furthermore appears that in addition to translatability, non-translatability is also a significant part in any act of communication, as it generates new information. Thus, translation is to be regarded as an essential participant in all the main functions of texts and *resp.* culture (cf. Lotman 1990, 11–19): the transmission, storage (memory), and creation of new information.

# THE TARTU-MOSCOW SCHOOL OF SEMIOTICS

## 5    Conclusion

From the early pronouncements of Revzin to Lotman's final works, TMS members have characterized the history of literary translation as a massive and monumental reservoir of experience in the workings and interaction of complex semiotic systems (Revzin 1968, 427). Translation, especially artistic translation, has been regarded as a laboratory *par excellence* for understanding the workings and interrelations of complex sign systems.

Thus, the phenomenon of translation has attracted the attention of TMS members as a fundamentally semiotic phenomenon due to its intimate connection with meaning, a central issue in TMS studies of any cultural phenomenon. Meaning is in turn understood as that what is conveyed in translation.[12] The heterogeneity among different translations of a source text highlights the importance of the invariant, or that which remains consistent across all of the source text's translations.

Meaning and translation are among central keywords of common interest to disciplines and subfields such as linguistics, machine translation, cybernetics, poetics etc. The translation-related interests of these disciplines instigated a more differential treatment of meaning among TMS members; for example, categorical and periphrastic meaning (see Revzin), the special question of poetic meaning (see poetic model; see Ivanov; Revzin), as well as attempts to clarify the concepts of adequate translation and equivalent translation (Lotman). One issue Lotman returns to several times is that of the opposition between translatability and untranslatability, both of which are seen as necessary and inevitable in the dynamics of culture. It must also be added that in general, TMS members' approaches to translation are characterized by adherence to the scientific rigor principle of structural research, as evident e.g., when Toporov describes Batyushkov's translation of Parny.

TMS synthesized a wide tradition of intellectual movement spanning from Russian Formalism to cybernetics, from structural linguistics to poetics, and devised influential means of analyzing culture as a process of meaning generation and storage. TMS was in close contact with the outstanding scholars on both sides of the Iron Curtain, including Andrei Kolmogorov and Mikhail Bakhtin from the Soviet Union, and Julia Kristeva and Roman Jakobson

---

12    This view is remarkably close to Charles Sanders Peirce's formulations, e.g.: "meaning [... is] in its primary acceptation the translation of a sign into another system of signs" (CP 4.127) or "the meaning of a sign is the sign it has to be translated into" (CP 4.132).

abroad.[13] With specific regard to translation, Jakobson's influence on the views of Lotman and other TMS members cannot be underestimated. Of course, it is obvious that TMS members also shared and/or elaborated many of Jakobson's views in several other spheres besides translation. TMS members and their colleagues around the world exchanged, synthesized and elaborated ideas towards their better application to the study of culture. Some TMS ideas, especially those of Lotman, have also infiltrated into mainstream translation studies. The polysystem theory devised by Itamar Even-Zohar is one such approach, which has been influenced to a significant extent by the "system thinking" of Russian Formalism and Prague dynamic functionalism (e.g., Even-Zohar 1990, 88), and ideas of the Tartu-Moscow school (e.g., Even-Zohar 1990, 2). For instance, the polysystem theory and TMS cultural semiotics both recognize the dynamic relations between the center and the periphery of a system (e.g., Even-Zohar 1990, 14–17, etc.). Furthermore, in a 1997 article, Even-Zohar acknowledges Lotman and TMS for introducing the concept of modeling the world, the semiosphere, and the semiotic approach to analyzing literature and culture in general (Even-Zohar 1997, 17). Additionally, the concept of 'oscillation' in polysystem theory, which refers to shifts in a system as a part of rather than violations of the system, is said to originate in Lotman's concept of 'ambivalence' (Even-Zohar 1990, 88). The initiator of descriptive translation studies Gideon Toury uses the TMS concept of "secondary modelling systems" (Toury 1980, 11–96), and his book *In Search of a Theory of Translation* (1980) in general testifies to (cultural) semiotic influence. Furthermore, Toury's 1986 article on translation for the *Encyclopedic Dictionary of Semiotics* explicitly designates semiotics of culture as the proper framework for the interpretation of translational facts (Toury 1994[1986], 1112).

Although the works of Lotman and his TMS colleagues began to be published in German, Spanish and Italian and other translations already in the 1960s, they were not introduced to the English-speaking audience until 1973 (see Kull 2011). Additionally, for a long time Lotman and most other TMS scholars were known in the West primarily in Slavistics circles, and in literary studies to a lesser extent. Thus, it is not surprising that TMS ideas have received limited attention in translation studies. This situation has been furthermore aggravated by the fact that translation is not an explicitly foregrounded topic or concept for the majority of TMS members. Nevertheless, the concept of translation has an important role in the thinking of several leading figures of TMS. For Ivanov and Revzin, the issue of translation is intimately connected to the

---

13    For an overview of Lotman's correspondence with scholars abroad see, e.g., Pilshchikov, Trunin 2016, 372.

# THE TARTU-MOSCOW SCHOOL OF SEMIOTICS

notion of meaning, as well as possibilities for identifying meaning of different kinds. For Lotman's work, translation had an even more fundamental significance, gradually evolving into a concept that elucidates the principal workings of both human consciousness and the semiosphere in its entirety: translation explicates and forms the core of the asymmetrical and dynamic relationship between two or more different systems. Without translation, no semiotic structure can emerge or operate. Thus it can be concluded that throughout the history of TMS, the concept of translation has gradually emerged from relative invisibility to the status of an exemplary case of complex sign operation, and finally, to the central mechanism of the workings of culture, which Tartu semioticians continue to study and develop in the present day.

### Acknowledgments

This work was supported by institutional research funding IUT2-44 of the Estonian Ministry of Education and Research, the institutional research grant IUT2-44 (Semiotic Modelling of Self-Description Mechanisms) from the Estonian Research Council and by baseline funding PHVFI17926 of the University of Tartu. The authors are grateful to Aynur Rahmanova for her help with proofreading the manuscript.

### References

Bar-Hillel, Yehoshua. 2003[1960]. "The present status of automatic translation of languages." In *Readings in machine translation*, edited by Sergei Nirenburg, Harold Somers, and Yorick Wilks, 45–76. Cambridge: The MIT Press.

CP = Peirce, Charles Sanders. 1931–1958. *Collected papers of Charles Sanders Peirce*. Cambridge: Harvard University Press. [Vols. 1–6 edited by Charles Hartshorne and Paul Weiss, 1931–1935; vols. 7–8 edited by A.W. Burks, 1958. In-text references are to CP, followed by volume and paragraph numbers.]

Even-Zohar, Itamar. 1990. "Polysystem studies". *Poetics Today* 11 (1).

Even-Zohar, Itamar. 1997. "Factors and dependencies in culture: A revised outline for polysystem studies." *Canadian Review of Comparative Literature* 24 (1): 15–34.

Gerovich, Slava. 2002. *From Newspeak to Cyberspeak: A History of Soviet Cybernetics*. Cambridge: The MIT Press.

Grabak 1967 = Грабак, Йозеф. "Иржи Левый." *Труды по знаковым системам* 3: 417–418.

Grishakova, Marina, and Silvi Salupere. 2015. "A school in the woods. Tartu-Moscow Semiotics." In *Theoretical schools and circles in the twentieth-century humanities: literary theory, history, philosophy*, edited by Marina Grishakova and Silvi Salupere, 173–95. New York, London: Routledge.

Ivanov 1968 = Иванов, Вячеслав. "О цветаевских переводах песни из "Пира во время чумы" и "Бесов" Пушкина". In *Мастерство перевода 1966*, 389–412. Москва: Советский писатель.

Ivanov 1976 = Иванов, Вячеслав. *Очерки по истории семиотики в СССР*. Москва: Наука.

Ivanov 1978 = Иванов, Вячеслав. *Чет и нечет. Асимметрия мозга и знаковых систем*. Москва: Советское радио.

Ivanov 2004[1961] = Иванов, Вячеслав. "Лингвистические вопросы стихотворного перевода." In *Сравнительное литературоведение. Всемирная литература. Стиховедение*. Vol. 3 of *Избранные труды по семиотике и истории культуры*, *by Вячеслав Иванов*, 570–582. Москва: Языки славянской культуры.

Jakobson, Roman. 1966[1959]. "On linguistic aspects of translation". In *On translation*, edited by Reuben Arthur Brower, 232–39. New York: Oxford University Press.

Kourdis, Evangelos. 2017. "The semiotic school of Tartu-Moscow: The cultural 'circuit' of translation." In *Going East: Discovering new and alternative traditions in translation studies*, edited by Larisa Schippel and Cornelia Zwischenberger, 149–168. Berlin: Frank & Timme.

Kull, Kalevi. 2011. "Juri Lotman in English: Bibliography." *Sign Systems Studies* 39 (4/2): 343–56.

Lotman 1970 = Лотман, Юрий. *Структура художественного текста*. Москва: Искусство.

Lotman 1972 = Лотман, Юрий. *Анализ поэтического текста: Структура стиха*. Ленинград: Просвещение.

Lotman 1992a[1978] = Лотман, Юрий. "Феномен культуры". In *Избранные статьи* by Юрий Лотман, 34–45. Таллинн: Александра.

Lotman 1992b[1983] = Лотман, Юрий. "К построению теории взаимодействия культур (семиотический аспект)". In *Избранные статьи* by Юрий Лотман, 110–120. Таллинн: Александра.

Lotman 1994[1964] = Лотман, Юрий. *Лекции по структуральной поэтике. In Ю. М. Лотман и тартуско-московская семиотическая школа*, edited by А. Д. Кошелев, 10–263. Москва: Гнозис.

Lotman, 2009[1992]. *Culture and explosion*. Translated by Wilma Clark, edited by Marina Grishakova. Berlin and New York: Mouton de Gruyter.

Lotman, Juri and Boris Uspensky. 1978. "On the semiotic mechanism of culture". *New Literary History*, 211–232.

Lotman, Juri Mikhailovich, Vjacheslav Vsevolodovich Ivanov, Aleksandr Moiseyevich Pjatigorskij, Vladimir Nikolayevich Toporov, and Boris Andreevich Uspenskij. 2013[1973]. "Theses on the semiotic study of cultures (As applied to Slavic texts)." In *Beginnings of the Semiotics of Culture*, edited by Silvi Salupere, Peeter Torop, and Kalevi Kull, 53–77. Tartu: University of Tartu Press.

Lotman, Jurij. 1977. *The structure of the artistic text*. Translated from Russian by Gail Lenhoff and Ronald Vroon. Ann Arbor: University of Michigan Press.

Lotman, Yuri M. 1990. *Universe of the mind*. Translated by Ann Shukman. London, New York: I.B. Tauris & Co. Ltd.

Lotman, Yuri. 1979. "Culture as collective intellect and the problems of artificial intelligence." In *Dramatic structure: poetic and cognitive semantics*, edited by Lawrence Michael O'Toole and Ann Shukman. Vol. 6 of *Russian Poetics in Translation*, edited by Ann Shukman, 84–96. Oxford: Holdan Books.

Mel'čuk, Igor Aleksandrovič. 2000. "Machine translation and formal linguistics in the USSR." In *Early years in machine translation: Memoirs and biographies of pioneers*, edited by William John Hutchins, 205–226. Amsterdam and Philadelphia: John Benjamins.

Monticelli, Daniele. 2017. "From modelling to untranslatability: Translation and the Semiotic Relation in Y. Lotman's Work (1965–1992)." *Acta Slavica Estonica* IX. *Стратегии перевода и государственный контроль. Translation Strategies and State Control*, edited by Lea Pild, 15–35. Tartu: University of Tartu Press.

Pasternak 1973 = Пастернак, Е.В. "Дополнение к публикации первых опытов Б. Пастернака: Переводы из Рильке." *Труды по знаковым системам* 6: 546–548.

Pilshchikov, Igor and Mikhail Trunin. 2016. "The Tartu-Moscow School of Semiotics: A transnational perspective." *Sign Systems Studies* 44 (3): 368–401.

Revzin 1968 = Ревзин, Исаак. "Семиотический комментарий к чешской книге о переводе." In *Мастерство перевода 1966*, 425–439. Москва: Советский писатель.

Revzin 1977 = Ревзин, Исаак. *Современная структурная лингвистика*. Москва: Наука.

Revzin, Rosenzweig 1964 = Ревзин, Исаак и Виктор Розенцвейг. *Основы общего и машинного перевода*. Москва: Высшая Школа.

Salupere 2008 = Салупере, Сильви. "О понятии перевод в трудах Юрия Лотмана." *Sign Systems Studies* 36(2): 417–436.

Sütiste, Elin (forthcoming). "The functional roots of Jakobson's plural concept of translation." In *Reconsidering Jakobson*, edited by Elin Sütiste, Remo Gramigna, and Jonathan Griffin. Tartu: University of Tartu Press.

Toporov 1969 = Топоров, Владимир. "'Источник' Батюшкова в связи с 'Le Torrent' Парни." *Труды по знаковым системам* 4: 306–334.

Toporov, Vladimir. 1992. "Translation sub specie culture." *Meta* 37 (1): 29–49.

Torop 1982 = Тороп, Пеэтер. "Процесс перевода и некоторые методологические проблемы переводоведения." *Труды по знаковым системам* 15: 10–23.

Torop, Peeter. 1999[1981]. "Metatekstide teooriast mõnede tekstikommunikatsiooni probleemidega seoses." In *Kultuurimärgid* by Peeter Torop, 27–41. Tartu: Ilmamaa.

Toury, Gideon. 1980. *In search of a theory of translation.* Tel Aviv: The Porter Institute for Poetics and Semiotics.

Toury, Gideon. 1994[1986]. "Translation. A cultural-semiotic perspective." In *Encyclopedic dictionary of semiotics,* edited by Thomas A. Sebeok, 2nd ed., Volume 2 N–Z, 1111–1124. Berlin, New York: Mouton de Gruyter.

Uspensky, B. 1987 = Успенский, Борис. "К проблеме генезиса тартуско-семиотической школы." *Труды по знаковым системам* 20: 18–29.

Uspensky, V. 1992 = Успенский, Владимир. "Серебряный век структурной, прикладной и математической лингвистики в СССР и В. Ю. Розенцвейг: Как это начиналось (заметки очевидца)." *Wiener Slavistischer Almanach* 33 (Sonderband).

CHAPTER 5

# Heeding the Call for Transfer Theory

*Shaul Levin*

## Abstract

Even-Zohar's 1981 call for transfer theory as a general framework for dealing with translation has been scarcely addressed and not yet answered. Part I of this paper offers a critical reading of four investigations into the relationship between translation and transfer carried out by Rachel Weissbrod (2004, 2010), Susanne Göpferich (2007), and Lieven D'hulst (2012). Strongly connected with Even-Zohar's theorization, the concepts of transfer employed by these scholars exhibit a sharp distinction between a Jakobsonian understanding of transfer and a socio-cultural one, potentially blurring the conceptualization of these relations in the discipline. Part II turns to Anthony Pym's (1992) markedly different understanding of transfer, and systematic conceptualization of its relations with translation as one of its possible responses. Part III suggests that combining previous insights with knowledge acquired outside of translation studies may lead at long last to a fruitful formulation of a general theory of transfer. Following Pym's categories, it is suggested that relations between transfer and its various forms can all be conceptualized along causal, economic, semiotic, epistemological—and functional—terms. Incorporating notions of temporality and continuity is also urged, and recontextualization identified as a universal characteristic of transfer processes.

In a seminal paper titled "Translation theory today: A call for transfer theory", read to a conference in Tel Aviv in 1978 and published in *Poetics Today* in 1981, Itamar Even-Zohar stated the following:

> Our accumulated knowledge about translation indicates more and more that translational procedures between two systems (language/literatures) are in principle analogous, even homologous, with transfers of various kinds within the borders of the system [...]. [T]he procedures by which textual models in one system are transferred to another [...] constitute a major feature of systems. This has been, at least generally, formulated before, notably by Jakobson (1959), but no consequences were ever drawn for translation theory. Can we stick to this practice, or would it be wiser to acknowledge the implicit practice whereby translation is

© KONINKLIJKE BRILL NV, LEIDEN, 2021 | DOI:10.1163/9789004437807_006

discussed in terms of transfer and vice versa? In other words, *would it be profitable to establish a transfer theory*, and if so, where will inter-systemic translation be located, and with what consequences?

My answer is that [...] sooner or later it will turn out to be uneconomical to deal with [translation and transfer, S.L.] separately [...] I am deeply convinced that at our present stage in translation theory, we simply do not have much choice.

EVEN-ZOHAR 1981, 2–3; my emphasis—S.L.

Developing transfer theory from translation theory, Even-Zohar concludes, will help in looking for the really particular in translation, and in determining what "translational procedures" consist of.

Four decades have gone by and attempts to rise up to the challenge have been relatively scarce. A general theory of transfer is yet to be formulated, and its various relations with translation—and other forms of transfer (such as adaptation, imitation, and borrowing)—are yet to be defined. What follows is an attempt in this direction. In the first part, I trace the trajectories of four investigations into the relationship between translation and transfer, carried out by three different scholars in the field in the past two decades: Rachel Weissbrod (2004, 2010), Susanne Göpferich (2007), and Lieven D'hulst (2012). As we shall see, the concepts of transfer employed by these scholars do not share a common core of meaning. They exhibit a sharp distinction between a 'narrow' Jakobsonian understanding of transfer on the one hand, and a 'wider' socio-cultural understanding of the concept on the other hand. Ignoring this distinction may well have contributed to the blurring of the conceptualization of relations between translation and transfer in the discipline, a blurring that is already found in Even-Zohar's own theoretical oeuvre, which serves as an important building stone for these approaches.

In the second part I turn to a markedly different understanding of the concept of transfer employed by a fourth, prominent scholar in the field, Anthony Pym (1992). While seeking inspiration in the same seminal call by Even-Zohar, Pym's idea of the relations between translation and text transfer stems from a different point of view, and his systematic conceptualization of these relations—in particular of the causality pertaining between the two phenomena—may serve as foundations for a theoretical bridge between the two.

In the third and concluding part, I return to Even-Zohar's call to suggest that establishing a theory of transfer is profitable insofar as it deals with translation in terms of transfer rather than vice versa. Treating non-translational transfers as if they were translations fails to utilize exactly those features which

# HEEDING THE CALL FOR TRANSFER THEORY

differentiate transfer in its multifarious forms and translation in its specific-ities as two distinct concepts and processes. The way is then outlined for a general theory of transfer, in which insights from within translation studies combine with conceptualizations developed in various other disciplines in order to devise proper categories for exploring the relations between transfer and its various processes and products, including translation.

## 1 The Relationship between Translation and Transfer

The gist of Even-Zohar's argument is this: it is neither logical nor profitable to treat one section of phenomena—translation—as an object of study, while the other section—non-translational transfer of texts, such as adaptation, imi-tation, and a "heap of [other] non-translational translations" is pushed outside the realm of translation theory (Even-Zohar 1981, 3–4). This is an inevitable conclusion of the analogy/homology hypothesis of translational and trans-feral processes. Put differently, it is a reverting to Jakobson's famous notion of intra-lingual, inter-lingual, and inter-semiotic processes as analogous cases of 'translation'. Indeed, this is exactly what Even-Zohar does when he insists that translation theory has "isolate[d] translated texts from too many other kinds of texts, rather than putting the former in the context of the latter" (Even-Zohar 1990a, 75). This is tantamount to saying, that in reading Jakobson, translation theorists have put so much effort into differentiating inter-lingual from intra-lingual and inter-semiotic processes, that they forgot to pay attention to the common basis which makes them all 'translations' in Jakobson's terms.

### 1.1 Rachel Weissbrod: From Translation to Transfer

This rationale (in its reformulation in Even-Zohar 1990a) has been taken up and followed by Rachel Weissbrod in her 2004 paper titled "From translation to transfer". In this article, Weissbrod aims to map and illustrate the forms of transfer implied by what she calls "Even-Zohar's definition of transfer". However, while relying completely on Even-Zohar's work, the definition she attributes to him is actually her own. It states that "transfer [is] the re-creation in cultural system A of a text or a model originating in system B" (Weissbrod 2004, 23), whether within the same macro-system or not. Weissbrod then takes Even-Zohar's rationale one step further, suggesting (once again in his name) that all the phenomena discussed by Jakobson could actually be labeled 'transfer'. The first stage of transfer's "coup d'etat" thus completed, Weissbrod proceeds to characterize the operation of transfer by several long-standing concepts of translation studies: obligatory and non-obligatory shifts, the important role played by target system norms and repertoire, and general laws or universals, such as the tendency toward standardization. Finally, the stage is set to "show that other forms of transfer 'behave' as translation does according to the translation theory described here" (ibid., 25).

Though Weissbrod's attempt seems to be driving Even-Zohar's call to a logical conclusion, it nevertheless appears to go against the most essential grain of Even-Zohar's rationale. Instead of reinstating translation in its wider transferal context in order to derive the real particularities of translation, she takes what translation studies had previously deemed to be particular to translation and applies it invariably to the wider context of transfer. While perhaps not implausible or futile in terms of dealing with transfer, her vector is quite the opposite to that of Even-Zohar's, in terms of what this move is expected to accomplish for translation theory.

Weissbrod here indeed takes a step in the direction of developing a transfer theory from translation theory. But even if she claims in closing that "one can [...] benefit from a theory whose power lies in the realization that there is a mechanism of transfer shared by translation and other cultural phenomena" (ibid., 38), her own attempt seems only to suggest that transfer and translation behave essentially in the same way. Clearly, substituting 'transfer' for every occurrence of 'translation' in Jakobson's categories will not bring us closer to a beneficial placing of one within the context of the other, nor to a better understanding of the relationship between the two.

### 1.2 Susanne Göpferich: A Plea for Widening the Scope of Translation Studies

Susanne Göpferich's "Plea for widening the scope of translation studies" (2007) appears to be of a completely different kind. This is certainly true insofar as her theoretical starting point is concerned. Working within the functionalist paradigms of the German and Finnish tradition, she pleads for the inclusion in translation studies of "any mediated transformation of offers of information performed to fulfill specific functions and meet the needs of specific audiences" (Göpferich 2007, 26), and claims this would bring translation studies closer to the newly established field of 'Transferwissenschaften' (Transfer Studies) which she deems beneficial to both.

That the notion of transfer employed by Göpferich is very different from that of Even-Zohar is immediately visible. Citing Antos, 'Transferwissenschaften' is here defined as the field which "investigates the conditions, principles, forms and strategies as well as problems and chances of creating meta-knowledge about knowledge" (ibid., 27) for the purpose of optimizing knowledge transfer

HEEDING THE CALL FOR TRANSFER THEORY

in order to eliminate inaccessibility to knowledge. The decisive feature of Göpferich's own transfer concept is likewise "to make, what is transferred, cognitively accessible in the target culture" (ibid., 33; see also Göpferich 2010).

This version of transfer seems a far cry from that of Even-Zohar's: a Skopos-based 'Transferwissenschaften' of practical, even prescriptivist tendencies, seems even further removed from the transfer theory he called for. However, within the terminology of her own working, Göpferich essentially shares Even-Zohar's most basic drive. Like him, she claims it does not make sense to exclude from translation studies intra-lingual transformations such as text adaptations, optimization and popularization, only because the competence required for intra-cultural transfers forms a less complex subset of the competence necessary for inter-cultural ones, including translation. In other words, she resorts to the same idea of the common denominator between Jakobson's original categories of translational phenomena.

Two further claims put forth by Göpferich show that her overall conception of the relations between translation and transfer is in fact much closer to Weissbrod's than it appears. First, the course of her call is parallel to Weissbrod's, positing that intra-cultural transfers should be regarded as inter-cultural ones, and so, as cases of translation. Thus, we once again have transfer as a form of translation rather than the other way around. Second, in finally comparing translation studies and 'Transferwissenschaften' based on her own concept of translation, Göpferich concludes that "in their core areas, the two disciplines are congruent" and the main tasks of the latter can be considered as genuine tasks of the former (ibid., 35). Thus, if in Weissbrod, translation theory seemed to metamorphose into transfer theory, in Göpferich, the two existing fields of translation studies and 'Transferwissenschaften' seem on the brink of merging. Differences in paradigms notwithstanding, neither approach appears to lead us towards a deeper understanding of the one concept within the wider context of the other.

### 1.3    *Two Incongruous Notions of Transfer*
Whereas Weissbrod's first attempt drew heavily on Jakobson along the lines of Even-Zohar's call for transfer theory, her 2010 paper titled "Translation and cultural transfer" takes a very different approach. Leaning closely once again on Even-Zohar, she now employs a markedly different notion of transfer, based on his later conception of the role of transfer in the making of culture repertoires, and on his laws of cultural interference (Even-Zohar 1997, 2005). Let us first state what this later notion of transfer amounts to, and how it differs from the one put forth in Even-Zohar's initial call for transfer theory.

As we have seen, Even-Zohar's 1981 paper called attention to the common transferal basis of the different translational phenomena defined by Jakobson. It spoke in semiotic and structuralistic terms, reaching its peak in formulating a set of nine hypotheses which strove to define the relations between translation and transfer 'procedures' (interestingly, this set of highly formalized hypotheses had been almost completely removed from the 1990 version of this paper).

In contrast, Even-Zohar's later notion of transfer deals exclusively with "the socio-cultural juncture where transfer plays a role" (Even-Zohar 2010[1997], 70). Developed in the 1990's, it seems very much in line with what has often been called the cultural and sociological turns in translation studies. While clearly inter-lingual and inter-cultural in the explicit context of "translation in its accepted sense" (ibid.), it never once mentions Jakobson, and overall does not refer much to translation *per se*. Its main interest lies in the relations between transfer—or 'interference'—and repertoire-making. Transfer is here defined as "the state of integrated importation into a repertoire" (ibid., 73), and interference as "a procedure emerging in the environment of contacts [relationship between cultures—S.L.], one where transfer has taken place" (Even-Zohar 2010[2005], 52). The formalization of hypothesized procedures linking transfer and translation in 1981 now gives way, most notably, to a range of sociological factors that need to be taken into account:

> What need be studied is the complex network of relations between the state of the receptive system, the nature of the transference activity [...] and the relations between power and market, with a special attention to the activity of the makers of repertoire who are at the same time agents of transfer.
>
> EVEN-ZOHAR 2010[1997], 76

### 1.4 Rachel Weissbrod: Translation and Cultural Transfer

It is this later notion of transfer of Even-Zohar's that Weissbrod employs in her 2010 paper. This is made obvious from the very title: "Translation and cultural transfer: Israeli law as a case in point". The current purpose is twofold: "to present the evolution of Israeli law as a product of intercultural transfer crossing the lines between East and West, and to examine the role of interlingual translation in this process" (Weissbrod 2010, 272). Transfer is here regarded as "a process that generates a multiplicity of repertoires originating in diverse and even disparate cultures and reflecting the power struggles, tensions and compromises between them" (ibid., 274). Doubtless, we have crossed over to a very socio-cultural sense of transfer, much wider and vaguer in scope than the Jakobsonian typology employed previously.

For the sake of fairness, it must be stated that Weissbrod had no intention of working towards a general theory of transfer in this paper. However, the manner in which she carries out her case study is an attempt to put to use such a framework in a way that is relevant to our current purpose. In essence, Weissbrod treats Even-Zohar's laws of cultural interference as if they were general laws of cultural transfer and uses historical research to highlight the interaction between interlingual translation and the intercultural transfer of models. In a sense, she is much closer to pursuing Even-Zohar's original goal of studying translation in the wider context of transfer than she had been in her previous, Jakobsonian attempt. However, since the notion of transfer she uses now has undergone a wholesale conversion into a socio-cultural frame of reference, we find ourselves somewhat at a loss as to what constitutes the relations between inter-lingual translation in its original, Jakobsonian terms, and transfer in its new, socio-cultural ones.

Indeed, it is in this sense that dealing with translation in the context of intercultural transfer seems to be straying away from translation studies and its goals (ibid.), and not because it marginalizes interlingual translation as an object of study, or obscures the discipline's boundaries, the dangers raised by Even-Zohar in 1981 and reiterated by Weissbrod here. It is rather because a general theory of transfer, if it is to succeed in providing a better understanding of translation within a wider context of analogous phenomena, must furnish a much subtler account of the relations between these phenomena on all relevant frames of reference. While Even-Zohar's initial call for transfer theory tried to do so in Jakobsonian terms, the latter notion of cultural transfer used by Weissbrod requires further development in order to do so in relevant socio-cultural terms.

1.5    *Lieven D'hulst: From Assumed Translation to Assumed Transfer*

An integrated approach linking the concepts of transfer and translation within a historical methodology is the declared goal of Lieven D'hulst's 2009 "Traduction et transfert: pour une démarche intégrée". Defining transfer in the English abstract as a "process of interaction between literary systems, their subsystems and their communication models" (D'hulst 2009, 150), he calls for expanding the study of translational norms and methods of analysis to other transfer procedures. While this may remind us of Weissbrod 2004 and Göpferich 2007, whom D'hulst indeed cites, his latter development of the prospective theoretical framework involves a stronger affinity to Even-Zohar's later notion of cultural transfer.

In "(Re)locating translation history: From assumed translation to assumed transfer" D'hulst first pays tribute to Even-Zohar's seminal call for transfer theory, citing a full key paragraph from its 1990 version (D'hulst 2012, 140). He then suggests the concept of "assumed transfer" (after Toury's "assumed translation", of course) as an umbrella concept encompassing all possible features of cultural exchange processes, of which explicitly-labeled verbal translation is only one. Furthermore, he sees it as "a tool to identify and describe the forms, meanings and functions of a broad spectrum of exchange activities taking place both between and within cultures" (ibid., 150). Thus, "assumed transfer" here could actually be viewed as an umbrella concept encompassing an entire Jakobsonian-like typology of transfer of the sort Even-Zohar seems to have called for in 1981. But importantly, for D'hulst, this typology is deeply embedded within a socio-cultural conceptualization of transfer. His "basic and specific features of transfer" thus include the whole range of socio-cultural players and institutions in the field of production and reception, as well as the specific category of mediators or agents manipulating these products. That this resembles Even-Zohar's 1997 range of sociological factors to be taken into account in the study of transfer need not surprise us: Even-Zohar's very paragraph is cited in full in an endnote (ibid., 142, 151 n. 3).

D'hulst's framework is the most developed attempt at theorizing transfer surveyed yet, integrating the notion of transfer in its systemic, Jakobsonian reading, with the latter notion of transfer in its highly socio-cultural reading. This integration is clearly manifest in the practical methodology for transfer histories that he devises, where the interrelations between different transfer techniques are sought to be analyzed while taking into account the specific configurations of agents involved. Even so, D'hulst continues to echo Even-Zohar in concluding that still "more work is needed to understand how translation relates to other transfer techniques and how this relation determines the specifics of translation" (ibid., 150). It therefore seems apt to recall at this stage an earlier attempt of a different order at defining these very relations between translation and transfer.

## 2　A Different Understanding of the Transfer Concept

In 1992, Anthony Pym set out to conceptualize the relations between translation and material text transfer in causal, economic, semiotic and epistemological terms. Seeking inspiration in Even-Zohar's call for transfer theory (1990 version)—and expressing optimism about its declared aims—he wished to achieve a useful and more complex understanding of what he termed "the discontinuity between translation and the non-translational results of transfer" (Pym 1992, 172).

Translation has its own inner discursive logic, which operates within the wider social logics governing material transfer. At the same time, translation situations derive their rationality in relation to other transfer alternatives. While it is not so easy to delimit translation from non-translational products of transfer, applying too general concepts concerning the wider generality of transfer to translational practice *per se* has its own dangers, since all of the advantages that Even-Zohar foresees in his general proposal "depend on a clear initial 'distinction' between transfer and translation" (ibid., 173, emphasis in original). Transfer analysis is Pym's suggested method to overcome these difficulties.

Pym's treatment of the causality pertaining between transfer and translation is most illuminating and may serve to exhibit in general the advantages that such conceptualizations hold in store. Transfer is considered by him to be the material moving of texts across space-time. Translations could then be described as one particular kind of displaced texts which are the products of transfer. Put in the form of a causal statement, transfer "set[s] up situations in which translation might be required, making translation one of several possible responses to transfer" (ibid., 184). Transfer can thus be approached "as a social conditioning of translation [...] the way a text is translated will be conditioned by the social reasons motivating the transfer in the first place" (ibid., 186).

Since transfer and translation are linked through fundamental causality, and since this causality is clearly directional—transfer (may) bring about translation, not the other way around—it follows that only within the context of transfer analysis can a comprehensive account of any individual case of translation be achieved. Pym uses transfer analysis to identify basic categories and principles which "go some way towards defining the nature and function of translation as a phenomenal form whenever and wherever it occurs" (ibid., 188). Transfer-derived categories such as implied receivers or reception situations, coupled with principles such as the value transformation inherent in transfer, can suggest why translation should occur in the specific times and places that it does, by what range of transformational possibilities, etc. Of particular importance is the fact that these categories stand in causal relation to translation, as opposed to the tautological relations found in other theories according to Pym. It is these transfer-derived categories, he concludes, that are "potentially able to locate the specificity of translation within a highly interdisciplinary framework" (Pym 1992a, 188).

Other kinds of relationships pertain between transfer and translation, and between translational-transfer and other kinds of transfer. Economic relations, though also of a causal nature, are nevertheless not mechanistic: social intervention often has priority over free-market or systemic liberalism. Semiotic relations between the two phenomena are grounded on distance and represented by translational paratexts, whose combination determines how close to or far from the receiver the source text is placed. Translational paratexts thus act as representations and (innocent or driven) misrepresentations of transfer, reflecting and signaling intercultural distance.

In epistemological terms, translational procedures both respond to transfer and represent transfer. Whereas translation analysis tends to generate answers based on the various factors concerning the translator's immediate situation, transfer analysis tends to look for social purposes for general cases. For instance, in the case cited by Pym, a 1991 advertisement in *Le Monde* in which the State of Kuwait seeks international contractors,

> a standard purpose-based translation analysis can ask "Why translate this text?" and then come up with some kind of general answer based on the various factors surrounding the translator. It could be supposed, for example, that the Kuwaiti text was translated into French because of Le Monde's general policy concerning foreign languages. But transfer analysis can ask the same question in a slightly different form: "Why should this text have been moved to a position where it should be translated?". That is, why should the Kuwaitis have had the English text sent to a French newspaper in the first place? This second kind of question leads to a different kind of answer, involving far more than the one-off factors concerning the translator's immediate situation. (ibid., 186)

Thus, any given translator's—and translation—situation is invariably situated within a wider transfer situation, and the purposes and methods of the former can only be assessed once the purposes and mechanisms of the latter have been explained. This "double epistemology", as Pym dubs it, points in two helpful directions: On the one hand, it should "connect translation studies with general transfer situations, and thereby with the wider social sciences bearing on the more general aspects of intercultural communication" (Pym 1992, 186). On the other hand, it should

> affect the way translated texts are perceived and evaluated within translation studies. In particular, it should show that translation is not a given need but an option causally determined at certain times and places; it

should reformulate the ethical problem of the way translations represent intercultural distances; it should promote a wide but centered interdisciplinary; and it should increase awareness that translation is a very particular mode of text transformation. (ibid., 187)

Both directions correspond to Even-Zohar's call, placing translation within the wider frame of transfer while increasing awareness to the particularities of translation itself. And the way is elegant, grounding both wider and narrower aspects in the (directional) causal and epistemological relations pertaining between the two phenomena. Pym's warning against the blurring of translation and transfer is clear enough: no crossing over of Jakobsonian categories, no translation as transfer or vice versa. His basic concept of transfer as the moving of a material object over space and time differs from Even-Zohar's later notion of transfer as the state of integrated importation into a repertoire, in that it sees this movement as being separate and independent of any rules for adaptation or interpretation, and certainly of any prospective integration. All these may come later in the frame of "inner transfer", procedures for adapting these moving structures to new interpretive systems, of which translation is one.

Pym's concept of transfer is nevertheless grounded in a sociocultural perspective, which is not incompatible with Even-Zohar's later notion: its very occurrence is motivated by social reasons, hence the tendency of transfer analysis to look for social purposes. Within this context, Pym's systematic conceptualization of the relations between translation and transfer presents us with ways by which the two phenomena may be conceptually linked. Rather than metamorphose one into the other, or point to a possible merger, his method lays down the foundations for a theoretical bridge between the two.

## 3 A General Theory of Transfer

"Would it be profitable to establish a transfer theory?" asked Even-Zohar in 1981, to discuss translation in terms of transfer and vice versa? The approaches surveyed above suggest a narrow and a wider sense in which these questions can be answered. Discussing transfer in terms of translation may offer some insights for studying the forms of transfer included in Jakobson's categories of intra-lingual and inter-semiotic translation. This is, in essence, what Weissbrod (2004) and Göpferich (2007) had offered. However, treating non-translational transfers as if they were translations seems ultimately the wrong path to take. It fails to utilize exactly those features which differentiate transfer in its multifarious forms and translation in its specificities as two distinct processes and concepts. While this may be profitable in the narrow sense of including such non-translational phenomena as objects of study in translation studies, it both fails to relate to the wider range of transfers conceptualized and dealt with outside of the discipline, and does not seem to offer much gain in terms of dealing with translation proper within it. (The latter is also true for the work carried out by the Göttingen School active in the 1990s, whose "transfer-oriented" model sought basically to enhance the analysis of the differences that "need to be mediated by an act of translation" via widening the scope into literary and cultural differences between source and target (Hermans 2020, 153)). It seems much more effective and logical to discuss translation in terms of a wider conceptualization of transfer, and it is in this wider sense that establishing a transfer theory may be most profitable. More specifically, I believe that combining insights and methods from D'hulst and Pym with knowledge acquired outside of translation studies may lead to a fruitful formulation of such theory. Let me state briefly what seems to me the key points in this undertaking.

First, taking translation to be one possible form of transfer (and not the other way around), Even-Zohar's notion of developing transfer theory 'from' translation theory has to be dropped altogether. A transfer theory may have much to gain from the insights and tremendous work carried out within translation studies for decades, but translation studies should by no means serve as the single source for its development. Whether we go along with Pym and see translation as one particular kind of displaced texts which are the products of transfer, or with D'hulst and see translation as one explicitly-labeled verbal outcome of cultural exchange processes, the actual pool of transfer processes and products and the possible ways of dealing with them is much larger than that which translation studies delineates. This view seems clearly endorsed by both Pym and D'hulst, the former taking general transfer situations to be part of the wider social sciences bearing on the more general aspects of intercultural communications, the latter enumerating the many disciplines in the humanities in which the concept of cultural transfer is being variously used. Establishing a general theory of transfer should be as interdisciplinary an endeavor as the actual research into concrete cases of transfer history (D'hulst), or into the highly interdisciplinary frameworks in which the specificity of translation is to be located based on transfer-derived categories (Pym).

Second, clearly, from the point of view of translation studies, two major types of relations have to be thoroughly explored and conceptualized in the frame of a general theory of transfer: the relations between translation and transfer, and the relations between translation and various forms of non-translational products/processes of transfer. Here, combining the methods put forth by Pym and

HEEDING THE CALL FOR TRANSFER THEORY

D'hulst could prove a powerful approach. Following Pym, we need to look into all possible forms in which these relations could be conceptualized, and devise transfer-based categories according to which transfer products/processes can be examined. This will provide us with stepping-stones of shared frames of reference and rid us of discrepancies such as putting a Jakobsonian concept of translation to work against a socio-cultural concept of transfer. At the same time, following D'hulst, setting up well-designed research programs into concrete cases of transfer histories would facilitate further theoretical reflection. Here, we must be very careful not to draw our theoretical conclusions upon the exclusive study of historically marked contexts of nation and culture building, as seems to have been the case rather frequently in translation studies, most notably in Even-Zohar's own work (see Levin, unpublished manuscript).

Third, the importance of interdisciplinarity can hardly be overemphasized. Anthropology, psychology, sociology, cultural geography, transnational history, systems theory, comparative literature, cultural studies, psychoanalysis, computer science, law, commerce, development economics, and translation studies—these are just the fields named by D'hulst and Pym in their respective articles in which various forms of transfer are being used and conceptualized; to which I would add at least management, organization, communication, and media studies. All of which deal in one way or another with questions of "how things [...] get from here to there" (Katz, 1999, 145), and what happens to them as they do. Objects and concepts, methods and practices, models and structures migrate, transfer, diffuse, circulate, disseminate, percolate, get transmitted, imported, exported, exchanged and transposed across boundaries, languages, cultures, systems, and networks through the actions of a host of transformers and intermediaries operating in contact zones, locales, transnational networks, and intercultures, getting recontextualized, redefined, reinterpreted, reinvented, reconfigured, rearticulated, reconstructed, reoriented, altered, optimized, framed, customized, emulated, modified, hybridized, creolized, adapted, adjusted, translated, and much more along the way. The frame of reference for dealing with transfer is clearly wider and more complex than the systemic-semiotic terms of Jakobsonian typology, or the terms of any specific literary, sociological, or cultural approach. Drawing on insights and methods developed in these diverse disciplines would greatly expand our understanding of transfer, and thus our ability to conceptualize its relations with its various products/processes and to devise proper categories according to which they could be explored.

As a first step, Pym's conceptualization of the relations between transfer and translation in causal, economic, semiotic, and epistemological terms may easily be taken to pertain to all forms of transfer: all manifestations of transfer have actual material transfer as their cause; economic factors are involved in their selection and distribution; all may be seen as semiotic representations of acts of transfer; and their production and reception are conditioned by the socio-cultural reasons motivating the actual transfer, and carried out by various socio-cultural agents. One important addition would be the conceptualization of these relations in functional terms as well. The social reasons motivating transfer may be discerned on either or both sides of the movement vector (such as Kuwaiti need of international expertise due to the structure of its market or *Le Monde*'s looking for income from advertisement in accordance with its readership and political standing, in Pym's example). While either or both may condition procedures employed in frame of the actual transfer mechanism, the intended function of the 'transferée' may condition the same mechanism in different ways (an ad intended to fit into a scheme for boosting a newspaper's feminist image, for instance, is likely to be translated differently than an ad that is not).

What would then differentiate between different forms of transfer would be the relations pertaining between transfer and its various possible manifestations. The actual 'mapping' of these relations onto specific circumstances for every given case, should hopefully lead to the possibility of answering the question why transfer had been carried out in the particular way that it had been rather than any other: Why were German books imitated in France in 1810–1840 (D'hulst 2012), a Kuwaiti ad translated into English and partially-translated into French when published in *Le Monde* in 1991 (Pym 1992), an Israeli court rule concerning international law and human rights quoted in US legal proceedings in the early 2000s (Weissbrod 2010), Russian principles of dialogue composition borrowed by a Hebrew writer in 1905–1913 (Even-Zohar 1990b), the German Catholic Party organization scheme copied by an 1870s Dutch leader (Velde 2005), and women's shelters and rape crisis centers adapted to fit specific political settings in the Netherlands in the 1980s (Roggeband 2007).

It seems fair to assume, that socio-cultural factors and circumstances facilitate and govern the selection of one semiotic-functional manifestation of transfer over another. Employing the notion of transfer mechanisms "as sets of rules or procedures for adapting structures to new interpretive systems" (Pym 1992, 172; in the case of translation, the 'transfer map' provided in van Doorslaer 2007, 226–227 may serve as a good overview), it is reasonable to suggest a two-step process, in which for every case of transfer, (1) the form of manifestation is first selected from a pool of available possibilities, followed by (2) selection of the actual strategies, procedures etc. of the mechanism(s) of transfer employed in the process of this particular form of transfer (D'hulst calls them 'techniques').

Of course, all manifestations of transfer are in fact forms of intended integration in a socio-cultural system across a boundary (however we define system, boundary, even integration), reflecting an intended function or way of being put to use in this culture. In this sense, even when a transferred 'it' (textbook, sit-com format, security scheme, car model) seems to be integrated "as is" some procedures of transfer are nevertheless carried out, at least at the semiotic-functional level. Recontextualization is not only a way of describing what agents of transfer are doing; it may very well be taken as a universal of transfer processes and procedures, simply by the nature of the fact that any transferred 'it' is instated in an inevitably different context.

Finally, two highly important characteristics of transfer processes should also find their way into our conceptualization: temporality and continuity. Time plays an important role in transfer and recontextualization, both in the selection of actual procedures within a particular transfer mechanism and in the selection of one form of transfer over another. Pym's discussion of value transformations which change with time and may be met with different translation strategies to withstand them (Pym 1992, 180–181) incorporates time into a conceptualization of the causal relations between translation and transfer. The diffusion of innovations theory (Rogers 2003), widely used in various fields in the social sciences, considers time to be of great pertinence to the diffusion process, and sees its inclusion as a variable in diffusion research as one of the framework's strengths. Scholars in relevant fields thus examine in depth relations between the time factor and the nature of change undergone by diffused items (see, for instance, Hays 1996; Roggeband 2007; Ansari, Fiss, and Zajac 2010). In the terminology used here, they all deal with various ways by which the time factor may condition selection of actual procedures within particular transfer mechanisms. They also offer various understandings of how the time factor may lead, under different circumstances, to the selection of different forms of transfer, such as early adopters opting for a faithful 'translation' (or copying) of a model whereas later ones may find greater incentives for adaptation (Roggeband 2007).

The notion of continuity is essentially the idea of transfer as an ongoing process, which may extend, in principle, for as long as the 'transferée' continues to move from one cultural system to the next. Even-Zohar's adherence to a formalistic, dichotomous view of center vs. periphery in systems, coupled with a strong emphasis on nation-building moments in history, led him to regard transfer processes between different polysystems (distinct cultures) as different in nature from ones taking place within a given polysystem. This ultimately meant regarding transfer as a fragmented process, made of separate segments behaving differently and dealt with differently by the theory (see

Levin, unpublished manuscript). However, conceptualizing transfer processes as continuous in principle seems to correspond more precisely to actual phenomena. This approach finds wide support in various disciplines, from Daneš's structuralistic conceptualization of a "continuous transitional zone" among inter- and intra-systemic levels (Daneš 1966, 14); to D'hulst's view of transfer as a continuous process where one product may give way to another using different carriers (D'hulst 2012, 140); to the view of diffusion as a continuous and dynamic process (Roggeband 2007, 249); to notions of cultural transfer as continuous in various branches of history (see Eisenberg 2005; Solomon 2008; Werner and Zimmermann 2006). Whatever the nature and level of the specific systems involved, whatever the specific modification undergone, the flow of elements in culture is always carried out according to the same dynamic principles governing a continuous transition in the frame of diffusive relations.

Translation studies deals with translational phenomena; one may claim, almost too obviously, that these are the objects of study to which its various theories apply. Relating translation to transfer complicates the picture, with several possible outcomes ranging from blurring the nature of the object of study, to blurring the terminology used to describe it and theorize about it, to blurring the boundaries of the discipline within which it is investigated. Approaching translation as one possible manifestation (or result) of transfer inevitably means recalibrating translational phenomena and the analytical tools used for understanding them within a (much) greater field of transferential phenomena and the analytical tools used for understanding them. It also means resituating the discipline in which they are investigated within a greater field of disciplines dealing with transfer.

In the most general terms, an umbrella-like theory of transfer would deal with how things get from here to there, and what happens to them as they do. Translation studies could hold a venerable position among the disciplines investigating the various manifestations of transfer and contributing to the ongoing development of the umbrella theory. Unearthing the nature of the relationship between translational and non-translational transferential phenomena would help delineate more clearly the position of translation studies and its object of study among its sister disciplines.

### References

Ansari, Shahzad M., Peer C. Fiss, and Edward J. Zajac. 2010. "Made to fit: how practices vary as they diffuse." *Academy of Management Review* 35 (1): 67–92.

HEEDING THE CALL FOR TRANSFER THEORY 103

D'hulst, Lieven. 2009. "Traduction et transfert: pour une démarche intégrée." *TTR: traduction, terminologie, rédaction* 22 (2): 133–150.

D'hulst, Lieven. 2012. "(Re)locating translation history: From assumed translation to assumed transfer." *Translation Studies* 5 (2): 139–155.

Daneš, František. 1966. "The relation of centre and periphery as a language universal." In *Travaux linguistiques de Prague, 2: Les problèmes du centre et de la périphérie du système de la langue*, edited by Josef Vachek, 9–21. Prague: Academia, Éditions de l'Académie tchécoslovaque des sciences.

Eisenberg, Christiane. 2005. "Cultural transfer as a historical process." In *Metamorphosis: structures of cultural transformations*, edited by Jürgen Schlaeger, 99–111. Tübingen: Gunter Narr Verlag.

Even-Zohar, Itamar. 1981. "Translation theory today: A call for transfer theory." *Poetics Today* 2 (4): 1–7.

Even-Zohar, Itamar. 1990a. "Translation and transfer." *Poetics Today* 11 (1), Special issue on Polysystem Studies: 73–78.

Even-Zohar, Itamar. 1990b. "Gnessin's dialogue and its Russian models." *Poetics Today* 11 (1), Special issue on Polysystem Studies: 131–53.

Even-Zohar, Itamar. 1997. "The making of culture repertoire and the role of transfer." *Target* 9 (2): 373–381. [Recollected in *Papers in culture research*. 2010. Tel Aviv: Unit of Culture Research, Tel Aviv University. 70–76.]

Even-Zohar, Itamar. 2010[2005]. "Laws of cultural interference." In *Papers in culture research*, 52–69. Tel Aviv: Unit of Culture Research, Tel Aviv University.

Göpferich, Susanne. 2007. "Translation studies and transfer studies. A plea for widening the scope of translation studies." In *Doubts and directions in translation studies. Selected contributions from the EST congress, Lisbon 2004*, edited by Yves Gambier, Miriam Shlesinger, and Radegundis Stolze, 27–39. Amsterdam: John Benjamins.

Göpferich, Susanne. 2010. "Transfer and transfer studies." In *Handbook of translation studies*, Vol 1, edited by Yves Gambier and Luc van Doorslaer, 374–377. Amsterdam: John Benjamins.

Hays, Scott P. 1996. "Influences on reinvention during the diffusion of innovations." *Political Research Quarterly* 49 (3): 631–650.

Hermans, Theo. 2020. *Translation in systems: Descriptive and systemic approaches explained*. 2nd edition. London and New York: Routledge—Taylor & Francis Group.

Jakobson, Roman. 1959. "On linguistic aspects of translation." *On Translation* 3: 30–39.

Katz, Elihu. 1999. "Theorizing diffusion: Tarde and Sorokin revisited." *Annals of the American Academy of Political and Social Science*, 566: 144–55.

Levin, Shaul. (unpublished manuscript). "The culture-making bias of interference in polysystem theory and DTS." Based on a paper read to the 12th Prague International Conference in Translation and Interpreting Studies, Charles University of Prague, September 2013.

Pym, Anthony. 1992a. "The relations between translation and material text transfer." *Target* 4 (2): 171–189.

Pym, Anthony. 1992b. "The relations between translation and material text transfer." https://usuaris.tinet.cat/apym/on-line/research_methods/1992_transfer.doc.

Rogers, Everett M. 2003. *Diffusion of innovations.* [5th edition]. New York: Free Press.

Roggeband, Conny. 2007. "Translators and transformers: International inspiration and exchange in social movements." *Social Movement Studies* 6 (3): 245–259.

Solomon, Susan Gross. 2008. "Circulation of knowledge and the Russian locale." *Kritika: Explorations in Russian and Eurasian History* 9 (1): 9–26.

van Doorslaer, Luc. 2007. "Risking conceptual maps: Mapping as a keywords-related tool underlying the online Translation Studies Bibliography." *Target* 19 (2): 217–233.

Velde, Henk te. 2005. "Political transfer: An introduction." *European Review of History* 12 (2): 205–221.

Weissbrod, Rachel. 2004. "From translation to transfer." *Across Languages and Cultures* 5 (1): 23–41.

Weissbrod, Rachel. 2010. "Translation and cultural transfer: Israeli law as a case in point." *Translation Studies* 3 (3): 272–286.

# PART 2

## *Localizing the Concept, the Object and the Discipline*

∴

CHAPTER 6

# Political Ideology in the Translation of Occidental Modernist Literature in China in the 1950s

*The Case of French Modernist Literature in Shijie Wenxue*

*Feng Cui*

### Abstract

According to André Lefevere, translation is a rewriting of an original text. All rewritings, whatever their intentions, reflect a certain ideology and poetics, and as such manipulate literature to function in a given society in a given way. Borrowing this concept, this chapter examines the translation of occidental modernist literature, with a focus on French modernist literature in *Shijie Wenxue* (World Literature)—the only official journal publishing translated literature in Mainland China in the 1950s, a period when China was dominated by Maoism and the unified communist ideology. During that time, China's alliance with the USSR, its antagonism against the Western capitalist camp, and Mao Zedong's mandate that "literature should reflect politics" all exerted ideological influences on the translation of occidental modernist literature in China. Taking a temporal and geographical approach, this chapter aims to examine the cultural behaviors of translators in the given cultural climate and timespans, the relationship between poetics and ideology in the polysystem of the target culture, the interaction among professional actors (such as reviewers, critics, teachers, and translators), mainstream ideologies and patronage, and the translator's subjectivity under the manipulation of ideology. Framing the case study in a specific historical period, the concepts of rewriting, subjectivity, and ideology in translation studies will be examined as well.

## 1    Introduction

Traditionally, the fidelity of the translated text to the source text was taken as the single, most important judgement criterion; everything else, ranging from the improvement in translation techniques, theoretical analysis, and comparisons between translated versions, were secondary. Translators, and by

---

© KONINKLIJKE BRILL NV, LEIDEN, 2021 | DOI:10.1163/9789004437807_007

extension, their works, were critiqued solely based on how close their translation is to the source texts—translations did not exist, nor were valued, independently of their sources. Yet, such an orientation—the source-oriented approach—could only be seen as an approach for translation criticism and not translation studies.

Translation studies emerged as an academic discipline in the Western scholarly circle circa the 1970s; it took the approach of a target-text orientation, 'liberating' the discipline from the "stronghold" of the original-text oriented model. This 'liberation' propelled the discipline forward and helped it gain a life of its own in academia. By the 1990s, with the adoption of the "cultural turn" in translation studies (Bassnett and Lefevere, 1990), the field took on the perspectives often focused on by scholars in Cultural Studies. With such a breakthrough, it then became apparent that translation was never an 'innocent' action—rather, it was and still is intricately linked with political ideologies (Wong 1999). This led to a heightened interest in studying ideologies; "many scholars worldwide began to explore issues of power and translation" (Gentzler and Tymoczko, 2002, xiii).

As the field continued to grow and evolve, Gentzler and Tymoczko (2002, xvi) note that the "*cultural* turn" in translation studies has become "the '*power* turn'". Every translation activity is, to some degree, manipulated by power and ideology; concomitantly, the translation activities are also involved in the construction of power structures and knowledge within a specific culture. The interactions between each and every component—translation and power, power and ideology, ideology and knowledge, knowledge and translation—come together to form a cyclical relationship, where each factor has some bearing on another, be it direct or indirect. In the words of Gentzler and Tymoczko (2002, xvi):

> [G]iven that we are always already formed by the discourses of the age in which we live, how can anyone effect cultural change? How can we bridge cultural gaps so as to experience anything new or different? How can we penetrate reified worldviews, particularly in the West, to allow real cultural difference to enter? Although in translation studies all now agree that translations are never fully homologous to the original—always containing shifts, errors, and subjective interpretations—it is also agreed that translations do nevertheless import aspects of the Other to the receiving culture. What sort of impact does translation have on cultural change? Under what circumstances do translations have the most impact? What forms of translation are most successful? And how does all this relate to cultural dominance, cultural assertion, and cultural resistance—in

THE CASE OF FRENCH MODERNIST LITERATURE IN *SHIJIE WENXUE* 109

short to power? In a sense such questions as these have meant that the "cultural turn" in translation studies has become the "power turn," with questions of power brought to the fore in discussions of both translation history and strategies for translation.

It is with such a perspective that this chapter chooses to focus on *Shijie Wenxue* as a case study, setting it against its historical and cultural contexts and exploring the relationships between translation, literature, and politics. As an investigation of the translation activities situated in 20th century China, this chapter not only pays attention to the synchronicity of translation activities in China, but also to other areas such as the cultural space in which these activities are carried out, the aims of the translators, and the types of foreign texts introduced into 20th century China via such translation activities. In doing so, this chapter aims to explain the ideologies underpinning literary translation and its effects on the translation itself and to discuss the relationship between translated literature and domestic literature in that specific cultural time and space.

Launched in July 1953 and discontinued on the eve of the Cultural Revolution in January 1966, 世界文学 (*Shijie Wenxue*), which literally means "World Literature", was the only journal publishing translated literature in Mainland China during the 1950s and the 1960s, serving as one of the main platforms for the Chinese people to keep abreast of foreign literature and the latest literary trends in the world. Hailed by almost all outstanding contemporary translators and foreign literature scholars nationwide, *Shijie Wenxue* published 2,827 translated works of various genres, including works from a total of 131 countries and regions. In its 134 issues, the journal had published works translated by a total of 850 translators. As a state-sponsored journal run by the Chinese Writers Association, *Shijie Wenxue* enjoyed a high political status for a long time.

Admittedly, the frequent political movements in the People's Republic of China (PRC) and its complex and uncertain diplomatic relations have had an important bearing on literary activities, especially literary translations. However, in-depth case studies of how translation activities have been affected by politics since 1949—when PRC was founded—are very limited, and this is especially so in the case of *Shijie Wenxue*. By controlling the selection process of source texts, *Shijie Wenxue* directly participated in, and also concurrently resisted the dominant ideology's construction of literary discourse in the two phases of translating the occidental modernist literature during the 1950s in Mainland China. This chapter examines the translation and the introduction of French modernist literature in *Shijie Wenxue* since France was the home of many influential modernist writers and literary works.

## 2 The First Phase: Absence of Translation and Presence of Selective Profiling (July 1953 Issue–March 1956 Issue)

Due to the Cold War and the antagonism between the socialist and capitalist camps at that time, the Communist Party of China (CPC), after it took power in 1949, adopted the policy of "leaning to one side [一边倒]", i.e., the Soviet Union, and made "learning from the Soviet Union" one of the major guiding principles of building and developing Mainland China. Meanwhile, CPC's literary norms also followed those of the Soviet Union, so the latter's principle of socialist realism entered the literary system of Mainland China. In the late 1940s and early 1950s, the Soviet literary world was in the midst of resolving literary issues by resorting to Zhdanovist political determinism, which preached "conflictless literature" (Moser 1992, 515–516) with the slogan of anti-capitalist ideology. The core concepts of Zhdanovism, like the emphasis on literature and the arts' service to political struggle, were also accepted by the literary world of Mainland China. The criteria and purposes of the selection, translation, and introduction of foreign literature by the translation circles of Mainland China at that time also echoed the widespread dominance of Zhdanovism in the literary world of Mainland China.

From the founding of *Shijie Wenxue* in July 1953 to the implementation of the policy of "let a hundred flowers blossom, let a hundred schools of thought contend" (also known as "The Double Hundred Policy" [双百方针]) by CPC in March 1956, *Shijie Wenxue*'s translation and introduction of foreign literary works focused on those of the Soviet Union and the socialist states in Eastern Europe. The characteristics of Zhdanovist literature were omnipresent in the selection of subject matter, the portrayal of characters, and the educational significance demonstrated in the plots. These works were considered "the most perceptive, noble and revolutionary literature" in opposition to "the dirty literature" of the capitalist class (Dementjev et al 1953, 209–234). Meanwhile, some literary works of capitalist states such as the United Kingdom, France, and the United States were also translated and introduced, with their quantity accounting for nearly one-fourth of the total output. It is conceivable that in the political environment of the period, the antagonism between ideologies meant that the conformity to socialist political ideology became the major criterion of translating and introducing capitalist literature. Occidental literary works under consideration for *Shijie Wenxue*'s translation and introduction were chiefly realistic works that ostensibly reflected "the decline" (Bianzhe 1954a, 215) and "most hideous reality" (ibid., 213) of the capitalist class, and their authors were mainly 'progressive' writers and members of the left-wing camp

# THE CASE OF FRENCH MODERNIST LITERATURE IN *SHIJIE WENXUE*

or the communist party. In sharp contrast to these literary works, American and European modernist literature was regarded as "degenerate, backward and decadent", and was excluded from selection as its themes were considered not pertinent to the highlighting of the superiority of the socialist system.

## 2.1 *Shijie Wenxue's Selective Introduction and Intentional Selection: A Perspective from the Translation and Introduction of Modernist Writers of the French Communist Party (PCF)*

The first half of the twentieth century witnessed rapid developments in the French communist movement, which started earlier and was larger in scale and more lasting in influence than that of most other major capitalist countries. It was because of this political setting that the number of PCF writers and their works translated and introduced in *Shijie Wenxue* was much larger than that of other capitalist countries. There was no lack of world-renowned literary masters among these translated and profiled writers. It is conceivably reasonable for *Shijie Wenxue* to favor such writers with the label of being both 'correct' in their political leanings and outstanding in their literary achievement. Of the fifteen French writers translated and introduced in this period, four are PCF members, i.e., Paul Eluard, George Cogniot, Louis Aragon, and Anatole France. We will examine the translation and introduction of Paul Eluard. He enjoyed an international reputation for his literary achievement and later joined the PCF because of his sympathy for the communist cause. Moreover, he was one of the representative writers of the French modernist literary movement. Therefore, it is reasonable to infer that when one modernist, 'progressive', and a Communist writer was translated and introduced by *Shijie Wenxue* in the first half of the 1950s, the selective introduction of his identity and intentional selection of their works were unavoidable.

*Shijie Wenxue* only published the translations of Eluard's six realism poems. "约瑟夫·斯大林" (Ode to Stalin) and "苏联—唯一的希望" (The Soviet Union: The Only Hope) are eulogistic poems just as their names imply. "路易斯·卡尔洛司·普列斯梯斯" (Luís Carlos Prestes) sings the praises of the Brazilians' struggle for independence, democracy, and freedom led by Brazilian Communist Party's General Secretary Luís Carlos Prestes. "布拉格的春天" (The Spring of Prague) relates that "Prague smashed her enemies under the shadow of death" (Eluard 1953b, 96). "亨利·马丁的信心" (The Confidence of Henri Martin) eulogizes Henri Martin, the famous French navy mariner who opposed the war in Indochina. "一篇该算的账" (An Old Score to Be Settled) was written for the famous Soviet journalist and writer Ehrenburg who "fights against wars" (Eluard 1953a, 98).

Readers are likely to deem Eluard a revolutionary and antiwar poet who believed in communism if they read only these realism poems. But the fact is that Eluard is also a representative of French surrealist poetry. His modernist poems, such as "To Live Here", "I Am Not Alone", "The Drowning Man", and "The Phoenix", are all representative of French Surrealist writing. However, *Shijie Wenxue* completely avoided mentioning features of his modernist writing and the representative works that demonstrated "he had been close to Dadaism and Surrealism" (Bianzhe 1954b, 194). These artistic techniques were deemed "decadent, pessimistic, and formalist" even though they had helped to build Eluard's literary fame. It says instead that "After 1936, [the poet] gave up his decadent, pessimistic, and formalistic inclinations and concerned himself with depicting the anti-fascist movement which preoccupied the progressive people of the time in his literary creation" (ibid.). By deliberately omitting certain facts about Eluard, *Shijie Wenxue* proceeded to portray Eluard as a revolutionary poet: "[The poet] joined PCF in its hardest times. In the postwar period, he always worked to safeguard world peace and fought against war agitators. Peace became the sole theme of his poetry" (ibid.). From the aforementioned representative Surrealist poems of Eluard, however, we can conclude that although he wrote many poems on the theme of peace, it is obviously not "the sole theme of his poetry". Published in the same issue with Eluard's six poems was "保罗·艾吕雅" (Paul Eluard), a study of Eluard by the Soviet critic Yakhotova. The author's examination of Eluard in this article begins with Eluard's participation in the labor movement and by completely avoiding Eluard's Surrealist literary practice, only closely analyzed poems that bear clear marks of communist ideology, such as in "The Worker", "The Victory of Guernica", "The Massacre", "The Poem of Power and Love", and "To the Comrade Print-Workers".

Manipulated by political ideology, *Shijie Wenxue*'s selective introduction and intentional selection made it impossible for mainland Chinese readers of that time to have a comprehensive grasp of Eluard's oeuvre as all of his major Surrealist works were absent from *Shijie Wenxue* in this period with the exception of the six revolutionary poems that appeared in the June 1953 issue.

*Shijie Wenxue*'s translation and introduction of Louis Aragon is largely similar. It deliberately glossed over Aragon's participation in Dadaist and Surrealist literary movements in his early years and neglects entire collections of his representative poems like *Fire of Joy* and *Perpetual Motion*, as well as his novels like *Anicet* and *Paris Peasant*. Only his anti-fascist poem "法兰西晨号" (Prelude to the French Reveille) was selected. Aragon took the road to communism and became an active antiwar propagandist in the 1950s. As

THE CASE OF FRENCH MODERNIST LITERATURE IN *SHIJIE WENXUE*    113

a result, he was introduced to Mainland China as "a progressive writer of the French Communist Party" who "broke away from the nihilism and disorder of Surrealism and turned to socialist realism" (Gold 1956, 100).

*Shijie Wenxue*'s translation and profiling model, exemplified in its selective introduction of Aragon and Eluard, demonstrates that the publication cleverly grasped the process of the two figures' change from being men of letters to 'revolutionaries' and while enhancing their socio-political traits or profiles in the target language context, *Shijie Wenxue* also deliberately downplayed and neglected their literary traits or profiles. Their social-political profiles had been formed by the selective reading provided by *Shijie Wenxue* to its readers and the translators and critics' judgments of their works. This way of profile-making usually adopts a utilitarian strategy that prioritizes the cultural or social needs of the country of the target language and is, therefore, to some extent, manipulation. Theoretically, this manipulative force consists of the external factors that influence or determine translation activities. It decides the translator's choice of source text/s and the translator or critic's unique understanding of the writer, which is bound to be constrained by various factors such as the translator or critic's perspective, position or context (Xu 2007, 120). The strong influence of social and cultural contexts on the creation and spread of such profiles is evident. After being translated and introduced to the cultural context of Mainland China, Aragon and Eluard's profiles as the Other were changed in the new historical space, and having gained the approval of Mainland readers, proceeded to merge into the target language context.

## 2.2    *Literary Identity and Political Position: Viewing Translation Criteria from the Translation and Introduction of Sartre*

Similarly manipulated by political factors in the target language context, the translation and introduction of Sartre by *Shijie Wenxue* changed dramatically in the first few years of the 1950s. In July 1952, Sartre was excluded from "the progressive French literati who use their pen as sword" and was regarded as a 'reactionary' advocate for 'existentialism'. (Xu and Song 2007, 89) The reason for this exclusion was that Sartre once remarked that "[the morality of Communists] had become conservative and it was the morality of petty bourgeois" (Sartre 1989, 254). Sartre's drama *Angzang de Shou* (*Dirty Hands*) that was first performed on stage in 1948 also tarnished the profile of the communist party (Xu and Song 2007, 89). However, in May 1954, Sartre visited the Soviet Union at the invitation of its writers; and in September 1955, he and Simone de Beauvoir visited Mainland China for one and a half months at the invitation of the Chinese People's Association for Cultural Exchanges with

Foreign Countries. During their stay, they were accorded high-level receptions by Chairman Mao Zedong and Premier Zhou Enlai. Around the time of Sartre's visit to China, in "世界文艺动态" (Literary and Artistic Activities in the World) of *Shijie Wenxue*'s August 1955 issue, Luo Dagang introduced Sartre's new work *Nekrassov* in detail, highlighting how "the author's sharp pen laid bare capitalist newspapers' same old tricks of starting rumors about and spreading slanders against PCF and the Soviet Union". Luo also praised Sartre for "progressing in recent years" and moving away from being an advocate for "idealistic and pessimistic existentialism" (Luo 1955, 244). Later in the same year, *Shijie Wenxue*'s November issue published Sartre's drama 丽瑟 (The Respectful Prostitute) after he ended his visit to China.

So, why did the reception towards Sartre change so dramatically amongst the literary world of Mainland China? The root cause was that Sartre participated in a series of activities in support of the PCF since the end of 1951 and thus became "a fellow-traveller" of the communist party. Sartre's pro-communist political position and his enormous international reputation made him a favorite in socialist countries. For *Shijie Wenxue*, whenever there was a contradiction between politics and literature, politics always prevailed: a foreign writer's political position was always far more important than his or her presumed literary achievement or experience. Even though Sartre had been a 'reactionary' modernist writer, his past 'reactionary' experience could be forgiven as long as he changed his political stance to a 'correct' one. His works, after intentional selection, could still be translated and introduced; and his personal profile, after selective introduction, could still be considered to be that of a 'progressive' pro-communist writer by Chinese who possessed little knowledge of the outside world beyond those that came from channels of propaganda.

In its November 1955 issue, *Shijie Wenxue* published Sartre's one-act play 丽瑟 (The Respectful Prostitute). In a period when modernist literary works were collectively 'absent' from *Shijie Wenxue* and even a writer's modernist background was either deliberately omitted or criticized in his or her allotted introduction, it would have been completely impossible for *The Flies*—the most representative work of Sartre as a dramatist and an existentialist work that aimed to arouse French people's free will—to get published in *Shijie Wenxue*. Instead, Sartre's 丽瑟 (The Respectful Prostitute) was labeled a model work which "mercilessly exposed the brutal and inhuman prosecution that the black people suffered in the so-called 'democratic and free' United States, as well as exposed the contemptible overbearing, ruthlessness of the reactionary class of the United States" (Bianzhe 1955b, 257).

As mentioned above, based on the introductions translated from French works, what requires our attention is how the absence of French modernist writers and that of modernist literary works were separate issues. The absence of French modernist literary works from *Shijie Wenxue* did not mean the synchronic absence of occidental modernist writers. While the Surrealist poems of Eluard and Aragon and the existentialist dramas of Sartre were rejected by *Shijie Wenxue*, the personal profiles of these writers could still appear in *Shijie Wenxue*. The only problem was that their profiles were not created by translating and introducing their modernist works, which would have meant approving their entry into the mainstream literary discourse of the source language context. Instead, their profiles were reconstructed in accordance with certain ideologies in the target language context. Reconstruction manifested itself in two ways. First, the editors and translators of *Shijie Wenxue* selectively introduced the literary experiences of these major French modernist writers in the postscript sections. In order to conform to the political discourse and ideology of the time, they regarded writers like Eluard and Aragon as representatives of those who had changed from being 'backward' to being 'progressive', i.e., they had abandoned the "decadent and pessimistic" modernist creative techniques of their early career and became 'revolutionary' and 'progressive' writers with antiwar and anti-capitalistic credentials. The second way of reconstruction was to intentionally select the works of these writers, including only those texts that showed their integration with "the antifascist movement of the progressive people" (Houji 1954b, 194), and in so doing, provide evidence for the arguments deployed in the postscripts written by various editors and translators. These two methods complemented each other and together reconstructed writers' profiles in order to meet the ideological norms of the target language context.

It can be seen that the intentional selection and selective introduction in target language context are used to rewrite and manipulate the literary fame in source language context and solidify local culture and values, fulfilling its purpose of educating and guiding target language readers in service of the mainstream ideology. As the only official journal that translated and introduced foreign literary works in Mainland China, *Shijie Wenxue* had a monopoly over the channels from which Chinese readers hoped to learn about foreign writers and works, thus depriving readers of their right to know the facts regarding the different literary experiences of a writer and his or her representative works. Beneath this practice of selective translation lie the culturally hegemonic inclinations of the Chinese society, emphasizing the superiority of socialism over capitalism. The Chinese readers' knowledge and even understanding of

116 CUI

many writers were confined to the official discourse in various "译后记" (post-scripts to translations), and these largely conformed to mainstream ideology. What's more, the intentional selection and the selective introduction reveal the translation as an act of rewriting, 'raping', and replacing of the source text and the reputation of the author. In the process of intentional selection and selective introduction, translators select specific aspects or texts to transpose and emphasize. Such a process serves to produce partial representations of the source texts.

## 3    The Second Phase: Aesthetic Translation (April 1956 Issue– July 1958 Issue)

After the mid-1950s, with the continuous progressions in the nation-building in Mainland China, the CPC leadership began to realize that "the Soviet Union had unwittingly exposed some of their shortcomings and mistakes in the midst of building their socialism" (Mao 1999, 23). Meanwhile, the emergence of divergence between China and the Soviet Union and the breakout of the Hungarian Revolution of 1956 directly and significantly raised the CPC leaders' consciousness of independence. CPC began a comprehensive self-examination of its developmental path and as a result, China subsequently detached itself from dependence on the Soviet Union. At the Enlarged Meeting of the Political Bureau of the CPC Central Committee held in April 1956, Mao Zedong officially proposed the policy of the Double Hundred Policy and pointed out that: "Literature and Art should be allowed to flourish freely, while different schools of thought in the Sciences should be allowed to contend; I think this should be our guiding principle" (Mao 1999, 54). The Double Hundred Policy exerted considerable influence on the literary and artistic world of Mainland China at that time.

The importance of the socialist ideology, which had previously been a primary priority and factor in *Shijie Wenxue*'s selection criteria, now showed signs of waning. The number of Soviet literary works translated and introduced by *Shijie Wenxue* dropped sharply during this period. *Shijie Wenxue* not only increased its translation and introduction of capitalist literature, but also for the first time introduced modernist literature, thought, and aesthetics which had been considered 'reactionary' and 'dirty' by the Chinese literary world.

Compared to the first phase, changes in the second phase were demonstrable in three respects. Firstly, some aspects of Wang Qi's captioning of several impressionist paintings in the April 1957 issue deserve special attention. The virtues of impressionist paintings were affirmed in a positive way, which is also in stark contrast to the previous negation and rejection of modernist literature and culture.

Secondly, the "Postscript to Translation" in the May 1957 issue marked the first time that *Shijie Wenxue* introduced the well-known Spanish modernist poet Rafael Alberti directly and positively.

Finally, the most striking example of changes between the first and second phase is in the July 1957 issue in which Chen Jingrong translated nine of Charles Baudelaire's poems in *E Zhi Hua* 恶之花 (*The Flowers of Evil*), i.e., "朦胧的黎明" (The Spiritual Dawn), "薄暮" (The Set of the Romantic Sun), "天鹅" (The Swan), "穷人的死" (The Death of the Poor), "秋" (Autumn Song), "仇敌" (The Enemy), "不灭的火炬" (The Living Torch), "忧郁病" (Spleen), and "黄昏的歌" (Evening Harmony). Although Chen had started to translate Baudelaire's poems as early as the 1940s, she translated these nine poems specifically for *Shijie Wenxue*. These poems were the only works translated and introduced by *Shijie Wenxue* in the 1950s and 1960s that are considered modernist in the source language context.

Mainstream literary criticism in the source language context had long reached a conclusion regarding Baudelaire, describing him as "the originator, pioneer, or founder of French Symbolist poetry" (Mein 1973, 154), and labeling *E Zhi Hua* as "Symbolist poetry" (Rhodes 1929, 444; Babuts 1997, 116). However, *E Zhi Hua* had now taken on "a different look" in the target language context: Firstly, the poetics were different from the poetics of socialist realism in the target language context. Secondly, in the introduction of *E Zhi Hua*, "the editor" vaguely dealt with the different interpretations of *The Flowers of Evil* between the source and target language contexts, an approach which alerts us to the translator/editor's resistance towards mainstream ideology. Thirdly, the Soviet critic Levik's paper "波特莱尔和他的'恶之花'" (Baudelaire and his *The Flowers of Evil*), which was published together with the translated poems, rewrote the work, or at any rate, rendered it into a more realist one that differed from its Symbolist aesthetic gloss in the source language context.

The above examination reveals that "knowledge does not necessarily precede the translation activity, and that the act of translation is itself very much involved in the creation of knowledge" (Gentzler and Tymoczko 2002, xxi). Translators, as much as creative writers and politicians, participate in the powerful acts that create knowledge and shape culture, and introduce occidental modernist literature and culture from the perspective of aesthetics into mainland China. We can further examine this through the lens of the polysystem theory, which sees various social symbols as being part of a large, open, and dynamic system made up of many sub-systems. Notably, the system of translated literature is regarded as part of the polysystem of culture; and its operation, position, and function in the latter are controlled by translation norms and ideology. The translation and introduction of occidental modernist literature and culture from the perspective of aesthetics in the second phase fully demonstrates how the translation subjects of the system of literary translation interact with the ideology of the polysystem. This theory can show us how translators express their subjectivities in the face of regularization from the mainstream ideologies of their times, that is, in this case, how the translators push back against the mainstream ideology covertly in their translation activities.

### 3.1 Poetics in E Zhi Hua

Despite the translator and the editor's ideological rewriting of *E Zhi Hua* in the target language context, readers could still perceive that the poetics—literary techniques and themes—in the translated poems were essentially different from those in socialist realism because the latter belonged to "festival literature" (Chen 2002a, 170), which typically had simple and similar plots and eulogized heroes and leaders. It can be observed that this set of poems are interrelated and the poet chose images such as "a woman forced into prostitution", "swollen purple" eyelids, "a poor woman", "ice-cold wizened breasts" and "the surge of blood" (Baudelaire 1957, 134) and other dark and repugnant images to boldly expose the ugly side of human nature and criticize the decadence of Paris society. The poems frequently adopt figures of speech such as symbolism and synesthesia, posing aesthetic questions through sensory stimulation and the construction of images. These are rarely seen in socialist realist poetry. Additionally, western religious and spiritual motifs like heaven, hell, angel, and Satan previously never appeared in socialist realist poetry that stressed leader worship and atheism. It is no wonder then that Levik described the novelty felt by readers in the socialist context as follows:

> [...] in terms of theme, images, verse form, and, above all, content, Baudelaire's poetry, compared with his predecessors, boasts something new and original. In addition to the abstract beauty and the phantom of ideality, it also exposes before us man's inner heart that has never been explored in poetry and depicts cities that are full of contradictions and urban life which is splendid on the surface but extremely ugly and even disgusting from within.
>
> LEVIK 1957, 162

In the 1950s when confrontations between different ideologies in China were at their height, the most important factor that led to *E Zhi Hua*'s introduction to the literary world in China was the relatively weakening of socialist ideology and the increasing importance attached to the aesthetic value of literary works after the implementation of the Double Hundred Policy. On the one hand, with the increase of national strength, the breakout of the Hungarian Revolution of 1956, and the exposure of Secret Speech at the 20th Congress of the Communist Party of the Soviet Union, China in the mid-1950s began to draw lessons from the problems of the Soviets. However, since China and the Soviet Union still shared the same ideology, the two countries continued to maintain the honeymoon phase of their relationship by implementing the Double Hundred Policy that marked the climax of the bilateral alliance. In this context, Soviet literature could still be viewed as the reference for the translation and introduction of foreign literary and cultural works into the Chinese literary world. On the other hand, Mao Zedong pointed out that: "'Let a hundred flowers blossom' would entail the emergence of both fragrant flowers and poisonous weeds and 'let a hundred schools of thought contend' meant permission to discuss idealism had been granted. But it did not really matter as long as poisonous weeds and wrong remarks were criticized." (Shen 2013, 321) Therefore, the overall trend in the Chinese literary world of that time was still characterized by the loosening of control. In the May 1957 issue, through "读者来信" (Reader's Letters) *Shijie Wenxue* proposed to "break away from rigid rules and conventions; forsake one's narrow worldview and embrace all the excellent literary works in the world"; "let the beautiful literary flowers of various schools, styles, and genres of all times and from different countries blossom in the garden of *Shijie Wenxue*"; and "publish more well-known works of various schools and styles from modern capitalist countries rather than publish socialist realist works exclusively" (Bianzhe 1957a, 196–97). From then on, the scope and genres of literary works that were translated and introduced began to break away from the influence of ideology.

## 3.2 Translator's Covert Resistance to Mainstream Ideology and the Construction of the Realist Identity of E Zhi Hua

Lefevere (1992, 61) suggests that the profiles of the translated literary works first and foremost depend on the translator's ideology, which can either be the ideology that the translator identifies with, or ideology imposed on the translator by the patronage. This is observed quite clearly in *E Zhi Hua*, where the poetics in the context of the target language differs from the poetics of socialist realism. It is, therefore, interesting to investigate, from which perspective, whether it be poetic or ideological, do professional actors in the target language context—including translators, editors, and reviewers—assess and analyze *E Zhi Hua*? How do they participate in the rewriting process of translation? Does the translator embrace his or her ideology or is the ideology imposed on the translator by the patronage? If the latter is the case, then how does the translator resist the imposition?

First of all, we shall examine the identity and background of translator Chen Jingrong. A representative poet of the Nine Leaves School, an important school for modern Chinese poetry in the 1940s, Chen was referred to as "a poet and translator profoundly influenced by classical poetry and western poetry" (Xin et al. 2000, 9). Having studied Baudelaire's works for a long time, Chen had a profound understanding of the poetic features and aesthetic significance of his works in the mainstream literary world of the source language. So, did Chen and the editorial committee of *Shijie Wenxue* assess *E Zhi Hua* from the standpoint of the mainstream literature of the source language?

A common practice of *Shijie Wenxue* is to attach a foreword or afterword to a piece of translation in the name of either the translator or the editor. A fore-word written by "the editor" appeared before the translated *E Zhi Hua* in *Shijie Wenxue*, and the first paragraph is as follows:

> "The flowers of evil" (Fleurs du mal), according to Charles Baudelaire, means "sick flowers". The dedication page of his book reads "[I] dedicate these sick flowers to …". In the past, the title of book was translated as "恶之花" (E Zhi Hua) in China. The character "恶" (E), which literally means ugly and evil, was often interpreted only as evil. Hence, the flowers of evil were deemed as poisonous flowers, poisonous weeds, or even poison.
>
> BIANZHE 1957b, 133

From the above quotation, we can observe that "the editor" did not present his/her interpretation of what Baudelaire meant by the title of the book. The wording of "the editor" apparently suggests that he or she was inclined to interpret the word "恶" (E) in "恶之花" (*E Zhi Hua*) as 'ugliness' rather than 'evil'. So, what is the difference between the two meanings? It seemed that "the editor" was rather critical of linking 'evil' to "poisonous flowers, poisonous weeds, and poison". However, as is well-known, "poisonous flowers, poisonous weeds, and poison" are the catchphrases frequently used in the mainstream discourse of the socialist context to refer to ideological struggles and criticism of capitalism. For example, when Mao Zedong expounded on the Double Hundred Policy in the Supreme State Conference in February 1957, he used the metaphor of "fragrant flowers and poisonous weeds" to describe the ideological struggle between socialism and capitalism throughout the conference. (Mao 2002, 162–163) *E Zhi Hua* was published in the July 1957 issue of *Shijie Wenxue* only five months after Mao Zedong's speech. In view of this, we can perceive "the editor's" overtone: it is inappropriate to interpret the word 'evil' in "the flowers of evil" through the lenses of ideology. Meanwhile, a study of Levik's "Baudelaire and *The Flowers of Evil*", which was published following *E Zhi Hua*'s appearance in *Shijie Wenxue*, reveals Levik's affirmation of Baudelaire, who expressed "his disgust at everything in the capitalist society" through his description of the 'ugly' and 'disgusting' "urban life" (Levik 1957, 162–163), and in this case, actually defines the precise meaning of "evil or malicious" in the socialist context. What deserves special attention is that Levik's definitions of 'ugly' and 'disgusting' were apparently different from what "the editor" believed them to be. The former favored the target language context's ideological interpretation of the word 'evil' in "the flowers of evil", whereas the latter favored the aesthetic interpretation predominant in the mainstream discourse of the target language. Thus, it becomes apparent that "the editor" had not agreed to the interpretation of the word 'evil' in "the flowers of evil" from the perspective of realism.

Although it is not clear who was "the editor", judging from the contents of the passage, "the editor" was someone very familiar with the original intention of *The Flowers of Evil* in the source language context, as well as the subsequent interpretation that surfaced after it was rewritten in the target language context. "The editor" mentioned that "'恶之花' (E Zhi Hua) had been in use as the title for *The Flowers of Evil* since the day the book was translated in China". This shows that "the editor" was also familiar with the history of the translation and the introduction of *The Flowers of Evil* to China "in the past". In addition, Chen was formally appointed as the leader of Editor Group for *Shijie Wenxue* in 1956, we may reasonably assume that the person who has a profound knowledge of Baudelaire and who is capable to write the foreword to *E Zhi Hua* in the name of the editor is very likely to be Chen. The key evidence for this assumption comes from the preface to Chen's book 图像与花朵 (*Images and Flowers*), in which she says, "The word 'evil' (*Mal*) in The Flowers of Evil can mean sickness or ugliness in French" (Chen 2002b, 6). This interpretation corresponds with the editor's interpretation in the July 1957 issue of *Shijie Wenxue* as both mention 'sickness' and 'ugliness' to be the meanings of 'evil' in the source language context.

After drawing the above conclusion, we need to explore how Chen, as a translator and an editor, dealt with the relationship between *E Zhi Hua* and the mainstream ideology. Let us first go back to one question asked previously: Does the translator embrace his or her ideology or is the ideology imposed on the translator by the patronage? Chen's background excludes the possibility of the first case. The two interpretations of the word 'evil' in the preceding part of the text show that Chen as "a translator" does not agree on an interpretation of *E Zhi Hua* in the target language context that is carried out from the perspective of realism. The obvious evidence is Chen's disagreement with Levik over Baudelaire's identity in the mainstream discourse of the source language. Levik says, "Progressive Russian critics have always correctly assessed the contradictions and complexities in Baudelaire's literary creation. On the contrary, only those who believe in literary decadence avoid mentioning his progressive side ... And it is here that the view that Baudelaire is the founder of Decadentism and Symbolism is formed" (Levik 1957, 164). Levik apparently inherited his realistic interpretation of Baudelaire from Russian literary traditions, which I will expound later in this chapter, and he did not see Baudelaire as a Symbolist writer. However, as early as the 1940s, Chen had already pointed out that "Baudelaire is different from other Symbolist poets, although he is, in fact, the founder of the school of Symbolism" (Chen 1946).

Nevertheless, Chen's view on the matter was implicit and words like 'modernism' and 'realism' did not appear in the foreword. The reason for this was twofold. On the one hand, Chen, as an editor, was bound to be constrained by the patronage. On the other hand, the state played the role of the patron in the literary system of translated literature in the 1950s, and *Shijie Wenxue* adhered closely to the mainstream official ideology in its selection of literary works.

First of all, during the implementation of the Double Hundred Policy, the loosening of socialist ideological control was relative rather than absolute. *Shijie Wenxue* did not reflect upon, let alone negate, the past practice of criticizing modernist literature from an ideological perspective, and socialist-realist literature remained the safest and most popular choice of literary style in the target language context. A case in point is the Conference on the Editorial Work of Literary Journals held by China Writers Association (CWA) in 1956. Although the conference stressed "being bold with the choice of literary works", it also made it clear that: "[The Double Hundred Policy] does not mean that we should furl the banner of ideological struggle [...] Our journals must share the advanced political thought of the Party and disseminate advanced ideology [...] to the public" (Benkan Jizhe 1956, 20).

We can see that CWA, a patron of all the journals, had specified the basic principles to be followed by all journals at the conference and had also clarified the bottom line of the reform. Therefore, the subsequent demonstration

THE CASE OF FRENCH MODERNIST LITERATURE IN *SHIJIE WENXUE* 123

of the practical significance of translated works to socialism in the target language context was in fact intended by the policy. That was why, under the constraint of ideology, "the editor" Chen could only implicitly hint at her literary and political position as "the translator" in the foreword. However, she did not rewrite the poetics to cater to the needs of realism but followed the artistic style of the original work, making it possible for Chinese readers to read a work that was poetically different from the works of socialist realism. She implicitly expressed her disagreement with the realistic interpretation of *E Zhi Hua*, and this, to some extent, proved the translator's subjectivity despite pressures from the mainstream ideology. By resisting the mainstream ideology of the target language, Chen managed to preserve the aesthetic values that were present in the source language context. At the same time, the prior conclusion that "the editor" is likely to be Chen further confirms the implicitness of her resistance—while "the translator" highlights individuality, "the editor" exercises the power of collective discourse. Therefore, it is politically safer and more tactful to implicitly disagree with the realistic interpretation of *E Zhi Hua* as "an editor" rather than directly interpret the work as "a translator". In doing so, ideologically sensitive topics can be handled in a way that allows for the editorial and translatorial responsibilities to be collectively shouldered, and this, in turn, reduces the tremendous pressure on the individual when the practice is considered politically 'incorrect'.

Secondly, during the implementation of the Double Hundred Policy, the fact that *Shijie Wenxue* published *E Zhi Hua*, the only modernist work in the source language context, showed that the editorial department was very cautious when dealing with modernist literature. After all, the relationship between modernist and socialist realists had for a long time been considered as ideologically contradictory. Through the publication of "Baudelaire and His *The Flowers of Evil*", an article that interprets the work from the realist perspective, *Shijie Wenxue* can incorporate *E Zhi Hua*, a work that looks so different from all previous works published in the journal in the literary realm of realism and in so doing, legitimize the translation and introduction of the book. Interestingly, both the editor's foreword and "Baudelaire and His *The Flowers of Evil*" mentioned that the first edition of *The Flowers of Evil* was abridged because it was accused of "being an insult to public decency" (Bianzhe 1957a, 133; Levik 1957, 162–163). Levik interpreted this as a result of bourgeois 'hostility', and the editor mentioned this incident again in the foreword as if to affirm that their translation and introduction of *E Zhi Hua* conforms to the mainstream ideology. Although as "a translator" Chen certainly did not agree with the realistic interpretation of *E Zhi Hua*, she, as "an editor", had to take the official ideological stance that had been embraced by the editorial department. Obviously, the editorial department had selected *E Zhi Hua* after careful consideration since other modernist works may not have been as rewritable as *E Zhi Hua*. Hence, the complicity between the translator and the editor (and the editorial department) is best exemplified in Chen.

In summary, differentiation between Chen's identity as "a translator" and as "an editor" is essential to the examination of the relationship between *E Zhi Hua* and the mainstream ideology of the target language. The first paragraph of "the editor's" foreword showed that after Chen "the translator" selected *The Flowers of Evil* for translation, she, for her political safety, tactfully made her poetic stand known by writing in the name of "the editor". Therefore, the resistance that Chen the translator expressed towards a realistic interpretation of the work does not conform to the ideology of the target language and should instead be read as a demonstration of her subjectivity. However, Chen "the editor" had to cooperate with the editorial department and endeavored to use the discourse of realism to interpret *E Zhi Hua*. This would explain why the second paragraph of "the editor's" foreword mentioned that the first edition of *The Flowers of Evil* had been accused of "being an insult to public decency" and the last paragraph deliberately wrote as follows, "In order to help readers know this great French poet, we have selected and translated [...] an article by Levik from the monthly Soviet journal *Foreign Literature* in addition to the nine poems from *The Flowers of Evil*". Obviously, this arrangement had to be made in the name of the editor and the editorial department.

The cultural identity and subjectivity of the translator propose an important research question since the cultural turn in translation studies and the studies conducted by scholars such as Itamar Even-Zohar, André Lefevere, and Theo Hermans. Both Hermans and Lefevere point out the importance of studying the translator's subjectivity. For example, Hermans says, "translations tell us more about those who translate and their clients than about the corresponding source texts" (Hermans 1999, 95). Lefevere even remarks that "translators could not only bestow life on the originals they translated, they could also decide what kind of life they would bestow on those originals and how they would try to inject them into the receiving literature" (Lefevere 1995, 7). Based on the existing understanding of subjectivity from the perspective of the translating process and philosophy, Zha Mingjian and Tian Yu give a more detailed explanation of the translator's subjectivity:

> The translator's subjectivity refers to the translator's subjective motivation towards translation goals. It is based on the premise of respecting

THE CASE OF FRENCH MODERNIST LITERATURE IN *SHIJIE WENXUE* 125

> the source text and is characterized by the translator's cultural conscious-
> ness, humanistic character, and cultural and aesthetic creativity.
>
> ZHA & TIAN 2003, 22

The above theories could be utilized when we use the polysystem theory to
examine the translator's subjectivity in the translating process. When examining the constraints of socio-cultural norms on the translator, such as mainstream ideology and patronage, in the framework of the polysystem theory,
the researcher should not neglect the translator's subjectivity that is demonstrated in the process of source text selection, translation and interpretation.
Although the ideology, as Lefevere has expounded, has an impact on the translator and is sometimes embraced by the translator and sometimes imposed
upon him or her by the patronage, the translator can disagree with and resist
mainstream ideology or refuse to accept the ideology imposed by the patronage. As the case of Chen's translation and introduction of *The Flowers of Evil*
demonstrates, Chen tactfully interacted with the mainstream ideology in
the process of translation and introduction because of subjective factors like
her cultural consciousness, humanistic character, and cultural and aesthetic
creativity, thus avoiding the intervention of politics in the creation of literature, which is very common in the research and writing of the history of translated literature.

Furthermore, Chen's role as an editor-cum-translator sheds light on how
translation negotiates with various powers. Instead of 'exploiting' her power as
an editor by overwhelming the reader with her explanation of the source text in
a top-down manner, Chen subtly injects her counterdiscourse into the translation, affecting the power structure in a bottom-up manner. Therefore, the role
of a translator is twofold: he/she could both be a part of the power structure as
an editor and be marginalized by the power structure as a translator.

Hermans has pointed out that "all translation implies a degree of manipulation of the source text for a certain purpose" (Hermans 1985, 11). Lefevere
takes the idea further by saying that translation is rewriting, and rewriting is
manipulation (Lefevere 1992, vii). Cultural manipulation is common in literary translation, but the specific means of manipulation differs. The case study
of Chen's translation and introduction of *The Flowers of Evil* showed how a
professional in the cultural polysystem of the target language rewrote and
manipulated the work via a postscript to the translation, the afterword, the
review, and the publication arrangement in order to meet the demands of the
mainstream ideology and conform to "the prevailing conventions" (Hermans
1985, 11) of the target language literature. In the study of the contemporary

history of translated literature, the examination of texts including the post-scripts of translations, the afterwords, and the reviews is of vital importance to our study of the development of translation norms and translation criteria. As Gentzler and Tymoczko point out, the representations of and commitments to source texts are not only evident "from analyses of translators' choices, word by word, page by page, and text by text", but are also "often demonstrable in the paratextual materials that surround translations, including introductions, footnotes, reviews, literary criticism, and so forth" (Gentzler & Tymoczko 2002, xviii). Therefore, *Shijie Wenxue*'s translation of *The Flowers of Evil* adopted a special strategy: the form is mainly foreignized, but the content is largely domesticated. On one hand, it foreignized the art form as the translation was faithful to the original's artistic techniques of "displaying beauty by describing ugliness" in the source language context; On the other hand, it domesticated the content as the editor's foreword and Levik's review rewrote the content of the original work, making it conform to the realist literary discourse approved by the mainstream ideology of the target language context. This strategy goes beyond the linguistic level and inspires us to study foreignization and domes-tication in translation from the perspectives of culture, poetics, and politics.

### 3.3 Baudelaire in the Socialist Context: Construction of the Profile of the Writer and His Work in the Target Language Context

Based on the previous discussions, we may further our inquiry by asking why *Shijie Wenxue* could not openly interpret *E Zhi Hua* when the control of socialist ideology had already been relatively loosening its grip. Also, did *Shijie Wenxue*'s aesthetic and poetic recognition of the work signify that the Mainland Chinese literary world would begin to give up its previous position on an ideological assessment?

Firstly, while *Shijie Wenxue* aesthetically and poetically recognized mod-ernism, it neither stated that Zhdanovist literary criticism would no longer be applied to modernist literature and culture nor did it attempt to redress its pre-vious judgment on modernism through an ideological reassessment of mod-ernism. In 1956 and 1957, although the tension between socialist ideology and literature had loosened, the Chinese literary sphere's evaluation of modernism generally maintained that of the first half of the 1950s. Modernist literature continued to be regarded as the opposite of realist literature and continued to be criticized and negated.

It is apparent that modernist literature occupied a very special position in the 1950s when the Cold War situation looked grim. Few modernist writers and works fell into the 'progressive' or left-wing category, and the characteristic traits of modernist form and content of expression made it difficult and unlikely for modernist literature to directly serve socialist politics. Therefore, when the Double Hundred Policy transitioned into the Anti-Rightist Movement in 1957, aligning socialist ideology to these political developments remained the guiding principle for *Shijie Wenxue*'s translation and analysis of the writers and their works. It is thus apparent that interpreting *E Zhi Hua* from the perspective of symbolist poetics and aesthetics would not have met the ideological demands of the target language.

It is worth noting that *Shijie Wenxue*'s construction of *E Zhi Hua* from the perspective of realism was definitely not a one-sided wish, and the classification of *E Zhi Hua* as realist literature in the socialist context of the target language was also definitely not an isolated case. As early as the nineteenth century, the Russian literary world had already started carrying out realistic interpretations of Baudelaire (Chu 2011, 131–144). By July 1957, the Anti-Rightist Movement had already formally started in Mainland China. Therefore, translation and introduction of a famous modernist work in the source language context had to be tactful. The realistic interpretation of *The Flowers of Evil* in the Soviet literary tradition became the most compelling justification and validation for *Shijie Wenxue*'s translation and introduction of *The Flowers of Evil*. This justification was not possible for other Symbolist poems that had not been given the same treatment in the Soviet literary sphere.

"Baudelaire and His *The Flowers of Evil*" was originally published in the March 1957 issue of the Soviet journal *Foreign Literature*. Two remarks in this paper deserve our attention. First of all, Levik was under the belief that the poems in *The Flowers of Evil* showed Baudelaire's disgust at everything produced by the capitalist society, and believed that Baudelaire was fined as a result of the publications' perceived insult to public decency. Levik saw *The Flowers of Evil* as the object of French authorities and public opinion's 'hate' (Levik 1957, 162–163). In this way, Baudelaire and his *The Flowers of Evil* were classified as members of the 'progressive' and left-wing camp of writers and literary works. In the context of the confrontation between socialist and capitalist literature, everything that was opposed by capitalism was embraced by socialism. Therefore, when Baudelaire was shaped into an opponent of the capitalist class, the socialist literary world naturally opened its doors to his translation and introduction.

Levik also skillfully handled the relationship between Baudelaire and the so-called decadentism. He distinguishes two kinds of decadentism: One is the Baudelairean decadentism, which is synonymous to exquisiteness, refinement, and delicacy, and is "an art that reaches great maturity, an art that emerges from old literature, and a refined, complex, delicate and exquisite style ...". Therefore, by this definition, "almost nothing especially refined, too novel or deliberately complicated could be found in Baudelairean style". On the contrary, the later form of decadentism is "full of affected clichés that are divorced from life". Levik maintains that 'progressive' Russian critics correctly assessed and addressed the contradictions and complexities inherent to Baudelairean decadentism, whereas the traditional view misconstrued Baudelaire by associating him with the "affected, dark, and morbid" decadents of later generations and by regarding him as the founder of decadentism and Symbolism, had fundamentally misunderstood Baudelaire and his style. (ibid., 164) Levik's differentiation between two kinds of decadentism shows that he tried to distance Baudelaire from the negative understanding attached to decadence in socialist literature at that time, and in doing so helped validate the translation and introduction of Baudelaire and his work in the target language context. The publication of his review in *Shijie Wenxue* further confirms that socialist ideology's control of capitalist literature was not loosened absolutely during that time despite the elevation of its aesthetic and artistic functions.

## 4    Conclusion

During the Second Plenary Session of the Eighth Central Committee of the CPC held in May 1958, the CPC leaders regarded class contradictions as the major contradiction in society again (Bo 1991, 624). Hence in August 1958, *Shijie Wenxue* released two papers, "修正主义是先进艺术的敌人" (Revision of Ideologies are Enemies of Progressive Art) and "德国文学界批判卢卡契" (The Criticism of Georg Lukacs by the German Literary Circle), reaffirming socialism as the mainstream ideology. Meanwhile, *Shijie Wenxue* defined modernism as a 'reactionary', 'defeated', 'pessimistic', and 'incorrect' means of expression by quoting Norwegian critic Martin Nag (Nag 1958, 159) and once again labeled modernism as the opposite of "progressive literature". With these, the temporary elevation of the aesthetic function of literature and arts that had been driven by the implementation of the Double Hundred Policy finally came to an end. It also foreshadowed *Shijie Wenxue*'s readjustment of its criteria for selecting works for translation and its complete exclusion of occidental modernist literature until January 1966 when *Shijie Wenxue* stopped publishing.

As the conflicts between China and the Soviet Union came to light in the late 1950s and as the struggle for decolonization in Latin American countries

# THE CASE OF FRENCH MODERNIST LITERATURE IN *SHIJIE WENXUE*   129

during the 1960s saw leaders of CPC scramble to propagate the idea of revolution in the third world, literary works from these countries began to gain recognition from *Shijie Wenxue* in a systematic way. Literature from the third world countries had long been disregarded as a target for translated literary work, but with the displacement of the Soviet Union from the central position of the target language context, a perceptible shift in how classical literature was being defined and accepted was reflected. As mentioned by Even-Zohar, with regards to the progress of the literary system and target culture, the concept of the canon is not static but rather a dynamic one (Even-Zohar 1990, 19). This leads to the eventual disappearance of the occidental modernist literature and writers, wiping out their respective translated works and introductions from *Shijie Wenxue*. Investigating these cases in translation can help us re-examine our current understanding of relevant translation theories and the methodologies we use in translation research, which can be summed up into the following four points.

First, it is apparent that situating the translated works in their historical contexts and understanding the motivations for translating these works and how the translators and editors balance the original and translated texts, is critical in investigating and analyzing the relationship between the social system and translation activities in the relevant periods of time. This is an attempt in understanding translation works and theories in the context of the cultural climates and timespans from which they emerge by resituating these works and theories in their relevant historical contexts.

Second, as observed by many scholars of translation, such as Hermans (1985, 11) and Lefevere (1992, vii), cultural manipulation is rampant in literary translation to serve various intents and purposes; the only differences lie in the means of manipulation. In the case of *Shijie Wenxue* in the 1950s to the 1960s, we see that manipulation of translations was no longer simply an addition or an ellipsis of the original, like how it was done in the late Qing dynasty. Instead, translations were manipulated through a combination of a careful selection of works to be translated and a critique of all the translated texts. For instance, in our investigation of Occidental Modernist Literature in *Shijie Wenxue*, we find that editors and translators will first exclude texts that conflict with the mainstream ideology and poetics of the time: they will, then, look at the remaining texts, and attempt to align them even nearer to the needs of the society at that time by adding post-scripts to the texts. Such acts of re-writing and manipulation "shore up and reinforce the prevailing conventions" (Hermans, 1985, 11), resulting in the "selective introduction" and "purposeful collection" that is characteristic of *Shijie Wenxue*. This 're-production' of the original works and authors in the target language is crucial to our analysis of the translation conventions and practices.

Third, as Even-Zohar (1978, 7–8) points out, "it is not sufficient that one recognizes that literary polysystems be discussed in their relationships with other literary polysystems. One has also to realize that whole literatures may behave *vis-à-vis* one another as various strata within a single whole, thus constituting an over-all literary aggregate, a kind of *megapolysystem*, the structure of which could explain relations hitherto neglected. Moreover, certain literatures may turn out to overlap some other literature(s), thus creating symbiotic structures". This mega-polysystem is essential for scholars of translation studies as it provides a theoretical framework and an analytic perspective that we can use in translation research. It helps to bring focus to the relationships between the factors within and without the system, including the impact of the polysystem on mainstream literary and translation theories and ideologies. It also serves to distinguish between issues relating to poetics and ideologies and to explain the relationship between the two. It also clarifies the kind of relationship between the patronage and the professionals involved in the translation activities. Again, using *Shijie Wenxue* as a case study, we have observed that translation conventions and regularization are intricately linked to the cultural backgrounds of the target language. For instance, it has been shown that the mainstream ideology has influenced the choices made when it comes to the types of literature being selected and has even affected the reception of these works in the target readers. At the same time, the formation of this ideology within the polysystem of translation in the target language is also tied to the political, economic, and cultural factors that exist outside of the system—the Russian literary views, for example, have swayed the Chinese translation conventions and practices; likewise, the global geopolitical climate has had the same kind of influence over the Chinese translation scene. These factors have all shaped the development and growth of the Chinese translation polysystem over the years. This development has, eventually, led to the formation of a literary taste amongst the target readers of the translation works.

Fourth, the mega-polysystem has also informed scholars of translation about the need to focus on not only the works that have been translated but also works that have been omitted from the translation activities, as omitted works often uncover how dominant cultures marginalize the other forms or interpretations of literary arts and of translation (Gentzler and Tymoczko 2002, xxi). It can also answer why these works have been omitted—by investigating how the authors of these omitted works are portrayed and perceived in the target language and culture, we can find out if these authors have been

THE CASE OF FRENCH MODERNIST LITERATURE IN *SHIJIE WENXUE* 131

purposefully left out due to an incompatibility between the authors and the target culture. In addition, the analysis of the omitted works can also reveal the changes in how the authors are perceived in the process of translation or non-translation, and why these changes have occurred. The reasons for the differences in the reception of the literary works between the target readers of the original language and the target language can also be accounted for if we situate the translations in the mega-polysystem of translation.

In sum, using the polysystem theory for studies on the history of translation of literature is beneficial not only for synchronic studies of translation activities but also for studies on the cultural space in which the activities occur. It also sheds light on behavioral patterns exhibited by the translators, their cultural motives, and the issues revolving translated and non-translated works in the Chinese translation polysystem. Through these investigations, future studies can, then, discuss the relationships between the translated works and the domestic literature in a specific timeframe, and investigate the influences that each has on the other.

### Acknowledgments

I would like to thank the Ministry of Education, Singapore AcRF Tier 1 Project (Translation and Politics in the People's Republic of China in the 1950s and 1960s: its Significance to Modern Translation Studies) for sponsoring the writing of this chapter.

### References

Babuts, Nicolae. 1997. *Baudelaire: At the limits and beyond.* London: Associated University Presses.

Bassnett, Susan, and Lefevere, André. 1990. *Translation, History and Culture.* London: Continuum International Publishing Group Ltd.

Baudelaire, Charles. 1957. "恶之花选译" (E Zhi Hua Xuanyi) [Selected translation of *The Flowers of Evil*]. Translated by Chen Jingrong. *Shijie Wenxue* 7: 133–143.

Benkan Jizhe. 1956. "办好文学期刊，促进 '百花齐放，百家争鸣" (Banhao Wenxue Qikan, Cujin "Baihua Qifang, Baijia Zhengming") [Publishing High Standard Journal and Promoting "Let a Hundred Flowers Blossom, Let a Hundred Schools of Thought Contend"]. *Journal of Literature and Art* 23: 20–21.

Bianzhe. 1954a. "后记" (Hou Ji) [postscript]. *Shijie Wenxue* 5: 212–216.

Bianzhe. 1954b. "后记" (Hou Ji) [postscript]. *Shijie Wenxue* 9: 192–198.

Bianzhe. 1955a. "世界文艺动态" (Shijie Wenyi Dongtai) [Literary and Artistic Activities in the World]. *Shijie Wenxue* (11): 214–230.

Bianzhe. 1955b. "后记" (Hou Ji) [postscript]. *Shijie Wenxue* 11: 253–260.

Bianzhe. 1957a. "读者意见综述" (Duzhe Yijian Zongshu) [A Summary of Readers' Opinions]. *Shijie Wenxue* 5: 196–200.

Bianzhe. 1957b. "恶之花" (E Zhi Hua) [The Flowers of Evil]. *Shijie Wenxue* 7: 133.

Bo, Yibo. 1991. 若干重大决策与事件的回顾 (Ruogan Zhongda Juece Yu Shijian De Huigu) [Recollection of Several Major Decisions and Events]. Vol. 1. Beijing: CPC Central Party School Press.

Chen, Jianhua. 2002a. 二十世纪中俄文学关系 (Ershi Shiji Zhonge Wenxue Guanxi) [The Relationship between Chinese and Russian Literatures in the Twentieth Century]. Beijing: Higher Education Press.

Chen, Jingrong. 1946. "波德莱尔与猫" (Bodelaier Yu Mao) [Baudelaire and the Cat]. *Wenhui Daily*, December 19.

Chen, Jingrong. 2002b. "题记" (Tiji) [Preface]. In Charles Baudelaire. 图像与花朵 (Tuxiang Yu Huaduo) [Images and Flowers]. Translated by Chen Jingrong. Changsha: Hunan Art and Literature Press.

Chu, Jinyi. 2011. "俄国现实主义文学视野中的波德莱尔" (Eguo Xianshizhuyi Wenxue Shiye Zhong De Bodelaier) [Baudelaire in the Context of Russian Realist Literature]. *Comparative Literature in China* 2: 131–144.

Dementjev et al. 1953. "苏联文学的基本特征" (Sulian Wenxue De Jiben Tezheng) [Basic Features of Soviet Literature]. Translated by Fang Turen. *Shijie Wenxue* 7: 209–234.

Eluard, Paul. 1953a. "一篇该算的账" (Yipian Gaisuande Zhang) [An Old Score to Be Settled]. Translated by Luo Dagang. *Shijie Wenxue* 8: 98.

Eluard, Paul. 1953b. "布拉格的春夜" (Bulage De Chunye) [The Spring Night of Prague]. Translated by Luo Dagang. In *Shijie Wenxue* 8: 96.

Even-Zohar, Itamar. 1990. "Polysystem Theory." *Poetics Today* 11: 1–94.

Gentzler, Edwin and Maria Tymoczko. 2002. *Translation and Power*. Amherst and Boston: University of Massachusetts Press.

Gold, Michael. 1956. "Aragon, poet-organizer." Translated by Bai Yuan. *Shijie Wenxue* 9: 100.

Hermans, Theo. 1985. *The manipulation of literature: Studies in Literary Translation*. London: Croom Helm.

Hermans, Theo. 1999. *Translation in systems: Descriptive and system-oriented approaches explained*. Manchester: St. Jerome.

Lefevere, André. 1992. *Translation, rewriting, and the manipulation of literary fame*. London: Routledge.

Lefevere, André. 1995. "Introduction: Comparative literature and translation." *Comparative Literature* 47 (1): 1–10.

Levik. 1957. "波特莱尔和他的'恶之花'" (Bodelaier He Tade E Zhi Hua) [Baudelaire and His *The Flowers of Evil*]. Translated by He Ru. *Shijie Wenxue* 7: 162–166.

Li, Qiaoning. 2007. 新中国的中苏友好话语构建 (Xinzhongguo De Zhongsu Youhao Huayu Goujian) [The Construction of Friendly Sino-Soviet Discourse in New China]. Beijing: Chinese Social Science Press.

Luo, Dagang. 1955. 萨特的新著:"尼克拉索夫" (Sate De Xinzhu: Nikelasuofu) [Sartre's New Work: *Nekrassov*]. *Shijie Wenxue* 8: 244–246.

M. Baskin. 1958. "修正主义是先进艺术的敌人" (Xiuzheng Zhuyi Shi Xianjing Yishu De Diren) [Revision of Ideologies are Enemies of Progressive Art]. Translated by Feng Xiang. In *Shijie Wenxue* (8): 146–149.

Mao, Zedong. 1991. "论人民民主专政" (Lun Renmin Minzhu Zhuanzheng) [On the people's democratic dictatorship]. In 毛泽东选集 Mao Zedong Xuanji [Selected Works of Mao Zedong]. Vol. 4, 1468–82. Beijing: People's publishing house.

Mao, Zedong. 1999. "在中共中央政治局扩大会议上的总结讲话" (Zai Zhonggongzhongyang Zhengzhiju Kuoda Huiyi Shang De Zongjie Jianghua) [The Summary Speech at the Enlarged Meeting of the Political Bureau of the CPC Central Committee]. In 毛泽东文集 Mao Zedong Wenji [Collected Works of Mao Zedong]. Vol. 7. 50–59. Beijing: People's Literature Publishing House.

Mao, Zedong. 1999. "论十大关系" (Lun Shida Guanxi) [On the Ten Major Relationships]. In 毛泽东文集 Mao Zedong Wenji [Collected Works of Mao Zedong]. Vol. 7. 23–49. Beijing: People's Literature Publishing House.

Mao, Zedong. 2002. 毛泽东文艺论集 (Mao Zedong Wenyi Lunji) [A Collection of Mao Zedong's Essays on Arts]. Beijing: Central Party Literature Press.

Mein, Margaret. 1973. "Baudelaire and Symbolism." In *L'Esprit Créateur* 13: 154–165.

Moser, Charles A., ed. 1992. *The Cambridge History of Russian literature*. New York: The Press Syndicate of the University of Cambridge.

Nag, Martin. 1958. "走向繁荣的道路" (Zouxiang Fanrong De Daolu) [Forward along the Path towards Prosperity]. *Shijie Wenxue* 8: 158–161.

Rhodes, Solomon Alhadef. 1929. *The cult of beauty in Charles Baudelaire*. Vol. 2. New York: Institute of French Studies, Columbia University.

Shen, Zhihua. 2013. 处在十字路口的选择:*1956–1957*年的中国 (Chuzai Shizi Lukou De Xuanze: 1956–1957 Nian De Zhongguo) [Choices at the Crossroads: China in 1956 and 1957]. Guangzhou: Guangdong People's Publishing House.

Wong, Wang Chi. 1999. 重释"信达雅":二十世纪中国翻译研究 (Chongshi "Xin Da Ya": Ershi Shiji Zhongguo Fanyi Yanjiu) [The Reinterpretation of "Faithfulness, Expressiveness and Elegance"—A Study of Chinese Translation in 20th Century]. Shanghai: Orient Publishing Center.

Xin, Di, et al. 2000. 九叶集 (Jiu Ye Ji) [Nine Leaves]. Beijing: Writers Publishing House.

Xu, Jun and Song, Xuezhi. 2007. 20世纪法国文学在中国的译介与接受 (Ershi Shiji Faguowenxue Zai Zhongguo De Yijie Yu Jieshou) [Translation, Introduction and

Reception of French Literature in China in the 20th Century]. Wuhan: Hubei Education Press.

Xu, Jun. 2007. 法朗士在中国的翻译接受与形象塑造 (Falangshi Zai Zhongguo De Fanyi Jieshou Yu Xingxiang Suzao) [The Translation and Reception of Anatole France in China and the Construction of His Image]. *Foreign Literature Studies* 2: 117–27.

Zha, Mingjian, and Tian, Yu. 2003. "论译者的主体性——从译者文化地位的边缘化谈起" (Lun Yizhe De Zhutixing: Cong Yizhe Wenhua Diwei De Bianyuanhua Tanqi) [On the Subjectivity of the Translator: Starting from the Marginalization of the Translator]. *Chinese Translators Journal* 1: 19–24.

Zha, Mingjian. 2003. 意识形态、诗学与文学翻译选择规范——20世纪50－80年代中国的（后）现代主义文学翻译研究 (Yishixingtai, Shixue Yu Wenxufanyi Xuanze Guifan: 20 Shiji Wushi Zhi Bashi Niandai Zhongguo De (Hou)Xiandaizhuyi Wenxuefanyi Yanjiu) [Ideology, Poetics and the Selection Norms of Literary Translation: A Study of (Post)Modernist Literary Translation in China from the 1950s to 1980s]. Ph.D. Dissertation, Hong Kong. Lingnan University.

CHAPTER 7

# The Art and Craft of Translation

*The Historical and Political Background of the Russian Translation Scholarship*

*Natalia Kamovnikova*

### Abstract

The article studies the development of the Russian-language Soviet translation scholarship in the twentieth century against the background of the political climate and social practices in the Soviet Union. The initial attempt to create a translation theory in the Soviet Union was made with an eye to the existing literary translation practices, which evolved under the influence of socially determined factors, including general orientation of arts and science towards education, the universally implanted principle of primacy of practice over theory, and the requirements of the Socialist realism. The focus on practice created favorable conditions for the application of comparative methodology to the study of existing translations and the wide spread of translation criticism. The groundbreaking work of Andrei Fedorov put linguistics in the focus of translation research and became a turning point in the development of the translation theory. The elevated interest of researchers to the translation theory continued to co-exist with the social requirements, such as the overtly imposed mandatory linkage of theory and practice and the covertly desired methodological orientation of translation studies.

## 1 Introduction

Translation as an activity within a social and cultural context has been studied widely by modern researchers (Baer and Witt 2017; Baer 2011; Pym, Shlesinger and Jettmarova 2006). Christina Schäffner and Susan Bassnett state that "linguistic interaction is embedded in and determined by socio-cultural, historical, ideological, and institutional conditions" and that "translation, although often invisible in the field of politics, is actually an integral part of political activity" (Schäffner and Bassnett 2010, 2–13). Maria Tymoczko notes that the ideology of translation is "a means of asserting dominance, deprecating or suppressing other cultures, manipulating representations so as to enhance power

© KONINKLIJKE BRILL NV, LEIDEN, 2021 | DOI:10.1163/9789004437807_008

hierarchies, preventing cultural infiltrations, and the like" (Tymoczko 2010, 255). Whereas existing social and cultural patterns and political conditions are able to define the general approach to literature and literary translation practice, as well as translation in the fields of journalism (Darwish 2010) and science (Montgomery 2000), it is quite natural that the translation scholarship as a constituent part of linguistic interaction also reacts to the existing socio-political conditions. In an ideologically charged social context, where language is seen as a means of social control, translation as a practice may be limited in its means and choice of authors and texts, whereas translation as a field of research may also be limited in the choice of subjects of study.

It should be noted that the development of literary trends, translation approaches, and, eventually, the development of translation scholarship in the Soviet Union was determined by the political course of the country, the general orientation of literature and translation practices, as well as by censorship, which alternately increased and loosened, but never disappeared. The impact of these factors on different spheres of the Soviet culture was described by Katerina Clark in her *Moscow, the Fourth Rome: Stalinism, Cosmopolitanism, and the Evolution of Soviet Culture* (Clark 2011). Detailed studies on Soviet literary translation were made by Samantha Sherry in *Discourses of Regulation and Resistance: Censoring Translation in the Stalin and Khrushchev Era Soviet Union* (Sherry 2015) and Brian James Baer in his *Translation and the Making of Modern Russian Literature* (Baer 2016). A variety of views upon literature, translation, and censorship, as well as interesting case studies can be found in *Contexts, Subtexts, Pretexts: Literary Translation in Eastern Europe and Russia* edited by Brian Baer (Baer 2011). Together with Natalia Olshanskaya, Baer also edited an anthology *Russian Writers on Translation* (Baer and Olshanskaya 2013). The most recent publication is the volume *Transnational Russian Studies* edited by Andy Byford, Connor Doak, and Stephen Hutchings, which is a comprehensive selection of articles including those related to translation (Byford, Doak, Hutchings 2020).

## 2    Political Situation as a Determinant Factor

The turn of the twentieth century held good promises for Russian researchers. These perspectives were particularly bright for the research in linguistics and language-related fields, for which the soil had been prepared by the groundbreaking activities of Russian linguists of the 19th century. Russian linguists of the 19th century addressed a wide range of problems, including the origin

THE ART AND CRAFT OF TRANSLATION 137

and classification of languages, their phonological differences, and structural features. Some of the observations concerned translation and transfer of texts. The key observation in this regard was made by the distinguished linguist Aleksandr Potebnia, who stated that the metaphoricity of any language implied the metaphoricity of any translation, therefore "we can only translate a metaphor into a metaphor" (Potebnia 1990, 304). Linguists Nikolai Krushevskii, Jan Baudouin de Courtenay, and Vasilii Bogoroditskii engaged in the studies of phonology, which were taken up by the Russian researchers of the 20th century. In 1909, Lev Shcherba organized the laboratory of experimental phonetics at St. Petersburg State University. Studies in comparative phonetics were also undertaken by Evgenii Polivanov. It was Polivanov who became one of the founders of OPOIAZ (Obshchestvo izucheniia POeticheskogo IAZyka, or Society for the Studies of Poetic Language), which alongside with the Moscow linguistic circle gave life to what is now known as the Russian Formalist movement. The formalists focused on the studies of the language material of poetic works, such as prosody, euphony, grammar, and wording; they also addressed the issues of translation. Concentrating on the "specifics of the researched material", adherents of Formalism did not see it as an "aesthetic theory; they saw their purpose as creating a separate literary discipline on the basis of specific features of the literary material" (Eikhenbaum 1987, 376).

One of the most distinguished members of OPOIAZ was Roman Jakobson, whose engagement in comparative studies in the theory of verse laid the foundation for his research in translation, which he conducted after his emigration from Russia in the 1920s. The comparative approach to language and text study was seen by Jakobson as a major method as early as 1926, when he defined it as the one that "permits us ... to appreciate fully the relationship between form and material" (Jakobson 1979a, 122). Later in his 1930 article *On the Translation of Verse*, Jakobson compared iambic tetrameters in the Russian and Czech languages to demonstrate how the hierarchical differences in the rhythmical structure of languages ensured fundamental differences in the structure, function, and effect of their iambics (Jakobson 1979b).

Theoretical issues in translation were also addressed by practicing literary translators. Thus, in 1916, poet, writer, and translator Valerii Briusov raised the issue of text aging, the impact of the temporal distance of the original on the reader of the translation, and the possible solutions to this problem in his article *A Few Reflections on Translating Horace's Odes into Russian Verse* (Briusov 2013). The article by Briusov came out five years before the 1921 article *Euripides and Professor Murray* by T.S. Eliot, which also addressed the dilemma of text aging and its perception in modern translation (Eliot 1998).

The activities of formalists continued in the 1920s despite rapid social changes, which drove a wedge between theoretical studies and practice-oriented activities. The third decade of the twentieth century was extremely heterogeneous in terms of types and purposes of translation-related projects. On the one hand, the new social situation set new tasks for linguists, literature specialists, and translators, reassigning them to practical tasks. The general focus shifted towards education. The project of universal education was one of the most successful Soviet projects throughout the entire Soviet history; it targeted the transfer of both the theoretical knowledge and of the ways this knowledge could be implemented in practice. Literature gained a special status in Soviet Russia: it came to be seen as the basis for education of new generations of the new monarchy-free state. This task was to be fulfilled by Russian literature, literatures of the Soviet republics, as well as foreign literatures. In 1919, writer Maksim Gor'kii initiated the publication project entitled *Vsemirnaia literatura* (World Literature). The series he planned for publication was supposed to consist of two parts—the main one, of 1500 volumes twenty printer's sheets each, and the so-called people's library of 2500 volumes two to four printer's sheets each. This ambitious plan required the participation of a vast group of translators of different backgrounds. The achievements they made, difficulties they faced, and the disagreements they had were widely discussed by readers and critics. Thus, by the end of 1919, writer, critic, and head of the Anglo-American section of *Vsemirnaia literatura* Kornei Chukovskii and poet Nikolai Gumilev published a brochure entitled "Principles of literary translation" (Chukovskii and Gumilev 1919). Published by *Vsemirnaia literature* publishing house, the brochure contained an article by Chukovskii devoted to the translation of prose and the article by Gumilev on the translation of poetry. In the preface, the publisher expressed the hope that the articles contained in the brochure would become a start in the construction of "if not a science, then, at least, practical guidelines to one of the most difficult and demanding arts— the art of literary translation" (ibid., 6). Based on the observations of contemporary literary translations, these two articles were rather of a practical nature. Both authors clearly worked towards the development of a methodology: Chukovskii dwelt upon different categories of problems faced by translators of literary prose (phonetical issues, style, vocabulary, syntax, and textual precision); Gumilev addressed the issues of creativity, phonetic effects and prosody, and individual style. It was at this point that Chukovskii described the translator as "an artist, a master of the word, a co-participant of the creative work of the writer he translates. He serves art the way an artist, a sculptor, or a painter does. The text of the original becomes the material for his difficult—and often

THE ART AND CRAFT OF TRANSLATION                                          139

passionate creativity" (ibid., 7). This degree of license was discreetly disputed by Gumilev, as he allocated the secondary role to the translator who was supposed to follow the original design and features of the original. The difference in views on translation, expressed by Chukovskii and Gumilev, was well known: they regularly engaged in disputes, which were referred to by Chukovskii in his diaries. "This talented craftsman", wrote Chukovskii about Gumilev, "has taken it into his head to compile a Set of rules for translators. To my mind, there are no such rules" (Chukovskii 2003, 109).

A year later, articles by Chukovskii and Gumilev were reprinted in a book together with two articles by the prominent philologist Fedor Batiushkov, who had died several months earlier in March 1920 (Batiushkov, Chukovskii, Gumilev 1920). The edition in memory of Batiushkov opened up with his article "Tasks of literary translation," in which he made acute observations on cultural approaches to rendering foreign texts. In Batiushkov's view, if the receiving culture sees itself as superior to the culture from which the literary work originates, looseness becomes the basic translation principle. Conversely, in case the receiving culture sees itself as inferior to the culture of the original, translations tend to copy their originals stylistically, lexically, and grammatically. Only if two cultures are recognized as equal, states Batiushkov, translations demonstrate both respect to the original and creativity in rendering (ibid., 7–9). Batiushkov quotes Potebnia when talking about the degree of proximity of originals and translations, repeating his words that in translations of poetry "the thought changes more than in a pencil copy of an oil painting" (ibid., 11).

Attempts to classify existing translation knowledge continued in the 1920s. Thus, the Russian formalist and OPOIAZ member Iurii Tynianov systematized his experience of translating Heinrich Heine's poetry into Russian. Like his predecessors, Tynianov addressed the problem of the impossibility of complete precision in the translation of verse. To resolve this problem, Tynianov highlighted the necessity of establishing correspondences in accordance with functions, which textual elements perform in the text (Fedorov 1983a, 91). Notably, Tynianov defined translation as a mode of genesis of literature (Tynianov 1977, 29). These observations were very much in line with the contemporary European findings, such as Rudolf Pannwitz's idea of translation as the means to enrich the language and increase its ability to change and transform (Pannwitz 1917, 242).

Another important publication came out in Leningrad (St. Petersburg) in 1930 under the title "The art of translation" by Chukovskii and the twenty-four-year-old literature specialist Andrei Fedorov, former student of Shcherba and Tynianov (Chukovskii and Fedorov 1930). Whereas Chukovskii in his article

"Principles of literary translation" remained true to the descriptive criticism of existing literary translations, Fedorov's article "Ways and tasks of literary translation" addressed the problematics of translation from the point of view of language and social context, highlighting the importance of such issues as structural differences of languages, purpose of translation, social expectations and requirements to translation, and the effect of foreign elements in the text of translation. Like Jakobson, who published his article on verse the same year, Fedorov paid close attention to the issue of differences in the systems of versification of different languages and the ways these differences affected the translation of poetry.

In the meantime, the Soviet government was working towards placing literature and press under close control. The official steps taken in the first postrevolutionary years included but were by all means not limited to the issuing of the Decree on Press in November 1917 (Dekrety 1957, 24–25), nationalization of publishing houses in 1919, and the 1922 establishment of the centralized censoring institution for literary and publishing affairs which would become universally known as Glavlit. Gradually, state control extended to educational institutions, research, and other social spheres, naturally affecting those engaged in translation practice, as well as in research. Gumilev was accused of taking part in a military conspiracy and shot in 1921; Jakobson emigrated. For disputing the officially promoted Japhetic theory and its author Nikolai Marr, Polivanov was suspended from work, deprived of the right to publish in Moscow and Leningrad, and had to move to Uzbekistan in the beginning of the 1930s. It was also in course of the 1920s that Briusov died, and Tynianov's health deteriorated. Still in his thirties, Tynianov had to abandon his academic career and focus on original writing both due to health reasons and to the increasing persecution of formalists, which started in the beginning of the 1930s.

The campaign against Formalism became an important point in the interpretation of the term as such and in the further attitude of the Soviet literature to the concept of 'form' in both original writings and literary translation. Formalism as a movement got severely criticized in the 1920s; the word 'formalism' gradually acquired pejorative meaning and came to be used to define, among others, the excessive keenness of translators to preserve the formal features of the original (Kashkin 1968b, 479). Also defining technical complexity, ponderosity of style, and lack of creative effort, the term 'Formalism' gradually became seen as synonymous to the cognate word 'formality' (Rus.: formal'nost') thus exemplifying the words of Viktor Shklovskii, one of the key figures and theorists of Russian Formalism, who in 1925 wrote not without irony, "All names are always false" (Shklovskii 1983, 80).

THE ART AND CRAFT OF TRANSLATION                                                    141

The semi-official struggle with Formalism turned into the openly declared war in Gor'kii's article "Upon Formalism" published in 1936 (Gor'kii 1936). The prosecutorial tone of the article is set by Gor'kii in the very beginning, the first paragraph starting with the words, "In the countries of class hierarchy, fascism is raging, which in its essence consists in selecting most vile scoundrels and villains to enslave all other people and make them domestic animals of capitalism" (ibid.). Gor'kii continues his passionate accusations of fascism in four subsequent paragraphs, when eventually in the fifth paragraph he describes formalism in literature as indifference to reality. The narrative becomes even more emotional as Gor'kii describes the formalist attitude from the first person, thus inviting the reader to rip away the literary formalists' mask of pretense. Gor'kii continues exposing literary Formalism by referring to fascist forms of sadism, deriding Plato's philosophy, dismissing Hegel's ideas, and mocking "Marcel Proust, Joyce, Dos Passos and different Hemingways" (ibid.). He concludes the article with the verdict which, given Gor'kii's position of the leading Soviet writer and critic, turned Formalism into a label that was able to tarnish any reputation.

> Formalism as a "manner," as a "literary means" mainly serves the purpose of covering up the emptiness and poverty of spirit ... Formalism is used in fear of the simple, clear, and sometimes rude word ... Some authors use formalism as a means of cladding their thought, so that their disgustingly hostile attitude to reality, their intention to distort the meaning of facts and events would not be noticed right away. But this already is not the art of writing, but the art of deceit.
>
> GOR'KII 1936—translated by N.K.

The denial of the concept of form on the official level contributed to the promotion of the clarity requirement to literature and translation pushed by official literary circles. Clarity of literature overtly answered the educational needs; covertly it automatically simplified control over creative writing. The importance of clarity in literature was much discussed during the First All-Union Congress of Soviet Writers in August 1934; in some contexts, the word 'clarity' in relation to literature was used as a synonym to the high quality (Pervyi Vsesoiuznyi S'ezd 1934, 49). Another important condition for any activities that defined the course of development of translation practices and theory was the primacy of practice over theory. This major principle of Marxist-Leninist philosophy was, among others, widely dwelt upon by Vladimir Lenin in 1908 in his main philosophical work *Materialism and Empirio-Criticism*

(Lenin 1977). Considered one of Lenin's most important works, *Materialism and Empirio-Criticism* was an integral part of the obligatory course on the history of the Communist party taught at all universities of the Soviet Union. Lenin defined practice, experiment and industry as criteria of the objective truth (ibid., 170). "The mastery of nature manifested in human practice is a result of an objectively correct reflection within the human head of the phenomena and processes of nature and is proof of the fact that this reflection (within the limits of what is revealed by practice) is objective, absolute, eternal truth" (ibid., 190). This relation of practice to objectivity and truth in Lenin's definition was gradually absolutized, and practice was eventually ascribed top priority.

The concept of truth in literature and arts was also much spoken about during the First Congress of Soviet Writers and its final resolution in 1934. As the main literary method, the Socialist realism targeted the "truthful, historically specific depiction of reality in its revolutionary development" in order to fulfill the task of "ideological remaking and education of the working people in the spirit of Socialism" (Ustav 1934, 716). The officially proclaimed Socialist realism, as well as other regulations of social life, posed a threat to the achievements of both practicing literary translators and to the existing findings of researchers who worked towards the potential construction of a translation theory. In the 1930s, many of the surviving formalists were persecuted: Polivanov, who persevered in his dispute with Marr, was shot for espionage; Viktor Vinogradov was arrested and exiled in 1934 together with other specialists in Slavic languages on charges of being part of the "Slavists' conspiracy". Any official steps towards the construction of a new theory therefore had to be made in accordance with the official requirements, which demanded the theory to cater for the needs of practice at all times. In the case of translation, approaches to practice were seriously recalibrated, and whatever translation theory there was to be constructed, it was supposed to provide for the new literary practice and to become a reality of the Soviet life.

## 3    Theory in the Service of Practice

The development and improvement of literary translation practices remained in the focus of attention throughout the entire history of Soviet literature. The increase of control over all spheres of life in the country directed public life and science towards centralization of activities. At the same time, the role of literature and translation was steadily growing. The importance of the transfer of knowledge through literature was regularly emphasized by Gor'kii, who by 1930s had become one of the main Soviet literary functionaries: he

# THE ART AND CRAFT OF TRANSLATION
143

was decorated with an Order of Lenin and later appointed Chairman of the Union of Soviet Writers. Gor'kii recurrently spoke about the importance of being acquainted to the works of world literature of all genres and subjects. As Gor'kii put it, "there is no weapon sharper than the knowledge based on … the studies of the past of humankind. The past is alien to us, but to strike the enemy dead, one needs to know the enemy well" (Gor'kii 1932, 14).

As a weapon of struggle, literature was supposed to follow a strict methodology based on the Socialist realism principles. The Socialist realism required literature and arts to be able to render the "national spirit" of the cultural situation described. Works of art were also supposed to correlate with the notion of the "ideological commitment" by representing of everyday life and activities of common people. Finally, arts and literature were supposed to conform to the requirement of specificity, which meant materialism and direct reference of art to reality (Ustav 1934). These requirements strongly affected the original creative writing; in the case of literary translation, they made the selection of some works of world literature impossible. The works, which passed the selection process, were somehow to conform to at least some of the Socialist requirements. This is why the role of a translator as a full-fledged co-participant of the creative process came to be a very convenient strategy. One of the main ideologists of the Soviet literary translation, Ivan Kashkin, later described this approach in the following way: "When translating a book, it is not an isolated word and its grammatical shape in the given language that one should translate, but the thought, the image, the emotion—all the specificity standing behind this word, with allowance for all expressive means, for all the variety of the sign or the polysemy of the word." (Kashkin 1968a, 377). Notably, Kashkin uses the word 'specificity' in relation to fuzzy concepts—"the thought, the image, the emotion"—whereas the "expressive means", "the sign" remain for allowances, despite their ability to construct the text and its form. Since the elevated interest to the form increased the risk of being branded as a "formalist," regular infringements on literary forms began to take place in translations quite regularly.

As both a literary translator and a translation theorist, Kashkin made a considerable contribution into the development of what is now known as the Soviet translation theory of the middle of the twentieth century. It was Kashkin who formulated the notion of the so-called "realistic translation theory". The career of Kashkin as a language specialist, translator, and critic experienced a rise when he was selected to chair a literary translation group created by the translation section of the Moscow Union of Writers in the 1930s. The group was expected to fulfill creative tasks and engage in discussions of the problems encountered in course of their work, thus contributing to the improvement of the quality of literary translations in the Soviet Union. Of all literary translation groups thus initiated in the 1930s, only Kashkin's group was destined to enjoy glory for their amazing literary achievements and high-quality translations widely read until nowadays. The success of his team-members turned Kashkin into one of the most influential figures of Soviet literature. However, long before it happened, still in the 1930s, Kashkin actively participated in the theoretical activities of the translation section of the Union of Soviet Writers.

The translation theory project, initiated in the 1930s, had primarily educational purposes. The initial idea of the translation activists of the Union of Writers consisted in creating a methodology that could be able to provide guidelines for practicing literary translators. This project was actively contributed to by linguists, translators, and literary critics. The translation section in Moscow regularly organized seminars and lectures by the leading specialists in the field of language and literature (RGALI b). It was in course of these events that Mikhail Lozinskii, the translator of Dante, Shakespeare, Lope de Vega, and Ferdowsi, read a lecture on the principles of poetry translation, where he dwelt upon the aesthetic value of translations and presented a detailed classification of the technical problems in verse rendering and the ways these problems could be approached (RGALI a, 3–6). An important conclusion Lozinskii made consisted in the equality of aesthetic value of the original and its translation and the 'objectivity' of the translation (RGALI a, 6).

Actively engaged in all public events devoted to translation, Kashkin's group initiated another project, which consisted in collecting practical materials that could serve the development of the translation theory. This project was an extremely elaborate one: Kashkin and the older members of his group engaged in writing out examples from existing translations and their originals on separate index-cards in order to demonstrate how different translation problems can be resolved. The index-cards were systematized according to the problems they related to: style, genre, lexical means, grammatical issues, sound rendering, etc. (RGALI b, 35). Compiled in this way, the catalogue of practical solutions, alongside with the materials of seminars and meetings' proceedings of the 1930s, formed the basis for Kashkin's theoretical conclusions.

A practical to theory was also taken by Chukovskii, who tended to see the analysis of existing literary translations, their merits, and failures as the basis for the theory. Having published several articles in the 1920s and 1930s, Chukovskii continued his work for almost half a century, rewriting chapters and adding new information, trying, as he himself admitted, to create a reference book for translators (Chukovskii 1941, 6). The book version of 1964 contained Chukovskii's views upon the contemporary literary translation requirements and included chapters on rendering different aspects of literary

THE ART AND CRAFT OF TRANSLATION 145

texts (style, lexicon, grammar, prosody), as well as on the Soviet literary translation history and achievements of Soviet translators (Chukovskii 1964). An important feature of Chukovskii's style was criticism, which was initially justified by his comparative methodology. In many cases, his critical comments verged with slander. Being part of the general rhetoric of the 1930s, relentless criticism became one of the features of the style used in publications devoted to translation even at the point when translation theory came to be recognized as a separate linguistic discipline (Gachechiladze 1964, 117–8; Levik 1987, 376; Rossel's 1984, 76–93).

As we can see from the above, active calls for the unified Soviet "translation theory" were, in fact, no calls for theory, but for a methodology. In the context of the educational orientation of literature and the new standards for literature, new translation methodology was in high demand, as it could provide guidelines for translators working under new political and social circumstances for a new target audience. For the Soviet translation theory, therefore, practice became both the point of departure and the purpose of existence.

4      The Advancement of the Translation Theory

Translation theory as a methodology in the service of translation practice was able to focus on immediate tasks faced by translators, as well as speculate on the degree of license translators could afford in their practical work. However, subjective literary criticism as a point of departure in the disputes over translation was clearly insufficient for a translation theory. Attempts to depart from criticism and purely empirical orientation of translation observations were persistently made by linguist and translator Aleksandr Smirnov (RGALI a, 17–20) and Andrei Fedorov, who continued active research in the field of translation and by 1941 wrote a monograph entitled *O khudozhestvennom perevode* [Upon literary translation] (Fedorov 1941). In 1941, Fedorov's monograph still largely related to "the art of translation, the achievements of this art, the paths leading to them, the ideological principles and practical means lying at their basis" (Fedorov 1941, 3). However, already in 1941, Fedorov described translation as a literary and cultural problem. Alongside the issues of methodology and rendering, he addressed the questions of literary genres, text aging, and the status of originals and translations in their cultures. Fedorov resumed his research after his return from the front and by the beginning of 1950 was the one to make a breakthrough in the Soviet discussions on translation by declaring the primacy of the linguistic approach to translation. The focus on linguistic issues, in Fedorov's view, offered much more objectivity in comparison to literary criticism, inspiration and other extra-linguistic phenomena. Fedorov's 1953 book *Vvedenie v teoriiu perevoda* [Introduction to the Translation Theory] (Fedorov 1953) demonstrated a tremendous evolution of ideas. It highlighted the importance of linguistics in the translation research, "for the content does not exist on its own, but in conjunction with the form, with the language means in which it is incorporated" (Fedorov 1953, 14). Fedorov's *Introduction to the Translation Theory* saw several editions and eventually evolved into another comprehensive monograph entitled *Osnovy obshchei teorii perevoda (lingvisticheskie problemy)* [Principles of General Translation Theory (Linguistic Problems)] (Fedorov 1983). As early as 1953, Fedorov spoke about translation theory as a separate discipline within the domain of linguistics. Opening up his book with the chapter entitled "Translation theory as a scientific discipline", Fedorov called for the linguistic approach to translation, which would enable researchers to establish grammatical and stylistic correspondences and analyze them with consideration to the psychological and social parameters related to translation.

> The linguistic approach to studying translation has an important advantage that lies at its very basis—the language, outside which no functions of translation are possible—neither social and political, nor cultural and cognitive, nor its artistic merit, etc. At the same time, the linguistic studies of translation, that is, its comparative studies of two languages, allow us to be specific, as we use objective factors of the language. Any research and speculation as to how the content of the original reflects in the translation and what role it played in the receiving literature would be groundless unless based on the analysis of the linguistic means employed in the translation. Translation theory as a special field of philology is primarily a linguistic discipline. In some cases, however, it is closely linked with literature studies—literary history and theory, where it borrows some data and ideas, and with the history of the nations, the languages of which take part in the translation process ... But the close linkage of the translation theory with these disciplines does not change its specifics as a linguistic discipline.
>
> FEDOROV 1953, 14—translated by N.K.

Dedicating a chapter to the importance of recognition of translation theory as a separate discipline, Fedorov also addressed a vast number of issues, which he thought were important in the construction of the translation theory. In his book, he gives the outline of the translation history in Europe and in the Soviet Union, and addresses the question of translatability. He also analyzes

THE ART AND CRAFT OF TRANSLATION                                    147

practical issues like lexical and grammatical correspondences, and translation approaches to different genres. Fedorov makes a special focus on literary translation by looking into such questions as the transfer of cultural realities, translation of historically remote texts, and individual style rendering. He maintains that the fulfillment of these practical tasks cannot follow a ready-made prescription or algorithm, because the cultural transfer of the original requires a careful study of both the original and the stylistic means of the target language (Fedorov 1953, 298). The translation of historically remote texts depends "on the correlation and correspondence of stylistic functions, performed in these languages by the elements of both similar and different formal categories" (ibid., 308). Finally, translating the individual style also requires the analysis of two language systems (ibid., 309). Thus, Fedorov draws the outline of the future research in the field of translation and departs from traditional viewpoints, creating a new basis for translation scholarship in the Soviet Union. He recognizes the potential of the comparative approach to the construction of translation theory, but unlike his predecessors, he takes this approach to a higher level in the linguistic hierarchy, calling for making a special focus on language structures, cultural phenomena, and historical backgrounds, and recognizing originals and their translations as single events in wider language and cultural contexts.

First published in 1953, Fedorov's monograph attracted universal attention not only due to its outstanding novelty, but also because *Introduction to the Translation Theory* was the first book on the subject published in the Soviet Union after World War II and was therefore separated by twelve years from Soviet pre-war publications on translation. Several manuals on translation practice were published after the war, but Fedorov was the first to address the theory, and the shift from the traditional literary-oriented course turned translation into the subject of thorough analysis, statistics, and argumentation.

Fedorov's approach provoked both approval and objection in the Soviet Union and in the West. Fedorov was criticized by Edmond Cary for the insufficient attention to philological issues (Cary 1957, 186). At the same time, in his review of the second edition of Fedorov's book, Cary highlighted the importance of the problematic raised by Fedorov and pointed out that the relations between linguistic and literary studies were an issue which required immediate attention (Cary 1959, 19). In the Soviet Union, Fedorov's call for the linguistic approach was criticized, among others, for the lack of sufficient grounds for the existence of the theory as such. Several months before the publication of Fedorov's book, the leading Soviet linguist Aleksandr Reformatskii argued that it was not possible for translation practice "to have its own theory" due to the variety of types and genres of translation (Reformatskii 1952, 12). Fedorov was also criticized by Kashkin and the adherents of the so-called realistic (or literary) approach for his seeming indifference to the aesthetic and emotional features of the original; the reaction of Fedorov's opponents was described in the notes of the Ukrainian scholar Oleksei Kundzich (Kundzich 1968, 219).

The positive response to Fedorov's monograph, however, by far surpassed its criticism. The impact of Fedorov's approach is tangible in the monograph *Poetry and Translation* by the distinguished Leningrad scholar Efim Etkind. Etkind addressed the issues of translatability, transfer of the implied meaning and formal features, and individual approaches to translation. "There is no universal criteria to evaluate the faithfulness of the translation to the original", states Etkind. "Faithfulness is a changeable notion" (Etkind 1963, 39). At the same time, Etkind declares the equality of form and content in literature; the unity of form and content, in Etkind's view, provides for the integrity of a literary work, and the interference with either of them invariably leads to the changes in the other.

Etkind severely criticized Kashkin's approach and disputed every argument of Kashkin's theory of realistic translation, in which the text was seen as a conditional verbal sign (ibid., 133–42). "It is insufficient to understand the reality 'in its directed development, in its revolutionary development', as Kashkin demands—it is also important to be able to read the original", ruthlessly summarized Etkind at the end of his ten-page long criticism of Kashkin's approach (ibid., 142).

In general, the debate about Fedorov's monograph on both sides of the Iron Curtain, as Brian Mossop observes, "unfortunately tended to be about the practice of translating rather than about theory ... What got lost in the debate was Fedorov's real achievement—an advance not in how to see practice but in how to go about theorizing" (Mossop, 2013). This acute observation can be applied to many other scientific debates and research projects in the Soviet Union. Soviet research in the humanities continued to demonstrate a slant towards the practical application of research results. Therefore, the practical orientation of the dispute over Fedorov's approach was a natural consequence of the existing views on theory and practice. Quite notably, the subsequent theoretical publications, including those with a strong theoretical basis, contained parts and chapters of purely practical nature, as the authors tried to ensure a linkage of theory and practice.

As the linguistic approach to translation was gaining influence, new researchers were coming into view. Thus, in 1950, Iakov Retsker published his article on the so-called "regular correspondences" (*zakonomernye sootvetstviia*). Regular correspondences, or natural correlations between the source and the target language units, in Retsker's view, could be established in course of comparative language studies in order to provide a stable linguistic basis for translation (Retsker 1950, 156). The translator's choice, in Retsker's definition, is far from being random, because natural correspondences limit the ways of text rendering. These naturally existing correspondences were divided by Retsker into three groups: equivalents, analogies, and adequate substitutions (ibid., 156–182). In 1974, Retsker published a monograph, in which he carefully studied the correspondences at different language levels (Retsker 1974).

The book entitled *Perevod i lingvistika* [Translation and Linguistics] by Aleksandr Shveitser came out in 1973 (Shveitser 1973). The book had a sub-title "Social press and military journalism translation", which accounted for the choice of examples and offered an alternative to the long-standing dispute over literary translation approach. Shveitser dwelt upon such theoretical issues as the relation of the translation theory to comparative linguistics, structural linguistics, generative grammar, as well as upon translation models, equivalence and its types, communicative aspects of translation, semantic and stylistic problems of translation.

In 1975, Leonid Barkhudarov published his monograph *Iazyk i perevod* [Language and Translation] (Barkhudarov 1975), where he addressed the issues of equivalence, extralinguistic context of translation, communicative situation, and semantics. He also paid close attention to translation practice, including translation typology, correspondence in translation, style, pragmatics, translation units, and levels of translation. Barkhudarov speaks about the controversy of literary vs. linguistic translation approach, quoting Chukovskii among other opponents of the linguistic approach. "These disputes by now ... have lost edge", concludes Barkhudarov. "The mere opposing of the linguistic and the literary approach to literary translation is incorrect, because literary translation, as well as any other, is nothing but transforming a text written in one language into a text written in another language" (ibid., 46).

Despite the impediments in the exchange of knowledge in the times of the Iron Curtain, both Western and Soviet researchers, as Ayvazyan and Pym note, were clearly aware "of what each side was doing, albeit often framed in the antagonistic terms of the Cold War" (Ayvazyan and Pym 2017). Thus, Fedorov, Retsker, Shveitser, and Barkhudarov actively cited both contemporary Soviet and Western researchers, including Catford, Chomsky, Kade, Nida, Mounin, and Vinay and Darbelnet.

The rapid development of translation scholarship in the Soviet Union made researchers go beyond linguistic issues and address interdisciplinary issues of translation. In the book *Obshchaia teoriia perevoda i ustnyi perevod* [General translation theory and interpreting] Riurik Min'iar–Beloruchev defined translation as a discipline related to linguistics, psychology, semiotics, and sociology, and spoke about translation and interpreting in the context of communication and semantics, introducing the term *informational theory of translation* (Min'iar–Beloruchev 1980). The detailed theoretical research of Min'iar–Beloruchev also included practice-oriented chapters on translation methods, including a big section on note taking in consecutive interpreting, as well as a separate chapter on military translation.

The necessitated linkage of practice and theory also created the basis for truly groundbreaking practical research projects. In this regard, there is much to be said about the Leningrad/St. Petersburg linguist Rajmund Piotrowski, who was one of the founders of machine translation in Russia. He published his seminal monograph *Tekst, mashina, chelovek* [Text, Machine, Human] in 1975 (Piotrowski 1975) and developed a rule-based machine translation system PROMT by 1991.

## 5 Conclusion

The Russian translation scholarship, as we have seen, was deeply rooted in the social and political practices of the Soviet Union. The practical orientation of translation theory was determined by educational needs, the social situation, and political requirements. The traditionally high status of literature in Russia and the Soviet Union also affected the process of construction of the Soviet translation theory. This theory in many respects was created with an eye to literary practices, including literary translation and literary criticism. The complete break with the existing tradition did not take place even after the adoption of the linguistic approach to translation studies. The further research sought to reconcile theory and practice and to apply theoretical observations to practical recommendations. At the same time, practical orientation of the Soviet translation scholarship made a substantial contribution to the education of several generations of literary translators whose translations channeled knowledge and ideas from beyond the Iron Curtain. In the context of the limited access to the Western culture in the Soviet Union, this increased focus of the translation scholarship on the practical achievements is quite natural. Practical aspects of translation were ascribed special value not only due to their compliance with the new socialist principles, but eventually because they provided substantial guidelines and methodology for translators who worked hard to bring the works of contemporary western literature to the Soviet readership. In the light of this, the efforts of the Soviet researchers in the development of a translation theory and their close attention to the theoretical works of their Western colleagues acquire even a higher value.

# References

Ayvazyan, Nune and Anthony Pym. 2017. "West enters East. A strange case of unequal equivalences in Soviet translation theory." In *Going East. Discovering New and Alternative Traditions in Translation Studies*, edited by Larisa Schippel and Cornelia Zwischenberger, 221–245. Berlin: Frank & Timme.

Baer, Brian James and Susanna Witt, eds. 2017. *Translation in Russian Contexts: Culture, Politics, Identity*. Abingdon: Routledge.

Baer, Brian James, ed. 2011. *Contexts, subtexts, and pretexts: Literary translation in Eastern Europe and Russia*. Amsterdam: John Benjamins.

Baer, Brian James, and Natalia Olshanskaya (eds). 2013. *Russian writers on translation: An anthology*. Manchester: St. Jerome.

Baer, Brian James. 2016. *Translation and the making of modern Russian literature*. New York and London: Bloomsbury.

Barkhudarov, Leonid. 1975. *Iazyk i perevod (Voprosy obshchei i chastnoi teorii perevoda)*. Moscow: Mezhdunarodnye otnoshenia.

Batiushkov, Fedor, Kornei Chukovskii, and Nikolai Gumilev. 1920. *Printsipy khudozhestvennogo perevoda [Principles of literary translation]*. Petrograd: Vsemirnaia literatura.

Briusov, Valerii. 2013. "A Few Reflections on Translating Horace's Odes into Russian Verse." In *Russian Writers on Translation: An Anthology*, edited by Brian James Baer and Natalia Olshanskaya, 69–71. Manchester: St. Jerome.

Byford, Andy, Connor Doak, and Stephen Hutchings (eds). 2020. *Transnational Russian studies*. Liverpool: Liverpool University Press.

Cary, Edmond. 1957. "Théories Soviétiques de la traduction." *Babel* 3 (4): 179–190.

Cary, Edmond. 1959. "Andrei Fedorov: Introduction à la théorie de la traduction." *Babel* 5 (1): 19–20.

Chukovskii, Kornei, and Nikolai Gumilev. 1919. *Printsipy khudozhestvennogo perevoda [Principles of literary translation]*. Petrograd: Vsemirnaia literatura.

Chukovskii, Kornei, and Andrei Fedorov. 1930. *The art of translation [Iskusstvo perevoda]*. Leningrad: Academia.

Chukovskii, Kornei. 1941. *Vysokoe iskusstvo*. Moscow: Khudozhestvennaia literatura.

Chukovskii, Kornei. 1964. *Vysokoe iskusstvo*. Moscow: Iskusstvo.

Chukovskii, Kornei. 2001. *Sobranie sochinenii. T. 3 [Collection of Works. Vol. 3]*. Moscow: TERRA—Knizhnyi klub.

Chukovskii, Kornei. 2003. Dnevnik 1901–1969. Tom 1. 1901–1929. [Diary. 1901–1969. Volume 1. 1901–1929]. Moscow: OLMA-PRESS.

Clark, Katerina. 2011. *Moscow, the fourth Rome: Stalinism, cosmopolitanism, and the evolution of Soviet culture, 1931–1941*. Cambridge, US: Harvard University Press.

Darwish, Ali. 2010. *A journalist's guide to live direct and unbiased news translation.* Melbourne: Whitescope Publishers.

Dashtents, Khachik. 1968. "Shekspir v Armenii" [Shakespeare in Armenia]. In *Masterstvo perevoda*, edited by Kornei Chukovskii, 60–68. Moscow: Sovetskii pisatel'.

*Decrety Sovetskoi vlasti. Vol. 1.* 1957. Moscow: Gosudarstvennoye izdatel'stvo politicheskoi literatury.

Eikhenbaum, Boris. 1987. "Teoriia formal'nogo metoda" [Theory of the Formal Method]. In *O literature* by Boris Eichenbaum, 375–408. Moscow: Sovetskii pisatel'.

Eliot, Thomas Stearns. 1998. "Euripides and Professor Murray." In: Eliot, Thomas Stearns. *The Sacred Wood and Major Early Essays*, 40–43. Mineola, New York: Dover Publications.

Etkind, Efim. 1963. *Poeziia i perevod [Poetry and Translation].* Moscow-Leningrad: Sovetskii pisatel'.

Fedorov, Andrei. 1941. *O khudozhestvennom perevode [Upon literary translation].* Leningrad: Goslitizdat.

Fedorov, Andrei. 1953. *Vvedenie v teoriiu perevoda [Introduction into Translation Theory].* Moscow: Izdatel'stvo literatury na inostrannykh iazykakh.

Fedorov, Andrei. 1983a. "Fragmenty vospominanii" [Fragments of memories]. In: Kaverin, Veniamin (ed). *Vospominaniia o Iu. Tynianove.* Moscow: Sovetskii pisatel'.

Fedorov, Andrei. 1983b. *Osnovy obshchei teorii perevoda (lingvisticheskie problemy) [Fundamentals of the General Translation Theory (Linguistic Problems)].* Moscow: Vysshaia shkola.

Gachechiladze, Givi. 1964. *Voprosy teorii khudozhestvennogo perevoda.* Tbilisi: Literatura da khelovneba.

Gor'kii, Maksim. 1932. "Preface." In: Shatobrian, Fransua, and Benzhamen Konstan. *Rene. Istoriia molodogo cheloveka*, 3–14. Moscow: Zhurnal'no-gazetnoe ob'edinenie.

Gor'kii, Maksim. 1936. "O formalizme [Upon formalism]." *Pravda*, April 9, no. 99.

Jakobson, Roman. 1979a. "Afterword of 1926." In: Jakobson, Roman. *Selected Writings. Vol. V. On Verse, Its Masters and Explorers*, edited by Stephen Rudy and Martha Taylor, 122–130. The Hague/Paris/New York: Mouton Publishers.

Jakobson, Roman. 1979b. "On the Translation of Verse." In: Jakobson, Roman. *Selected Writings. Vol. V. On Verse, Its Masters and Explorers.* Ed. by Stephen Rudy and Martha Taylor, 131–134. The Hague/Paris/New York: Mouton Publishers.

Kashkin, Ivan. 1968a. "Lozhnyi printsip i nepriemlemye rezul'taty (O bukvalizme v russkikh perevodakh Ch. Dikkensa)" [The False Principle and Unacceptable Results (Upon Bukvalism in the Russian Translations of Ch. Dickens)]. In *Dlia chitatelia-sovremennika (Stat'i i issledovaniia)* by Ivan Kashkin, 377–410. Moscow: Sovetskii pisatel'.

THE ART AND CRAFT OF TRANSLATION 153

Kashkin, Ivan. 1968b. "V bor'be za realisticheskii perevod" [In the Struggle for the Realistic Translation]. In *Dlia chitatelia-sovremennika (Stat'i i issledovaniia)* by Ivan Kashkin, 473–513. Moscow: Sovetskii pisatel'.

Kundzich, Oleksei. 1968. "Perevodcheskii bloknot" [The Translator's Sketchbook]. In *Masterstvo perevoda*, edited by Kornei Chukovskii, 199–238. Moscow: Sovetskii pisatel'.

Lenin, Vladimir. 1977. *Collected works. In English. 1908*. Vol. 14. Moscow: Progress Publishers.

Levik, Vil'gel'm. 1987. "O tochnosti i vernosti" [Upon preciseness and faithfulness]. In: *Perevod—sredstvo vzaimnogo sblizheniia narodov*, edited by Anatolii Klyshko, 358–377. Moscow: Progress.

Min'iar–Beloruchev, Riurik. 1980. *Obshchaia teoriia perevoda i ustnyi perevod [General translation theory and interpreting]*. Moscow: Voenizdat.

Montgomery, Scott Lyons. 2000. *Science in translation: Movements of knowledge through cultures and time*. Chicago and London: University of Chicago Press.

Mossop, Brian. 2013. "Andrei Fedorov and the origins of linguistic translation theory." http://www.yorku.ca/brmossop/Fedorov.htm.

Pannwitz, Rudolf. 1917. *Die Krisis der europäischen Kultur* [The crisis of the European culture]. Nürnberg: Hans Carl Verlag.

*Pervyi Vsesoiuznyi S'ezd Sovetskikh Pisatelei 1934: Stenograficheskii otchet*. 1934. Moscow: Sovetskii pisatel'.

Piotrowski, Rajmund. 1975. *Tekst, mashina, chelovek [Text, Machine, Human]*. Moscow: Nauka.

Potebnia, Aleksandr. 1990. *Teoreticheskaia poetika [Theoretical poetics]*. Moscow: Vysshaia shkola.

Pym, Anthony, Miriam Shlesinger, and Zuzana Jettmarova, eds. 2006. *Sociocultural aspects of translating and interpreting*. Amsterdam and Philadelphia: John Benjamins.

Reformatskii, Aleksandr. 1952. "Lingvisticheskie voprosy perevoda." [Linguistic issues of translation]. *Inostrannye iazyki v shkole* 6: 12–22.

Retsker, Iakov. 1952. "O zakonomernykh sootvetstviiakh pri perevode na rodnoi iazyk" [Upon regular correspondences in translation into the native language]. In *Voprosy teorii i metodiki uchebnogo perevoda*, edited by K.A. Ganshina and I.V. Karpov, 156–183. Moscow: Izdatel'stvo Akademii pedagogicheskikh nauk SSSR.

Retsker, Iakov. 1974. *Teoriia perevoda i perevodcheskaia praktika [Translation theory and translation practice]*. Moscow: Mezhdunarodnye otnoshenia.

RGALI (a) [Russian State Archive of Literature and Arts], f. 631, op. 21, ed.khr. 9.

RGALI (b) [Russian State Archive of Literature and Arts], f. 631, op. 21, ed.khr. 12.

Rossel's, Vladimir. 1984. "Znanie, talant, trud" [Knowledge, talent, labor]. In *Skol'ko vesit slovo: Stat'i* by Vladimir Rossel's, 44–126. Moscow: Sovetskii pisatel'.

Schäffner, Christina and Susan Bassnett. 2010. "Politics, media, and translation: Exploring synergies." In *Political discourse, media, and translation*, edited by Christina Schäffner and Susan Bassnett, 1–29. Newcastle upon Tyne: Cambridge Scholars Publishing.

Sherry, Samantha. 2015. *Discourses of regulation and resistance: Censoring translation in the Stalin and Khrushchev era Soviet Union*. Edinburgh: Edinburgh University Press.

Shklovskii, Viktor. 1983. *O teorii prozy* [*Towards the Theory of Proze*]. Moscow: Sovetskii pisatel'.

Shveitser, Aleksandr. 1973. *Perevod i lingvistika. Gazetno-informatsionnyi i voenno-publitsisticheskii perevod* [*Social press and military journalism translation*]. Moscow: Voenizdat.

Tymoczko, Maria. 2010. *Enlarging translation, empowering translators*. Manchester, UK and Kinderhook, USA: St. Jerome.

Tynianov, Iurii. 1977. "Tiutchev i Geine" [Tiutchev and Heine]. In: Tynianov, Iurii. *Poetika. Istoriia literarury. Kino*, 29–37. Moscow: Nauka.

"Ustav Soiuza Sovetskih Pisatelei SSSR" [Charter of the Union of Soviet Writers of the USSR]. 1934. In: *Pervyi Vsesoiuznyi S'ezd Sovetskikh Pisatelei 1934: Stenograficheskii otchet*. 712–713. Moscow: Khudozhestvennaia literatura.

CHAPTER 8

# Travelling Theories in Translation Studies
## *Rediscovering Fedorov*

*Anastasia Shakhova*

## Abstract

Andrei Fedorov (1906–1997) elaborated the first consistent theory of translation based on the linguistic approach that concerned itself not primarily with the translation of literature, but also with other text types, and provided the scholars with translatological text type taxonomy. Designed according to the needs of the Soviet system, it used to be perceived through the prism of ideological incompatibility with the Western discourses of translation studies. But was Fedorov's work a theory based on ideology, or a theory developed despite ideological pressure? Did he anticipate the development of modern translation studies and contribute to the development of the discipline? Do translation studies need to learn to translate themselves through time, space, language and ideological borders? The analysis of Fedorov's work and its further editions as well as a review of some critical articles concerning Fedorov propose controversial answers to these questions and allow to join a vibrant conversation on reshaping translation studies temporally, geographically, and ideologically.

## 1    Introduction

In 2014, the annual EST Translation prize was awarded to Brian Baer for his proposal to translate *Vvedenie v teoriju perevoda* [*Introduction to the Theory of Translation*] by Andrei V. Fedorov (1953) into English. Being a well-known work in Russian-speaking discourse of translation studies and having remained virtually invisible for the non-Russophone readership for more than six decades, this work is supposedly being rediscovered now. This 'missing theory' might redefine the boundaries of translation studies (TS) and would definitely enhance our knowledge of the historical development of the discipline, as scholars are no longer reluctant to acknowledge the pioneering role of

© KONINKLIJKE BRILL NV, LEIDEN, 2021 | DOI:10.1163/9789004437807_009

Fedorov's theses, which appear to be quite similar to some ideas of his Western colleagues.

The present article aims to draw attention not only to the particular case of Fedorov's theory and its rearrangement in the frame of the global discourse of TS, but also to the phenomenon of 'rediscovery' as such, to its ideological nature and its potential impact on the discipline, as well as to its correlation with the circulation of knowledge. The migration of theories in general and of scientific theories in particular always takes place in a certain socio-political context and under specific circumstances and represents a complex cultural phenomenon, which has a performative character. Such migration is the symptom and the result of a certain political constellation within and outside the scientific system, closely connected to its discursive politics. Theories of translation obviously travel within the global TS as well, and evidently may become lost on their way, being unable or unwanted to cross the discursive borders of the scientific field. The phenomenon of 'rediscovery' can be regarded as one of the phases of the travelling process and is closely connected with the variability of factors influencing this process, such as the principles of scientificity within the target discipline, external mechanisms regulating the text production (including ideological issues), the participation of mediators, who enable the process of travelling and facilitate or hinder the 'rediscovery' of theories, the purpose of its new use, the image of a travelling theory designed according to this purpose, as well as the needs and expectations of the target audience.

Being part of a travelling process, the rediscovery of a theory presupposes rewriting in its various forms, such as reviews, criticism, summarizing, anthologies, and translation. As far as the rediscovery of Fedorov is concerned, the particularity of this case lies in the fact that the rediscovery is taking place prior to the release of the full-text translation. Consequently, the role of other forms of rewriting (comprising selective translation) in reshaping the image of the 'rediscovered theory' is becoming more important.

The present article investigates this case of rediscovery in progress, testifies to continuous changes in the global discourses of TS, and raises a series of questions concerning not only its past, but also its present and future. The analysis of previously existing rewritings (including several re-editions of Fedorov's work in the source language) highlights some of the ideological issues, which have influenced the reception of Fedorov's theory. While this investigation offers a preliminary insight into this particular case of rediscovery, the future of Fedorov's theory in the global discourses of TS remains an open question, as a translation of it and a reaction to it are still to come.

TRAVELLING THEORIES IN TRANSLATION STUDIES 157

## 2    Missing or Abandoned?

Fedorov's theory was "strangely trapped in a very particular time capsule," claim Pym and Ayvazyan in the article "The case of missing Russian translation theories."[1] "Could we really have ignored the Russians so completely?" the authors wonder as they state that ideas similar to the translation theories of Western authors were already pronounced in the early 1950s by Russian authors, such as Sobolev, Smirnov, Retsker, and Fedorov (Pym and Ayvazyan 2014, 1). According to Pym and Ayvazyan, Soviet scholars "developed a translation concept that united foreignization and domestication, that named the priority of purpose, [...] that developed a catalogue of translation solutions" and "posited that translation was a fact of target cultures" already in the 1950s (ibid.). The authors raise another vibrant question:

> If all that is true, how is it that our more narrowly Western translation theories attribute Skopos theory to Vermeer, text-type theory to Reiss, solution types to Vinay and Darbelnet, target-side priority to Tel Aviv and Vermeer, Translation Studies as a discipline to Holmes, and still prolong millennial binarisms that offer just two main ways of translating? (ibid.)

Pym and Ayvazyan do not give a clear-cut answer. They suggest that the theories of Sobolev, Retsker and Fedorov were "associated with the final years of Stalinism and were thus strangely cut off from the development of translation studies in most other languages" (ibid.). If that is true, there is nothing strange in the fact that they were excluded from the discourses of Western TS for ideological reasons and are well-known in the post-Soviet area. However, one could not say that Fedorov's work was completely excluded from the discourses of the non-Soviet TS. Pym and Ayvazyan paradoxically prove it themselves as they collect fragmentary pieces of information concerning Fedorov's theory. They introduce some examples illustrating how Fedorov's work was criticized (for example, by Cary, Brang, etc.), or reduced to "the idea that linguistics might

---

1   Pym and Ayvazyan's article was consciously chosen for analysis and reference as it reveals how the research was conducted and what factors and personalities influenced the perception of Fedorov's theory and shaped the authors' attitude to it. The accomplished version can be found in Pym's book *Translation Solutions for Many Languages: Histories of a Flawed Dream*, 2016. In the book the information concerning Fedorov's biography, his previous publications, his reception worldwide, and similarities between his ideas and some ideas of the Western authors was updated with the participation of Russian-speaking colleagues.

provide a banal 'common denominator' (gemeinsamer Nenner) beneath all text types" (for example, by Jumpelt) (Pym and Ayvazyan 2014, 14).

Pym and Ayvazyan formulate a hypothesis according to which "in the days of dark Stalinism, some scholars thought about translation in formalist terms, absorbing the kinds of systemic text analyses that would elsewhere be called stylistics" (ibid., 18). Due to the fact that the publication of their pioneering theories coincided with the final years of Stalinism, they "were so strongly associated with Stalin and his legacy that they would be questioned both within and outside the Soviet Union, and thus never really move beyond Russian" (ibid., 19).[2] Meanwhile, the editors of the 5th edition of Fedorov's work would be surprised to learn that Fedorov's theory was called 'missing' in the Western discourse, as they claim in the preface that Fedorov's book has been a basic textbook on translation in Russia for years and is a well-known work abroad (Fedorov 2002, 3–5).

The authors then suggest that "it was easy enough to airbrush Stalin out of later editions and reflections, allowing the formalist tradition to produce a series of theories and textbooks" while outside Russia the negative reception of the Soviet theories has persisted till the present day (Pym and Ayvazyan 2014, 19). Quotations from Stalin and references to his work indeed visually disappeared from later editions of Fedorov's book, however, his ideas remained encoded in the text as well as in the discourse of Russian linguistics and TS in the shape of what Sériot calls "crypto-citation" (Sériot 1986), or hidden reference.

A rather sarcastic response to the thorough investigation, conducted by Pym and Ayvazyan, came soon from Sergey Tyulenev beginning and ending with the phrase "Elementary, Dr. So-and-So" which alludes to the image of Sherlock Holmes and his deductive method as well as to Dr. Watson, who, from Sherlock's point of view, tends to overlook the obvious. Tyulenev points out how "arduous and tortuous the way to the success was" (Tyulenev 2014). The authors were looking for the missing pieces of information all over the world except for Russia. They contacted neither St. Petersburg University, where Fedorov had been teaching for years, nor Fedorov's daughter, who was still alive and even participated in the annual conference *Fedorvskie chtenija* in St. Petersburg (ibid.).

Tyulenev underlines the discrepancy between the role and contents of philology as such in the Russian system of education and in the West and argues that there was nothing bizarre in Fedorov's biography, contrary to what Pym and Ayvazyan suggest. Fedorov's profound linguistic knowledge was due to

---

2　The authors mean here not only Fedorov's theory, but also the works of Sobolev, Retsker, and Smirnov.

TRAVELLING THEORIES IN TRANSLATION STUDIES 159

the fact that he was a student of Shcherba, Tynianov, Vinogradov, Zhirmunskii and other outstanding linguists of that time. Knowing this, one would not be surprised by how and why he approached translation from the linguistic perspective (ibid.). He wonders how the authors could have omitted mentioning Gorkii's project "Vsemirnaja Literatura" ["World Literature"] and its impact on the development of TS in the USSR. "Soon after launching the project, it was realized that certain common principles of translating had to be formulated and a new generation of translators needed to be trained" (ibid.). The development of Soviet TS as a discipline traces back to the conflict between 'craftsmanship with rules' (Gumilev) and 'creation' (Chukovskii), which finally brought both opponents to the "necessity to formulate some principles to be observed while doing literary translation," Tyulenev explains. According to him, Fedorov "continued the line of harnessing artistry and approached this as a scholar and philologist" (Tyulenev 2014). Tyulenev mentions that Pym and Ayvazyan have not considered "existing translations of Russian translatologists," such as Palma Zlateva's book (1993), as well as publications explaining the theories of some Russian authors, such as Peter Fawcett's work (1997). Though Tyulenev agrees with Pym's statement that Stalin's intervention played a crucial role in the Soviet science system in the 1950s, he doubts that it actually freed the science from any dogma and fostered its further development (including the development of TS) (ibid.).

Pym and Ayvazyan's article as well as Tyulenev's response do not only pay tribute to Fedorov's theory, but also highlight some issues concerning the interaction between the discourses of Russian and Western TS and the peculiarities of the scientific communication in general. The first issue concerns the networks within the scientific field, which might help to accumulate knowledge and provide a better communication between the discourses of TS. At the very beginning of their article, Pym and Ayvazyan refer to the difficulties of cooperation within the discipline:

> Translation Studies is performed through an international network of relations between largely isolated scholars, many of whom cooperate in order to create knowledge. The sparse nature of the relations, however, coupled with the difficulties of relatively opaque languages and hard-to-assemble materials, means that the cooperative production of knowledge is often fraught with difficulties: the network only vaguely discerns its international extension (rarely reducible to the West vs. the Rest) and has a very sketchy awareness of its own origins.
>
> PYM AND AYVAZYAN 2014, 1

The second issue concerns the remaining ideological tension between the discourses of Russian and Western TS. The fact that Tyulenev prefers a sarcastic publication to a potentially helpful private comment on Pym's forthcoming book highlights this tension. The ideological nature of his critique doesn't remain unnoticed in Pym's "A response to the response to 'The case of the missing Russian translation theories'" (2015). Pym points out that Tyulenev's remark on "unwilling distortion" indeed "implies that the critic somehow has access to the undistorted, true history, about which outsiders can only be taught by insiders" (Pym 2015, 347).

Pym explains that the term 'linguist' and 'linguistics' had ideological connotation in the 1950s and in 1960s:

> The term "linguist" was used ideologically to position Fedorov on just one side of that debate, opposing literary studies, in the 1950s, and that is the thing that does not fit in with the biography, that was the great historical injustice.
>
> PYM 2015, 349

Pym also indirectly acknowledges that the term 'linguist' negatively affects the contemporary Western understanding of Fedorov's role in the development of TS: "When I consulted several experts on the possibility of translating Fedorov into English", Pym says, "I was told he was not the one we should translate, because "he was a linguist". One expert advised we would do better to render Kashkin, a theorist of literary translation" (Pym 2015, 349).

The fact that calling Federov a 'linguist' becomes a subject of debate in contemporary publications proves that 'linguist' and 'linguistics' still have an ideological connotation and that these terms are likely to be partially incommensurable in the discourses of Russian and Western TS (due to their ideological past).

## 3    Enhancing Said's Notion of Travelling Theory

A further problematic issue that both articles touch on concerns the way theories and ideas circulate between the discourses of TS, in other words, the way how and why they travel and how and why they sometimes become lost on their way. A model illustrating how theories and ideas travel from culture to culture, from one scientific field to another, being metamorphosed and adapted to the needs of the target system, was developed in Edward Said's work in 1983. The notion of "travelling theories" has become a travelling theory itself and has

# TRAVELLING THEORIES IN TRANSLATION STUDIES 161

a rich history in the humanities discourses. Thanks to Mieke Bal's *Travelling Concepts in the Humanities* (2002) and Susam-Sarajeva's *Theories on the Move* (2006), it managed to drop anchor in the discourse of TS as well.

Said's original four-stage model of a travelling process includes the point of origin (that is simultaneously the moment of departure), then "a passage through the pressure of various contexts as the idea moves from the earlier point to another time and place where it will come into a new prominence," then acceptance or rejection of the imported theory, and finally its transformation and adaptation (Said 1983, 126). This model was criticized by Susam-Sarajeva for neglecting the crucial role of translation in such migration processes. Translation as a form of rewriting in Lefevere's terminology plays a formative role in the migration processes, shaping the travelling theory to the needs of the target system, and an indicative role, showing the needs and expectations of the target system (Susam-Sarajeva 2006, 1). It also reveals the power constellation between the source and the target system which characterizes any intercultural contact where interference takes place (see Even-Zohar 2008, 117–18). Bassnett and Lefevere point out that "all rewritings, whatever their intention, reflect a certain ideology and a poetics" and refer to rewriting as to "manipulation, undertaken in the service of power" (Bassnett and Lefevere 2003, xi).

Though there are no published full-text translations of Fedorov's work into English, German, French[3] or Spanish, which would make his ideas accessible to the wider scope of readers, his theory can be regarded as a travelling theory of translation rather than a missing theory.[4] Since their point of origin,[5] some Fedorov's ideas indeed have travelled into the discourses of non-Russian TS through such forms of rewriting as reviews, criticism, anthologies, and

---

3   There is indeed a translation of Fedorov's work (1958) into French. According to Irene Weber Henking, the work was translated in 1968 by R. Deresteau and A. Sergeant under the aegis of Institut supérieur de traducteurs et d'interprètes de Bruxelles. The typewritten translation includes over five hundred pages and remains confidential (Weber Henking 2019, 312). See Weber Henking, Irene. 2019. "Une nouvelle science á partir de 1960". In *Histoire des traductions en langue française, XXᵉ siècle*, edited by Bernard Banoun, Isabelle Poulin and Yves Chevrel, 277–324. Verdier.

4   It should be mentioned that Fedorov's book was translated into Chinese in 1954 (see Mossop 2013/2019 referring to Jin 2004 (1987), 141). Mossop points out the considerable influence of Fedorov's work on Chinese TS, while Jin who acknowledges this fact also adds that despite it, translation was still considered as an art rather than a domain of linguistics (Jin 2004, 141).

5   The point of origin of Fedorov's theory did not coincide with the publication of *Vvedenie v teoriju perevoda* (1953). He had already expressed similar ideas in his earlier publications, such as Fedorov, Andrej V. 1952. "Osnovnye voprosy teorii perevoda" ["The Fundamental Questions of the Theory of Translation"], 1952, and *Iskusstvo perevoda*, [*The Art of Translation*], 1930, co-authored by Chukovskii. However, the 1953 publication drew much more attention to his theory.

selective translation. They were interpreted differently by different scholars and adapted according to the expectations of the target system. The reception of Fedorov used to have a sporadic nature; in most cases it was facilitated by works of acknowledged scholars in target disciplines, such as Cary, Mounin, García Yebra, Brang, Jumpelt, etc. Many contemporary scholars created a fragmentary image of his theory, which did not promote its further integration (see Pym and Ayvazyan 2014, 14).

Pym and Ayvazyan also point out that one of the main sources of information about Fedorov's theory and Soviet TS in general was Edmond Cary, whose appreciation of Fedorov was rather low (ibid.).

As a translation is still missing, this form of reception continues to prevail. For example, Anna-Maria Corredor Plaja explains Fedorov's ideas giving references not to Fedorov's book, but to the translation of Mounin's work, where Mounin comments on Fedorov (Corredor Plaja 1994). Bolaños underpins his own theses with Mounin's and García Yebra's judgments as well (Bolaños 1998). It should be mentioned, however, that this form of circulation of ideas between the TS discourses is a widespread phenomenon in cases of a missing translation. Similarly, post-Soviet scholars writing about the Skopos theory generally give references to Komissarov's summary of Reiss and Vermeer's book (1999) instead of referring to the original work, which they obviously do not have access to.

Thus, an English translation of Fedorov's book will become a crucial point in the process of travelling from the Russian-speaking discourse into the global discourses of translation. Nevertheless, it will signify neither the beginning of the travelling process, not its end. The fact that the translation is coming after more than six decades since the first publication of the work demonstrates, on the one hand, the willingness of the Western system of TS to reconsider its discursive politics and to revise its own history. On the other hand, the temporal gap signals the persistence of specific barriers or borders between Russian and Western systems of TS.

The migration of scientific theories from one discourse to another may be motivated by the inner discursive politics of the discipline and the applicable principles of scientificity as well as external factors, the interaction of which can be described as 'patronage' in Lefevere's terminology. Describing the mechanisms of control in literary systems, Lefevere mentions that poetics and ideology represent two major forces controlling the text production within the discourse. While ideology prescribes what the world should look like, poetics prescribes what the literature should look like (Lefevere 2009, 65).

Two mechanisms of control can be derived from poetics and ideology: poetics is reserved for literary scholars, critics, reviewers, as well as translators and

# TRAVELLING THEORIES IN TRANSLATION STUDIES

controls the text production from inside, while the second mechanism of control, that affects the text production from outside, can be designated as patronage and has an ideological nature (Lefevere 2009, 74–75). Dizdar suggests that Lefevere's terminology, which primarily referred to the text production in literary systems, can be equally applied to the text production in general (Dizdar 2006, 357). Consequently, it can be assumed that similar mechanisms of control affect different forms of text production within a discourse of a discipline, including TS.

The observation of text production in scientific systems proves that ideology here maintains a similar function, while poetics can be substituted by the principles of scientificity (Shakhova 2017, 110). According to Foucault, "a discipline is defined by a domain of objects, a set of methods, a corpus of propositions considered to be true, a play of rules and definitions, of techniques and instruments" (Foucault 1981, 59). Foucault continues:

> It is always possible that one might speak the truth in the space of a wild exteriority, but one is 'in the true' only by obeying the rules of 'policing' which one has to reactivate in each of one's discourses. (ibid., 61)

These rules of policing can differ from culture to culture, from discipline to discipline, and can change as every discipline develops and changes. Unchanged remains the presence of certain norms of text production, which set the limits of the discourse. Flatau, having researched the Western scientific discourses of the 19th–20th centuries (focusing on works of Einstein, Mommsen, Freud, and Sauerbach) comes to the conclusion that the "scientificity binds the author to its laws and sets limits beyond which scientific authorship cannot take place" (Flatau 2015, 401—Translated by A.S.). This statement is applicable to the norms of text production within the discipline in the later period of time as well. The principles of scientificity continue to form a scientific tradition within the discipline. As far as ideology is concerned, it influences the text production in scientific systems from outside, as a component of patronage, but it can affect the principles of scientificity as well. Consequently, the migration of translation theories always takes place in the context of a discipline-specific discursive policy, which enables and controls the flow of new ideas.

Susam-Sarajeva, Neumann and Nünning, as well as Menzel and Pohlan point out that the travelling process inevitably requires mediators or a network of mediators. (Susam-Sarajeva 2006, 206; Neumann and Nünning 2012, 8; Menzel and Pohlan 2013, 7). If mediators are required to enable the process of travelling and help the travelling theories to cross the borders of discourse, who are those mediators within TS? On the micro level, there are translators and scholars as transporters, on the macro level, there are institutions, such as universities, publishing agencies and patrons. In many cases scholars perform a dual role, being professional translators themselves and integrating translated passages into their discourse. The scholars working in a certain field are likely to be responsible for the reception, integration and development of travelling theories in TS. They play a pivotal role in shaping the image, which a transported theory and its author would have in a new context, by putting the theory into a new paradigm, choosing certain parts for translation and presentation while omitting some other aspects that might seem less relevant in the new context. This is how they ensure that the image of new theories and their authors formed in the recipients' culture finds its place in the scientific discourse. Through their approval or critique as well as through the selective translation the travelling theory is changed or adapted to the needs of the domestic system of science. The formation of the image of theories or their authors is essential for their acceptance and integration; inevitably, it suggests that they will be compared with the domestic theories concerning their similarities and differences: As Beller remarks, "Valorizing the Other is, of course, nothing but a reflection of one's own point of view" (Beller 2007, 6). Consequently, voicing and stance of the scholars in translation, summarizing or criticism may reflect ideological issues concerning the ideas or theories introduced into the discourse (see Tymoczko 2003, 183, see also Dizdar 2006, 332–333).

Scientific writing, which usually comprises rewriting, is always carried out with a certain purpose in mind, according to the norms of text production and principles of scientificity within the discipline, and in the context of a certain ideology. To specify the meaning of 'ideology', one might refer to the taxonomy of the definitions of this term, elaborated by Peter Tepe. Tepe summarizes the manifold meanings of the term and arranges them into five basic definitions:

- Ideology[1] = desires, needs, interests, illusory thinking
- Ideology[2] = ideas and value systems (germ. Weltanschauung)
- Idology[3] = sociopolitical program
- Ideology[4] = definitely false ideological or socio-political consciousness
- Ideology[5] ("the ideological") = the process of conveying certain ideologies[2/3] by institutions and organizations (Tepe 2013, 17–29—Translated by A.S.).

In this taxonomy, the concept of ideology[4] presupposes a conflict of at least two ideologies,[1/2] for example, the ideologies of the source and target culture. Rewriting becomes a borderline where ideologies[1/2] encounter each other, as the rewriter may represent one of them, or a third ideology.[1/2] This confrontation may result in the ideologization of theories and ideas introduced into the discourse. The potential of a text to be written, translated, positioned or read ideologically (compare Dizdar 2006, 332–333) is unleashed by the purpose of production and new contextualization. As Eagleton notices:

TRAVELLING THEORIES IN TRANSLATION STUDIES

> You could not decide whether a statement was ideological or not by inspecting it in isolation from its discursive context [...]. Ideology is less a matter of the inherent linguistic properties of a pronouncement than a question of who is saying what to whom for what purposes.
>
> EAGLETON 1991, 9

Calzada-Pérez is even more assertive: "All language use is, as CDA [Critical Discourse Analysis] contenders claim, ideological. Translation is an operation carried out on language use. This undoubtedly means that translation itself is always a site of ideological encounters" (Calzada-Pérez 2003, 2). Ideologization is closely connected to the fifth concept of ideology in Tepe's taxonomy, namely the ideological, which stresses the performative character of ideologization, as the mediation of certain ideologies[2/3] by institutions and other organizations requires active involvement of a network of mediators that facilitate the mediation (Tepe 2013, 29).

Consequently, rewriting as a form of transporting a theory or idea into the target discourse can not only reveal the existing ideological discrepancies between the source and target discourse, but also create, amplify as well as soften or even efface them, depending on the purpose of rewriting and the needs of the target scientific discourse.

## 4      Fedorov's Case

It is worthwhile approaching Fedorov's theory relying on Said's model and sketch its way through the Western discourses, starting with its point of origin and then proceeding to the image formation in order to find out, how its image was formed in different discourses, how some ideological issues concerning Fedorov's book were handled, and how it contributed to its present status.

The image of Fedorov in the discourses of the Eastern Bloc will not be analyzed here, as Fedorov's theory was neither missing nor consequently rediscovered there. However, it should be mentioned that this image has always been a very positive one. For example, East German scholars, such as Otto Kade and other representatives of the so-called Leipzig School, often used quotations from Fedorov's book to justify their own statements. His theses were summarized and repeatedly referred to in their scientific writing, especially when some ideological issues were concerned. Nevertheless, Fedorov's work was not translated into German by East German translation scholars due to the fact that most of them could read in Russian and perceived Fedorov's ideas in the original. Also, a translation would have required an adaptation to the needs of the target system, as Fedorov's book focused primarily on the Russian language and reflected the politics of translation into Russian in the USSR, which was different from the translation politics from Russian and other languages into German in the GDR.

### 4.1 *Linguistic Discussion and New Principles of Scientificity*

The point of origin of the Soviet TS indeed coincided with the omnipresence of ideological pressure in the academic milieu and was influenced by the theses of the so-called Linguistic Discussion. In 1950, both Soviet linguistics and TS experienced a shock. Stalin's essay "Marxism and the Problems of Linguistics" originally published in the newspaper Pravda, turned the contemporary science upside down, by denying that language was a superstructure on the base and criticizing the theory of Nikolay Marr, which used to be an ideologically approved and acknowledged linguistic theory despite its pseudoscientific approach to the problems of linguistics. The essay represents a remarkable example of ideological patronage over text production in scientific discourses, as Stalin virtually translated himself and his new political program of building the Great Russian Nation and the Great Russian Language into the discourse of science.

Although the ideas of the Linguistic Discussion, including Stalin's theses, did not form a unified linguistic or translation theory, their interpretation and further development in the works of the Soviet scholars created the base on which the linguistic approach in the Soviet TS emerged. The social and political context in which these theses came to birth facilitated their circulation in scientific discourses. The ideological pressure on Soviet society forced the scientific discourses to accept them without questioning. A new function was attributed to the science; it had to be ideological and to promote ideology (see Shakhova 2017, 106). Stalin's intervention into linguistics and indirectly into TS abolished previous discursive restrictions within the discipline, but immediately set new rules and norms, restricting and controlling the text production in the Soviet discourse. Reflection of the Soviet ideology became one of the major principles of text production; the validity of Stalin's theses was indisputable, and any proposition had to conform to them in order to remain "in the true". In other words, his theses constituted a restrictive principle of scientificity (Shakhova 2017, 110).

It is worth mentioning that the consequences of Stalin's intervention were indeed as controversial as their interpretations in contemporary works are now. Baer sees in Stalin's rejection of Marr's ideas a reflection of the turn from internationalism to nationalism in the Soviet discourses (Baer 2016, 53). He notes that the consequences of this turn influenced Soviet TS in general and Fedorov's work in particular, enabling Fedorov to offer "a view of language that

# TRAVELLING THEORIES IN TRANSLATION STUDIES

comes very close to linguistic relativism" (ibid., 57), despite Fedorov's critique of Sapir-Whorf hypothesis. Also, Stalin's intervention into linguistics caused a paradigm shift within the discipline and made possible the emerging of the linguistic approach in the Soviet TS. "[...] It can be said that an intervention of a nonscientific authority triggered a non-scientific revolution, which however resulted in a breakthrough in linguistics and translation studies" (Shakhova 2017, 119). The term "non-scientific revolution" refers to Kuhn. According to his ideas, "scientific disciplines develop in a natural way only if the choice between paradigms remains in the hands of the scientific community; [...] if a nonprofessional authority forges a paradigm shift in a scientific discipline, this kind of 'revolution' wouldn't be a scientific one" (Shakhova 2017, 109, in reference to Kuhn 1970, 167).

It should be mentioned that not only Soviet linguistics and TS were affected by Stalin's intervention. Through immediate institutionalized translation, Stalin's essay reached the discourses of the Eastern Bloc, including the East German discourse of the humanities. Here are some examples of how intensively the work was reprinted in German: 1950, publishing company Stern; 1950, publishing house Einheit; 1951, publishing house Neues Leben; 1951, 1952, 1953, 1954, 1955, publishing house Dietz; 1968, 1972, publishing house Rogner und Bernhard.

During the conference of the Socialist Unity Party of Germany in 1951, Stalin's ideas were discussed at the governmental level. Consequently, the science in general and the humanities in particular obtained the same missionary ideological function as in the USSR (Maffeis 2007, 101; Schulz 2010, 27). The examples of how Stalin's theses were to be interpreted and applied in linguistics were also immediately translated into German and published in Eastern Germany in 1952 by Kuczynski and Steinitz (see Shakhova 2017, 116–117). The articles included in this compendium were selected according to the needs of the target system and to the ambitions of the source system; they reflected the current development of the Soviet discourse and introduced new patterns of text production. There were not only articles belonging to the Linguistic Discussion, but also articles dating half a year later, showing the establishment of Marxist linguistics and the way Stalin's theses should be applied. A positive image of the theses of the Linguistic Discussion was designed by selective translation, paratexts, reviews, and criticism (Shakhova 2017, 116).

Consequently, the ideas of the Linguistic Discussion left an imprint on the discourses concerning translation. In the book *Zur Frage der Übersetzung von schöner und wissenschaftlicher Literatur* (1953), edited by C.E. Matthias, there is an essay by Topjor (translated from Russian), which focuses mainly on the ideological aspect of translation and on the interpretation of Stalin's ideas.

There are also two articles by East German authors, namely Fickenscher and Hoeppener, which deal with translation as well. Both authors use a similar pattern of text production and base their argumentation on the theses of the Linguistic Discussion. However, it should be mentioned here that the Marxist TS in the GDR differed from the Marxist TS in the USSR by the spectrum of scientific tasks. The Soviet TS focused almost exclusively on linguistic aspects of translation, whereas the East German authors tended to take into account the organizational and action-oriented aspects of translational activity as early as in the 1950s.

The comparative analysis of the publications mentioned above as well as the comparative analyses of publications in the Soviet journal *Voprosy jazykoznanija* [*Problems of Linguistics*] (first issued in January 1952) from that time reveal that Stalin's essay indeed set new norms of text production in the discourse of linguistics and TS not only in the USSR. To be published, Fedorov's book had to fit into the new frame and meet the demands of the contemporary readership. Fedorov integrated Stalin's theses into his theory as it was expected from every Soviet scholar from that time and devoted a separate chapter to Stalin's essay. He proclaimed the notion of general translatability concerning all developed national languages, underpinning his argumentation with Stalin's theses. He modelled a new image of the translator—the translator as an ideological fighter, while the ideological loyalty was assumed to be the main condition for a proper and successful translation. The ideological responsibility of the translator had to be reflected "in the text selection, the quality of the translation and in the veracity of the translation" (Fedorov 1953, 3—Translated by A.S.).

Classical Marxist theoreticians were mentioned in Fedorov's work as experienced translators, whose attitude towards the original and the translation should be mimicked just like their strategies of translation. Quotations from Marx, Engels and Lenin, and, of course, Stalin, served as a relevant means of argumentation for the translator's decisions (Shakhova 2017, 114). The text type taxonomy elaborated by Fedorov also reflected the ideological mission of science in the sense that it suggested that political texts, especially Communist texts and speeches by the party leaders, constituted a separate subgroup. This suggestion was incompatible with the Western discourses, which were based on the opposite ideological premises. Nevertheless, it was not only the visible presence of the Soviet ideology, that made Fedorov's work incompatible with the Western discourse of TS, but also the visible or hidden presence of an anti-Soviet ideology in the discourse of Western TS. Leerssen suggests that "the default value of humans' contacts with different cultures seems to have been ethnocentric, in that anything that deviated from accustomed

TRAVELLING THEORIES IN TRANSLATION STUDIES                                    169

domestic patterns is 'Othered' as an oddity, an anomaly, a singularity" (Leerssen 2007, 17). This oddity resulting in incompatibility became one of the major aspects of criticism concerning Fedorov in the Western discourse.

However, during the period of de-Stalinization, the principles of scientificity changed. The Communist ideology still had to be reflected, but references to Stalin's work could not serve as a means of scientific argumentation any longer and were removed from the further editions of Fedorov's work. Nevertheless, the circulation of theories and ideas between the Soviet and Western TS was impeded by their ideological discrepancies. But was Fedorov's theory of translation indeed that ideological? What would remain of the theory if the ideological frame were removed? Would it be possible to remove it?

### 4.2    *Some Ideological Issues in Progress*

A thorough analysis of Fedorov's work (1953), comprising its correspondence to the works of contemporary authors and some relevant ideological issues is represented in Pym's book *Translation Solutions for Many Languages: Histories of a flawed dream* (2016); and the existence of this book proves that Fedorov's ideas are engaged in the process of travelling into the global discourse of TS. I would therefore like to focus on some ideological constants and variables in Fedorov's work throughout its long history of re-editing (1st edition-1953, 2nd edition-1958, 3rd edition-1968, 4th edition-1983, 5th edition-2002).

Fedorov's work is featured in Peter Fawcett's article "Ideology and translation", where Fawcett refers to its ideological aspects[6] and its reflection of Marxism:

> Fedorov's book is probably one of the very few books on translation theory to contain an entire chapter devoted to 'Marx, Engels, Lenin on Translation' and to make such statements as 'enormous interest and extreme value for the theory of translation are presented by the remarks of V.I. Lenin on translation and language' (Fedorov 1958: 91; translated) [...]. This pressure to mention the right people (a trait by no means confined to Communism) is just one of several ideological pressures found in Marxist-oriented translation theory. Communism had to reach as many people as possible, and therefore had to adopt appropriate translation strategies. Fedorov says of Lenin's own translational method that "he

---

6    Fawcett refers, however, to the second edition of Fedorov's work, where Stalin's presence is not so visible.

achieves full accessibility of content for the widest circle of readers"
(ibid., 98; translated).

FAWCETT 1998, 109–10

The idea of accessibility for the widest circle of readers is aligned with Fedorov's statement concerning his own style of narration. In the preface to the 4th edition he mentions that he adheres to his previous simple and comprehensible manner of narration, though contemporary authors are prone to an excessive use of terminology, which makes their works less accessible to the readership (Fedorov 2002,[7] 11).

In the preface to the 4th edition, Fedorov states that he is aware of the fact that the 4th edition bears the impress of the epoch when the previous editions appeared. However, he does not change its contents and structure because he is still faithful to the principles according to which the book was designed. Besides, a contemporary reader might be interested in the discussions on TS that took place in the 1950s–1960s (Fedorov 2002, 10). Fedorov probably hints at the Linguistic Discussion and refers to the era of Stalinism that influenced his work. The principles that Fedorov has in mind could be at the same time ideological principles or/and the scientific principles of approaching the translation. In his review of the history of translation, Fedorov himself points out that the ideology and aesthetics of the translator were closely connected with the principles of translation and that the application of certain methods and principles of translation played a certain political role from the historical perspective (Fedorov 2002, 81–82). The above statement can be read in terms of the Manipulation School and reveals certain similarity with Lefevere's ideas already highlighted in the present article.

The preface to the first edition, beginning with forced praise for Stalin's essay, has never been reprinted. While this reflects the ideological changes within the Soviet system, the titles of the five editions reflect the historical development of TS. The 1st and the 2nd edition had the title *Vvedenie v teoriju perevoda* [*Introduction to the Theory of Translation*]; the further editions were entitled *Osnovy obščej teorii perevoda* [*The Fundamentals of the General Theory of Translation*]. The new title proved that TS had already been established as an independent discipline and that Fedorov's division in the general and special theory of translation had been acknowledged in the discourses of TS. The 3rd edition had the subtitle *Lingvističeskij očerk* [*Linguistic Essay*], the second and

---

7   The preface to the 4th edition (1983) can also be found in the 5th edition of the book (2002). The 5th edition appeared after Fedorov's death and is a copy of the previous one, except for the editors' introduction.

the last edition had the subtitle *Lingvističeskije problemy* [*Linguistic Problems*]. As Fedorov explains in the preface to the 4th edition, the subtitle underlined the fact that translation involved many other aspects beyond linguistics, while his book covered primarily the linguistic aspects of translation.

The concept of the book, its structure and contents basically remained unchanged, though each edition of the book reflected the contemporary tendencies in TS. Such pivotal publications for the development of global linguistics and TS as Jakobson's essay, Revzin and Rosentsweig's work on machine translation, as well as series of publications of Soviet authors criticizing the Sapir-Whorf hypotheses appeared between the 1st and the 3rd editions, while a large number of works in stylistics,[8] text linguistics, and psycholinguistics appeared between the 3rd and the 4th edition (1983). Many of them are featured in the later editions of Fedorov's book. Some examples underpinning Fedorov's theses were updated too (mostly examples concerning news reports and scientific texts). Several passages justifying the establishment of the linguistic approach were also removed as there was no need to legitimize this already developed and acknowledged approach.

Fedorov sticks to the idea that to translate means to express accurately ('točno') and completely ('polno') by the means of one language what was already expressed by the means of another language. The accuracy and the completeness of translation are two criteria which help to distinguish translation from retelling, summary or any other kind of adaptation (Fedorov 1953, 7; 1968, 15; 2002, 14–5). Being the "major instrument of human communication" (a reference to Lenin), language maintains a similar function in translation. Consequently, the idea of the original should be expressed in the target language as completely, distinctly and functionally as it was expressed in the source language. To be comprehensible to the recipient, the translation should correspond to the norms of the target language (Fedorov 1953, 7–8; 1968, 17; 2002, 16). In the 1st edition, the above statement was underpinned with Stalin's thesis about the inseparability of language and thinking, the later editions contained only references to Lenin, as this ideological premise could hardly be airbrushed.

The main goal of the translation theory remains the same: to study the regularities concerning the correlation between the original and the translation, to generalize the conclusions based on empirical material, and to support the translational practice (Fedorov 1953, 12; 1968, 21; 2002, 19–20).

---

8  Fedorov suggests that stylistics is the most closely related discipline to TS (1953, 17; 1968, 29; 2002, 25).

The full value of a translation in Fedorov's works is used as a synonym to adequacy and means the accurate transfer of the semantic content of the original and functional and stylistic correspondence to the original (Fedorov 1953, 112–114; 1968, 151; 2002, 144). Fedorov's text type taxonomy remained unchanged through all five editions, though some examples were updated and replaced with corresponding contemporary texts. It should be recalled that Fedorov distinguished between three text types, namely (1) news reports, documentary and scientific texts; (2) social-political texts, such as journalism, literary criticism, and public speech; (3) literary works (Fedorov 1953, 198; 1968, 251; 2002, 227). It is remarkable that the similarity with the taxonomy of Katharina Reiss, which was noticed by contemporary authors including Bolaños and Pym, was acknowledged neither by Fedorov, nor by Reiss. In the 5th edition of his monography, there is a passage where he criticizes the text taxonomy elaborated by Katharina Reiss. Her article "Möglichkeiten und Grenzen der Übersetzungskritik" (1971) was translated into Russian and published by Vilen Komissarov in 1978. Komissarov's selection of works of foreign scholars working in the field of TS included a large variety of crucial texts of that time and offered to the readership an opportunity to get acquainted with the theories of Jakobson, Mounin, Kade, Catford, Nida, and many others. Fedorov points out that his own text taxonomy was criticized by Reiss (Fedorov 2002, 281). He defends his taxonomy and says that he is not persuaded by the division of text types into informative, expressive, operative, and audiovisual types. He claims that the mere existence of a text which has no informative function is scarcely possible (ibid.). Being familiar with Reiss's work through the translation, Fedorov points out that Reiss herself used only Peter Brang's summary of Fedorov's book (ibid.). It should be mentioned here that Fedorov was aware of the fact that Brang's review was rather negative (see preface to the 4th edition).

Fedorov also sticks to his criticism of Humboldt's idealistic and pessimistic approach to translatability (Fedorov 1953, 25–26; 1968, 43–45; 2002, 37–38). In the later editions, he also criticizes Sapir and Whorf as well as Leo Weisgerber (Fedorov 1968, 44–45; 2002, 38). His criticism is based on the incompatibility of their ideological premises with the Soviet discourse of TS. Fedorov claims that the "idea of untranslatability is common in bourgeois philology as a proof that the cultural values created in politically dominating countries cannot become the property of other nations" (Fedorov 1953, 26—Translated by A.S.). In the later editions "bourgeois philology" was replaced with "capitalistic philology" (2002, 39); "politically dominating" was replaced with "developed and politically dominating" (1968, 45; 2002, 39); "cannot become" was replaced with "cannot and should not become" (2002, 39). The above examples prove that ideological discrepancies between the Soviet and Western discourses of TS

TRAVELLING THEORIES IN TRANSLATION STUDIES — 173

remained sharp at least till the 1980s, and even at the edge of the 21st century editors had reasonable grounds not to soften or remove that statement. It is remarkable, that in a prefatory essay to his monography Fedorov expressed a similar explicit disapproval of any non-Marxist approach to translation. He claimed that any false/wrong political, aesthetic, historical, and literary approach to the translation leads to an erroneous perception and misunderstanding of the original, and to its distortion through translation (Fedorov 1952, 20–1). A correct/right ideological approach (presumably the Marxist one) is, on the contrary, a condition of a correct/right solution to a translational problem (Fedorov 1953, 11–12; 1968, 19).

The antithesis false/wrong vs. right/correct proves that Fedorov's understanding of a non-Marxist ideology and of a non-Marxist approach to translation corresponds to the concept of 'ideology'[4] in Tepe's terminology, namely definitely false ideological or socio-political consciousness, and underlines his own ideological identity.

As ideological pressure decreased, Fedorov did not abandon his principles, his terminology, and his manner of writing. He did not replace examples of translation strategies borrowed from the works of the Marxist Classics; he did not revise his attitude to the problem of translatability and did not reconsider the text type taxonomy. The ideological premises, which were suggested to be valid in the Soviet TS, were reflected in each edition of Fedorov's book, including the post-Soviet edition.

## 5 The Image of Fedorov and His Theory Outside the Soviet Discourses

### 5.1 *Fedorov's Theory and Ideology*

One of the first images of Fedorov and his theory within the West European discourses was sketched by Peter Brang. In the article published in the West German journal *Sprachforum* in 1955, Brang summarized some ideas of Fedorov's work, making its content partly available to his German speaking colleagues.[9] Due to the absence of a full-text translation, the image of Fedorov and his ideas was rather fragmentary, as Brang selectively translated several abstracts from Fedorov's work. Translation was used as an instrument of exploring Fedorov and as a means of constructing a certain image of his theory. In his critical review, which Pym and Ayvazyan call "a simplistic reading"

---

9  Fedorov's name and his theory were familiar to the East German theoreticians thanks to the scholars of the so-called *Leipziger Schule* [Leipzig School].

(Pym and Ayvazyan 2014, 8), Brang paid attention primarily to the ideological components of Fedorov's theory and pointed out that Stalin's theses were adapted to the needs of TS and served as a foundation for Fedorov's argumentation (Brang 1955, 127). This sort of criticism was natural and predictable in that period of time and in that type of scientific discourse. Nevertheless, Brang indeed pointed out that Fedorov's book paved the way to the development of TS as an academic discipline with its own specific object of studies (ibid., 126), and explained Fedorov's theses concerning translatability, functional correspondence in the source and target languages, text typology, and the practical tasks of translators.

Brang reproached Fedorov for neglecting the idea that language reflects a particular world view (Weltbild), a thesis contradicting Fedorov's notion of general translatability (Brang 1955, 128). It is not surprising to find such criticism in an article included into Leo Weisgerber's collection. This reproach makes ideological borders between the discourses much more visible than the statement that Fedorov's entire work is adapted to the Soviet needs and is not applicable in other situations. It reveals the basic antithesis—translatability vs. untranslatability, both derived from conflicting ideological premises and incompatible linguistic-philosophical views. Brang indeed had many reasons to criticize Fedorov's work for its ideological connotations. The patterns of text production in Fedorov's work including his narrative style and argumentation obviously deviated from the approved patterns of text production in the West German discourses, and Brang underlines this difference creating the opposition "we/us/West German scholars/West German TS vs. Fedorov/he/Soviet scholars/Soviet TS" (Brang 1955, 125–126).

### 5.2 *Fedorov as a Precursor of Modern Translation Studies*

A totally different image of Fedorov and a very positive assessment of his work is presented in the article "Vigencia de la teoría de la traducción de Andrei Fedorov", 1997, by Sergio Bolaños Cuéllar. Bolaños stresses the importance and validity of Fedorov's ideas, which are still significant and applicable after several decades, and regrets that such a pioneering work as Fedorov's was almost excluded from the non-Soviet discourses and was not translated into Spanish. He notes that Mounin (1977) and García Yebra (1983) already pointed out that contemporary TS actually began with Fedorov's work[10] (1953), in which translation was claimed to be a distinct object of study that could and should be

---

10      Bolaños mentions that according to Mounin and Garcá Yebra the other pioneering work that triggered the development of the discipline was *Stylistique comparée du français et de l'anglais. Methode de traduction* by Vinay and Darbelnet.

TRAVELLING THEORIES IN TRANSLATION STUDIES                    175

studied scientifically (Bolaños 1997, 53), while other famous scholars in the field of TS such as Nida, Taber, Newmark did not even mention Fedorov in their works.

Bolaños translates large passages from Fedorov's work concerning his ideas about the reconciliation of theory and practice of translation, the scientific status of translation, and about translation as a linguistic operation, and linguistic problems of translation. He compares some of Fedorov's statements with the ideas of Western scholars and notices that "the priority of the audience over the forms of the language" in the work of Nida and Taber (1969, 31) was already expressed by Fedorov (Bolaños 1997, 59). Wilss' proposal to distinguish between the general theory of translation, the descriptive theory of translation, and the applied theory of translation coincides surprisingly with Fedorov's ideas as well (ibid.). Bolaños points out that many authors referring to Fedorov erroneously attribute to him the idea that translation is 'exclusively' or 'simply' a linguistic operation. Again, he quotes Mounin who explains that translation for Fedorov was not only a linguistic operation, but primarily and consistently a linguistic operation (Bolaños 1997, 60). Bolaños also pays attention to Fedorov's and Sobolev's text type taxonomies and draws parallels with the taxonomy by Katharina Reiss (ibid., 70–71).

It is remarkable that Bolaños does not refer to the ideological aspects of Fedorov's theory and concentrates on its validity and applicability. For him, Fedorov is a precursor of modern TS, who anticipated the actual development of the discipline and whose work received undeservedly little attention outside the Soviet discourse. As in the previous case, the absence of a full-text translation of Fedorov's work allows Bolaños to construct a certain image of Fedorov's theory through selective translation and analysis of the chosen aspects. Again, translation serves as a means of image construction and as a tool of rediscovering.

Mossop[11] also creates the image of Fedorov as one of the so-called Founding Fathers of the TS. He acknowledges the crucial role of Fedorov's work and calls it "the first sustained argument [...] for a language-based rather than a literary theory of translation" (Mossop 2013/2019). He undermines Cary's criticism concerning Fedorov's view of the language as a common denominator:

> Now what Fedorov saw, I think, is that viewing translation in terms of fields and genres is highly problematic for any enterprise of 'scientific study'. For if drama translation is part of theatre work and the translation of news stories is part of journalism, then there can be no *general*

---

11    Bolaños's article is also included into Mossop's list of references.

*theory* of translation. For that purpose, a common denominator had to be found, and the most obvious common denominator was language (ibid.).

Mossop mentions Stalin's impact on Fedorov's book, but this fact does not diminish its value for him. He points at "a certain thematic resemblance between the notion that language is common to all social classes" (a statement coming from Stalin's essay) and "Fedorov's idea that language is the common denominator for all the social frameworks within which translation takes place (journalism, theatre, etc.)", but also suggests that Stalin's intervention into linguistics could have allowed Fedorov to publish the ideas he already had before (Mossop 2013/2019). Pym and Ayvazyan agree with this statement, though their suggestion that "thanks to Stalin, language could again be studied more or less on its own terms" (Pym and Ayvazyan 2014, 6–7), deserves a separate discussion.

Mossop openly stresses Fedorov's pivotal role in the development of European TS in general:

> A final word on Fedorov: Translation had traditionally been regarded in the European tradition as a useful practical activity but hardly ever as something of intellectual interest. [...] This changed with Fedorov, at least among those who could read him or learned about him from others. There was now a book-length argument conveying a sense that translation, in all fields, is worth studying for itself.
>
> MOSSOP 2013/2019

The opposition "we/Western science vs. Fedorov/Soviet studies/other" that can be observed in Brang's article is no longer valid as Mossop places Fedorov within the European TS without dividing it into East and West European or Soviet and non-Soviet branches.

It is worth mentioning that Mossop in his review of Pym's book *Exploring Translation Theories* (2010) notices the absence of information about Russian theories of translation:

> As usual, Western does not include Russian, presumably because like most West Western theorists, Pym does not read Russian, and the works in question have not been translated into a West European language. Pym refers the reader to Fawcett's *Translation and Language* (St Jerome 1997), which looks at Shveitser, Retsker and Komissarov, though it does not cover the remarkable 1953 introduction to the theory of translation by Fyodorov. (sic!).
>
> MOSSOP 2010

According to Pym and Ayvazyan, it was also Brian Mossop, who recommended translating Fedorov's work into English to Brian Baer (Pym and Ayvazyan 2014, 2). This case illustrates how the construction of a positive and appealing image of a theory and its author promotes its travelling into the discourses of TS and paves the way to the next crucial step—translation into the global academic lingua franca.


## 6      Conclusion

The fact that Fedorov's theory used to be excluded from the Western discourse of TS proves the existence of certain discursive borders between the Russian and Western systems of TS, closely connected to the principles of scientificity and ideological premises valid within the discipline. Indeed, the ideological played a pivotal role in Fedorov's work, having an effect on its contents and structure as well as on Fedorov's judgments concerning major problems of translation. But if so, how can some of his ideas be so similar to the ideas of the Western authors who proceeded from opposite ideological premises? This could be explained by the suggestion that the Soviet and Western scholars approached the same object, namely the phenomenon of translation, with a similar purpose, with similar 'tools' of investigation, and with similar willingness to find solutions to translational problems. At the same time, ideological discrepancies prevented them from acknowledging the fact that a proposition based on different ideological premises could also be valid.

A rediscovery of a missing theory is not a rare phenomenon in TS. Menzel and Pohlan point out that some modern tendencies in post-Soviet linguistics, translation, and cultural studies, such as 'kul'turologija' ('culturology' or cultural anthropology), 'lingvokul'turologija' ('linguocultural studies' or cultural linguistics) and 'ėtnopsiholingvistika' ('ethnopsycholinguistics'), which promote the concept of untranslatability, closely connected to the enigmatic "Russian soul" were able to emerge after the rediscovery of the Sapir-Whorf hypothesis and the ideas of Leo Weisgerber (Menzel and Pohlan 2013, 13–14). Again, the image of these theories was reshaped according to its new use, as their previous negative image, which can still be found in Fedorov's works, was no longer considerable. It goes without saying that in this case rewriting also played a pivotal role in reshaping the image of the rediscovered theories. Another phenomenon, similar to the rediscovery of Fedorov's work, would be the rediscovery of Reiss and Vermeer's Skopos theory and its integration into the post-Soviet discourses of TS. Probably, this will also happen prior to the release of a full-text translation, as the premises to that can be already found in works of contemporary scholars, such as Irina Alekseeva, Nikolai Garbovskiy, etc.

Though there is no unified image of his theory outside the Russian discourses and no unanimous attitude towards the validity of Fedorov's theses or their role in the development of TS, the changing image of Fedorov and his theory in the Western discourses paves the way not only to the expected translation of the work, but also to its re-integration into the historical paradigm of the global TS. Rediscovering Fedorov's work would involve a temporal and geographical reshaping of TS through the revision of its history. Moreover, the reaction to this work, which might follow after the first translation into English, would highlight the contemporary ideological borders between the discourses of the Russian and the Western TS. Hopefully, this will result in more discoveries and more translations, as TS does apparently need to translate itself in order to overcome time, space, language, and ideological borders.

### References

Alekseeva, Irina. 2004. *Vvedenie v perevodovedenie.* Moscow: Akademija.

Baer, Brian James. 2016. "From international to foreign: packaging translated literature in soviet Russia". *The Slavic and East European Journal*, 60/1: 49–67. Accessed January 26, 2020. https://www.jstor.org/stable/26633217.

Bal, Mieke. 2002. *Travelling concepts in the humanities: A rough guide.* Toronto: University of Toronto Press.

Bassnett, Susan and André Lefevere. 2003. "General editors' preface." In *Translation/history/culture. A sourcebook*, edited by André Lefevere, xi–xii. Taylor & Francis e-Library. https://www.taylorfrancis.com/books/translation-history-culture-andr%C3%A9-lefevere/10.4324/9780203417607.

Beller, Manfred. 2007. "Perception, image, imagology." In *Imagology. The cultural construction and literary representation of national characters. A critical survey*, edited by Manfred Beller and Joep Leerssen, 3–16. Amsterdam: Rodopi.

Bolaños Cuéllar, Sergio. 1997. "Vigencia de la teoría de la traducción de Andrei Fedorov." *Forma y Función* 10: 51–72.

Brang, Peter. 1955. "Das Problem der Übersetzung in sowjetischer Sicht." *Sprachforum: Zeitschrift für angewandte Sprachwissenschaft zur überfachlichen Erörterung gemeinwichtiger Fragen aller Lebensgebiete* 1: 124–134.

Calzada-Pérez, María. 2003. "Introduction." In *Apropos of ideology: Translation studies on ideology—Ideologies in translation studies*, edited by María Calzada-Pérez, 1–22. Manchester: St Jerome.

Cary, Edmond. 1957. "Théories soviétiques de la traduction." *Babel* 3 (4): 179–190.

Cary, Edmond. 1959. "Andrei Fedorov: Introduction à la théorie de la traduction." *Babel* 5 (1): 19–20.

TRAVELLING THEORIES IN TRANSLATION STUDIES 179

Corredor Plaja, Anna-Maria. 1994. "La traducción en la historia de la lingüística." In *La Lingüística francesa. Situación y perspectivas a finales del siglo XX*, edited by J.F. Corcuera, M. Djian and A. Gaspar, 111–116. Universidad de Zaragoza. https://dial net.unirioja.es/descarga/articulo/4033999.pdf.

Dizdar, Dilek. 2006. *Translation. Um- und Irrwege.* Berlin: Frank & Timme.

Eagleton, Terry. 1991. *Ideology. An introduction.* London and New York: Verso.

Even-Zohar, Itamar. 2008. "Gesetzmäßigkeiten der kulturellen Interferenz." In *Ästhetik und Kulturwandel in der Übersetzung*, edited by Maria Krysztofiak, 117–134. Translated by Katarzyna Lukas. Bern: Peter Lang.

Fawcett, Peter. 1997. *Translation and language. Linguistic theories explained.* Manchester: St. Jerome.

Fawcett, Peter. 2001. "Ideology and translation." In *Routledge encyclopedia of translation studies*, edited by Mona Baker, 106–111. London and New York: Routledge.

Fedorov, Andrei Venediktovič. 1952. "Osnovnye voprosy teorii perevoda." *Voprosy jazykoznanija* 1952/5: 3–22.

Fedorov, Andrei Venediktovič. 1953. *Vvedenie v teoriju perevoda.* Moscow: Izdatel'stvo literatury na inostrannyh jazykah.

Fedorov, Andrei Venediktovič. 1968. *Osnovy obščej teorii perevoda. Lingvističeskij očerk.* Moscow: Vysšaja škola.

Fedorov, Andrei Venediktovič. 2002. *Osnovy obščej teorii perevoda. Lingvističeskie problemy.* Moscow: Folologija tri.

Fickenscher, Wilhelm. 1953. "Einige Bemerkungen zur Übersetzung wissenschaftlicher Texte aus dem Russischen." In *Zur Frage der Übersetzung von schöner und wissenschaftlicher Literatur*, edited by C.E. Matthias, 63–80. Berlin: Kultur und Fortschritt.

Flatau, Elke. 2015. *Der wissenschaftliche Autor. Aspekte seiner Typologisierung am Beispiel von Einstein, Sauerbruch, Freud und Mommsen.* Wiesbaden: Springer Fachmedien. http://link.springer.com/chapter/10.1007/978-3-658-08141-6_2.

Foucault, Michel. 1981. "The order of discourse." In *Untying the text. A post-structuralist reader*, edited by Robert Young, 48–78. Translated by Ian McLeod. Boston: Routledge.

Hoeppener, Christine. 1953. "Bemerkungen zur Übersetzung belletristischer Werke." In *Zur Frage der Übersetzung von schöner und wissenschaftlicher Literatur*, edited by C.E. Matthias, 49–64. Berlin: Kultur und Fortschritt.

Jin, Di. 2004 (1987). "The debate of art vs. science (1987)". In *Twentieth-century Chinese translation theory. Modes, issues and debates*, edited by Leo Tak-hung Chan, 141–146. Translated by Priscilla Yip. Amsterdam/Philadelphia: John Benjamins.

Komissarov, Vilen, ed. 1978. *Voprosy teorii perevoda v zarubežnoj lingvistike.* Moscow: Meždunarodnye otnošenija.

Komissarov, Vilen. 1999. *Obščaja teorija perevoda: Problemy perevodovedenija v osveščenii zarubežnyh učonyh [General Theory of Translation. Translatological Problems in Works of Foreign Scholars].* Moscow: ČeRo.

Kuczynski, Jürgen and Wolfgang Steinitz, eds. 1952. *Beiträge aus der sowjetischen Sprachwissenschaft, Folge 1*. Berlin: Kultur und Fortschritt.

Kuhn, Thomas. 1970. *The Structure of Scientific Revolutions*. Second edition, enlarged. The University of Chicago Press.

Leerssen, Joep. 2007. "Imagology: History and method." In *Imagology. The cultural construction and literary representation of national characters. A critical survey*, edited by Manfred Beller and Joep Leerssen, 17–32. Amsterdam: Rodopi.

Lefevere, André. 2009. "Interpretation, Übersetzung, Neuschreibung: Ein alternatives Paradigma." In *Deskriptive Übersetzungsforschung. Eine Auswahl*, edited by Susanne Hagemann, 63–92. Translated by Susanne Hagemann. Berlin: Saxa.

Maffeis, Stefania. 2007. *Zwischen Wissenschaft und Politik. Transformationen der DDR-Philosophie 1945–1993*. Frankfurt/M: Campus.

Matthias C.E., ed. 1953. *Zur Frage der Übersetzung von schöner und wissenschaftlicher Literatur*. Berlin: Kultur und Fortschritt.

Menzel, Birgit and Irina Pohlan. 2013. "Vorwort." In *Russische Übersetzungswissenschaft an der Schwelle zum 21. Jahrhundert*, edited by Birgit Menzel and Irina Pohlan, 7–24. Berlin: Frank & Timme.

Mossop, Brian. 2010. "Review of Anthony Pym, exploring translation theories, Routledge 2010 by Brian Mossop, York University School of Translation." Accessed September 3, 2017. http://www.yorku.ca/brmossop/PymExploring.htm.

Mossop, Brian. 2013/2019. "Andrei Fedorov and the Origins and Fate of Linguistic Translation Theories." Accessed September 12, 2017 and January 2, 2020. http://www.yorku.ca/brmossop/Fedorov.htm.

Neumann, Birgit, and Ansgar Nünning. 2012. "Travelling concepts as a model for the study of culture." In *Travelling concepts for the study of culture*, edited by Birgit Neumann and Ansgar Nünning, 1–22. Berlin: de Gruyter.

Pym, Anthony and Nune Ayvazyan. 2014. "The case of the missing Russian translation theories." Last modified June 2, 2014. Accessed July 14, 2016. http://usuaris.tinet.cat/apym/on-line/translation/2014_russian_web.pdf.

Pym, Anthony. 2015. "A response to the response to 'The case of the missing Russian translation theories'". *Translation studies* 8/3: 347–351. http://dx.doi.org/10.1080/14781700.2015.1011221.

Pym, Anthony. 2016. *Translation solutions for many languages: Histories of a flawed dream*. Bloomsbury publishing.

Said, Edward W. 1983. *The Text, the world and the critic*. Cambridge: Harvard University Press.

Schulz, Tobias. 2010. Sozialistische Wissenschaft: Die Berliner Humboldt-Universität (1960–1975). Köln: Böhlau.

Sériot, Patrick. 1986. "De l'amour de la langue à la mort de la langue." Essais sur le discours soviétique 6: 1–19. Accessed September 3, 2016. http://crecleco.seriot.ch/recherche/biblio/86.EDS6.html.

Shakhova, Anastasia. 2017. "Paradigm shifts in Soviet linguistics and translation studies: the case of the Linguistic discussion of 1950". Acta Slavica Estonica IX. Translation Strategies and State Control: 106–121.

Susam-Sarajeva, Şebnem. 2006. *Theories on the move. Translation's role in the travels of literary theories*. Amsterdam and New York: Rodopi.

Tepe, Peter. 2012. *Ideologie*. Berlin: de Gruyter.

Topjor, Pavel. 1953. "Grundsätzliches zur künstlerischen Übersetzung." In *Zur Frage der Übersetzung von schöner und wissenschaftlicher Literatur*, edited by C.E. Matthias, 9–47. Berlin: Kultur und Fortschritt.

Tymoczko, Maria. 2003. "Ideology and the position of the translator. In what sense is a translator 'in between'?" In *Apropos of ideology. Translation studies on ideology—Ideologies in translation studies*, edited by María Calzada-Pérez, 181–201. Manchester: St Jerome.

Tyulenev, Sergey. 2014. "Elementary, Dr. So-and-So!" Last modified October 12, 2014. Accessed July 14, 2016. http://translation.tyulenev.org/#post90.

Weber Henking, Irene. 2019. "Une nouvelle science á partir de 1960". In *Histoire des traductions en langue française, XXᵉ siècle*, edited by Bernard Banoun, Isabelle Poulin, and Yves Chevrel, 277–324. Verdier.

Zlateva, Palma, ed. 1993. *Translation as social Action. Russian and Bulgarian perspectives*. Translated by Palma Zlateva. London/New York: Routledge.

CHAPTER 9

# Appropriation of Central Discourses versus Local Tradition

*Translation Studies in the Greek-Speaking World*

*Georgios Floros and Simos Grammenidis*

## Abstract

Translation studies as an academic discipline in its own right have only emerged in the Greek-speaking world over the past decades. Despite the recent emergence, sufficient time has passed for an attempt to take stock of the directions into which translation studies in Greece and Cyprus is now developing. The main aim of this paper is to explore the epistemological profile of translation studies in Greece and Cyprus. The examination of the Greek context as a 'peripheral' one might offer interesting insights into the processes by which translation knowledge is distributed and diffused, but also into the ways new translation knowledge is positioned against the existing situation. In order to sketch the epistemological profile of translation studies in Greece (TS in Greece), a corpus-based approach was adopted to analyze two sets of data by using the classic framework by Holmes (1988[1972]) and Gile's scientometric method (2000; 2006). The findings suggest that TS in Greece are, for the time being, mainly descriptively oriented and that the adoption of mainly western theoretical discourses in the last two decades has led to a reconsideration and re-interpretation not so much of the concepts and methodologies which were 'imported', but mainly of the very own local tradition.

## 1 Introduction

In the Greek-speaking world (i.e., Greek and Cypriot universities), translation studies (TS) have grown into an independent academic discipline over the last two decades. The systematic study of translation is ever growing, and new theoretical and practical courses are being introduced at university level. A considerable number of scholars operate in this new scientific field and a considerable number of seminal texts written in other languages, mainly English, have been translated into Greek. Within this optimistic context, the aim of this paper is to explore the epistemological profile of translation studies in

© KONINKLIJKE BRILL NV, LEIDEN, 2021 | DOI:10.1163/9789004437807_010

## APPROPRIATION OF CENTRAL DISCOURSES VERSUS LOCAL TRADITION 183

Greece and Cyprus—in short, TS in Greece.[1] The reason for focusing on the specific topic is twofold: first, sufficient time has passed since the early days of TS in Greece, so as to start taking stock of and evaluating the orientation TS in Greece have adopted as well as the level of maturity. Second, the examination of the Greek context, being a rather 'peripheral' one (as will be discussed further down), might offer interesting insights into the processes through which translation knowledge has been distributed and diffused so far and into the ways more recent translation knowledge is positioned against the existing situation. In other words, one of the main reasons for taking stock of trajectories within TS in Greece is to examine the degree to which there is a tendency to assimilate central discourses at the expense of a Greek, local tradition which had been formed before the Greek-speaking world attempted an epistemological opening to international debates, as well as the way(s) in which such assimilation is manifested.

Thus, the paper will attempt to identify the research trends which are prevalent in various studies of the translation phenomenon and to outline the epistemological characteristics of translation studies in Greece and Cyprus, by analyzing a large corpus of academic publications of Greek translation scholars of the last two decades. More specifically, the issues this paper seeks to explore include: (a) the main research questions Greek translation scholars address and the extent to which these questions reflect contemporary concerns at international level; (b) the (international) theoretical trends which have informed local contributions; (c) the interaction—if any—of international discourses with the local tradition in terms of theorizing translation. In doing so, this paper also examines the way translation is conceived and conceptualized in the Greek-speaking world, by examining to what extent Greek contributions to translational theory and practice are influenced by the etymology of the Greek term for translation μετάφραση [> meta + phrase] or by foreign terms such as *translation/traduction*. In other words, the results of questions (a) and (b) will serve as a basis for attempting to answer question (c) regarding the situatedness of the local tradition, understood as the degree of re-contextualization and/or re-interpretation of international discourses, in order to see, along with the examination of the etymology of the Greek term for translation, what might remain 'hidden' in contemporary TS in Greece.

---

1  It needs to be clarified that 'TS in Greece' does not refer to any well-established concept, but only stands for the academic activity by mainly Greek-speaking translation scholars in Greece and Cyprus (of any nationality). Henceforth, *Greek-speaking scholars* and *Greek scholars* will be used interchangeably to denote Greek-speaking scholars residing in Greece or Cyprus.

Questions (a) and (b) will be examined in the first two parts of the paper, while question (c) will be discussed in the third part.

## 2 Current Situation in the Greek-Speaking World

As far as the Greek-speaking world is concerned, the need and an attempt to explain the phenomenon of translation and predict choices were first recorded in the 16th century. At that time, special emphasis was put on intralingual translation, i.e., on the translation of Ancient Greek texts into the modern idiom.[2] According to Kakridis (1948, vi), the history of translation theory in Greece begins in 1544 with Nikolaos Sofianos' preface to his translation of Pseudo Plutarch's *On the Education of Children*. Following Koutsivitis (1994, 112–113), the year 1784, when the Greek translation of Real de Curban's *La Science du Gouvernement* by Dimitrios Katartzis was completed, can be considered the year in which translation theory was born in modern Greece. In the prologue of that translation, Katartzis examines in a systematic way several questions dealing with the 'type' of Greek language that needs to be used in translated texts and the method of translation to be adopted. Among others, he proposes rules and changes to guide the transfer procedure and he also points out the linguistic and educational usefulness of translation (Koutsivitis 1994, 103–11; Connolly and Bacopoulou-Halls 1998, 423). Ever since, various other approaches to translation, based on individual understandings, have been proposed and extensive translation activity has taken place, albeit mainly in the domain of literary translation. Today, the Greek-speaking world could be considered a translation-dependent culture in the sense that a large number of foreign literature works has been translated into Greek (albeit a much smaller number of Greek works translated into foreign languages), and Greece and Cyprus are fully integrated into the globalized market of the translation of so-called pragmatic texts (also including the news production industry).

Despite the long translation tradition (for a detailed discussion see Connolly and Bacopoulou-Halls 1998) and the particularly significant role of translation for the Greek-speaking world, the development of translation studies as a discipline in its own right is still at an embryonic stage in Greece. A rather inflexible legal framework governing the operation of universities and, possibly, the common misconception that translation is a fairly easy project undeserving of

---

2 Intralingual translation from the ancient to the modern idiom is still practiced and debated in Greece, but mainly in an educational/philological framework, in which—rather unfortunately—translation studies scholars have not systematically been involved.

# APPROPRIATION OF CENTRAL DISCOURSES VERSUS LOCAL TRADITION

specialized studies[3] are among the most obvious reasons why only few Greek universities, compared to other European countries, offer translation studies in their curricula. The current academic landscape in Greece could be considered problematic, full of paradoxes and contradictions which up to a certain degree reflect the broader Greek *status quo* state-wise. At undergraduate level, the following public education institutions offer theoretical and practical courses in Translation:

a) The Department of Foreign Languages, Translation and Interpreting at the Ionian University on the island of Corfu (Kerkyra), which is the oldest institution to offer a translation and interpreting program in Greece. It was established in the mid-eighties, a few years after Greece joined the then European Community,

b) The Department of Applied Foreign Languages in Management and Commerce at the Epirus Technical University in Igoumenitsa (Northwestern Greece), where students are offered language and translation courses (meanwhile discontinued),

c) The Translation Section of the School of French Language and Literature at the Aristotle University of Thessaloniki,

d) The Translation and Cultural Studies Section of the School of English Language and Literature at the Aristotle University of Thessaloniki,

e) Various other foreign language departments at the Universities of Athens and Thessaloniki, which offer theoretical and practical courses in translation as part of their overall curriculum.

At postgraduate level, there are three public institutions offering MA and PhD programs in translation and interpreting:

a) The Department of Foreign Languages, Translation and Interpreting at the Ionian University on the island of Corfu,

b) The Department of French Language and Literature, the Department of English Language and Literature and the Department of Turkish and Asian Studies at the University of Athens, each offering an MA in Translation,

c) The Aristotle University of Thessaloniki, offering an interdepartmental MA in Translation (jointly by all foreign language and literature departments of the School of Philosophy).

---

3   Such common perception comes along with another common misconception in Greece: That knowing a foreign language should be sufficient in order to practice translation—a misconception which translation studies as a discipline is still arguing against. Needless to say that this phenomenon is not specifically Greek, but it is still ongoing and very persistent in the Greek-speaking world.

At the same time, it should be noted that some private training/educational institutions such as the Metafrasis School of Translation Studies and the Hellenic American College have started offering training courses/programs in translation and interpreting.

Nevertheless, there seems to be an imbalance between offer and demand. As opposed to the very small number of translation programs offered, the number of people wishing to study translation keeps increasing. In Cyprus, the development of translation studies and the offer of translation courses lag even more, despite the existence of meanwhile seven universities on the free territories of the island (three state universities and four private ones). At undergraduate level, only the newly established Translation Studies Section within the Department of English Studies at the University of Cyprus (state university) offers a relatively solid specialization in translation studies through theoretical and practical courses in translation across the four years of study. Unfortunately, it has still been impossible to offer an MA program in translation, mainly because of the budget cuts due to the 2013 financial crisis.[4]

To return to the Greek-speaking world as a whole, it is noteworthy that, despite the small number of undergraduate and postgraduate programs offered, there has been intense research activity especially during the last two decades. Particularly in recent years, an even more important increase in the research output by Greek scholars in the field of translation studies could be documented. To a great extent, this increase is due to the fact that translation studies has been introduced in higher education institutions as a distinct specialty, which has led to the creation of teaching and research positions in this particular field of study (for a detailed discussion, see also Kassapi 2009). The research carried out, the conferences organized, and the publications in journals and special issues demonstrate beyond doubt that there is a core of researchers who remain systematically active and, despite the rough times, strive against all odds to maintain and develop this particular field of research within Greek-speaking universities and institutions. Some indicative examples of the increasing interest in and importance of translation research in the Greek-speaking world include the founding of the Hellenic Society for Translation Studies[5] in 2011, the high number of papers submitted to the biannual Meeting of Greek Translation Scholars, organized by the Translation Section of the School of French Language and Literature at the Aristotle

---

4   The only exception has been a Masters in Conference Interpreting, which was offered with the support of the European Commission and the European Parliament between 2004 and 2007.

5   *Ελληνική Εταιρεία Μεταφρασεολογίας* (http://www.hs4ts.gr).

APPROPRIATION OF CENTRAL DISCOURSES VERSUS LOCAL TRADITION          187

University of Thessaloniki, as well as the number of doctoral theses carried out on various topics around translation by Greek researchers in Greece and abroad. For example, between May and December 2012, eight doctoral theses addressing various theoretical topics in translation were defended at the University of Thessaloniki alone.

Last but not least, another aspect that is worth mentioning is the relatively big number of important theoretical works on translation rendered into Greek over the last years. Some standard literature in translation studies, including works by Mounin (2002), Munday (2004), Ladmiral (2007), Cronin (2007), Gouadec (2008), Williams and Chesterman (2010), Nord (2014), Ammann (2014), Benjamin (2014), and Schleiermacher (2014),[6] has been translated into Greek in an attempt to make standard literature accessible to Greek students and scholars working in languages other than those of the originals, so as to disseminate thought produced in discourses other than those in which some Greek scholars and researchers were educated. It is true that most of the researchers in the field of translation are competent in more than one foreign language, but this is still not sufficient to cover all needs. Beyond this—rather—practical reason for translating such works into Greek, this fact provides proof of the concern shown by the Greek academic community to safeguard a scientific approach to translation and to promote research activity beyond the merely practical one. It also manifests a solid academic positioning of translation studies in the Greek-speaking world and the crystallization of translation studies as an academic discipline in its own right. At the same time, however, the translation of standard literature from other languages and academic discourses also provides proof of a tendency to immediately adopt (*quasi* appropriate), rather than re-contextualize[7] foreign academic thought through discussions in theoretical works such as introductions and textbooks originally written in Greek. Such attempts are not totally missing, but they are much fewer than the translated works.

To sum up, we feel it is regrettable that translation studies in the Greek-speaking world did not emerge as early as in other countries and that quite a number of practical problems still persist. However, a much more optimistic landscape has started to be formed and the time seems right to explore the

---

6   The dates in brackets refer to the Greek publications.

7   Of course, this does not entail that a translation cannot be seen as a re-contextualization and that only academic works originally written in Greek could provide a re-interpretation of foreign academic thought. The juxtaposition of "translation as adoption" and "original works as re-contextualization" only points to the grounded assumption that these translations mainly aim at importing new knowledge and filling gaps rather than participating in an ongoing debate which might very well contest or confirm local understandings and traditions.

epistemological profile of TS in Greece and to start taking stock of the directions into which TS in Greece are now developing. The next section of the paper will present research carried out in order to define the basic research trends in TS in Greece, in an attempt to record the current profile and draw some preliminary conclusions regarding the relationships between the local and the international landscapes.

## 3 Prevalent Research Trends in the Greek-Speaking World

In order to identify the research trends which are prevalent in the study of various aspects of the translation phenomenon and outline the epistemological characteristics of translation studies in Greece and Cyprus, a corpus-based approach was adopted. Since the only period which allows for systematic study of epistemological characteristics seems to be confined to roughly the last two decades (see Section 1 of the paper), we restricted our research to publications between 1990 and 2015. This restriction was opted due to the fact that it was only after 1990 that academic positions in translation studies started to be announced in Greek universities and a more systematic academic activity started to take place. At the same time, we did not opt for a further breaking down of this period, as 25 years were deemed a rather short span of time for any further periodization to be meaningful. A large corpus of publications was compiled as an almost exhaustive list (Corpus A). The compilation was based on a project undertaken at the Aristotle University of Thessaloniki under the supervision of Simos Grammenidis (2015,[8] see also Filippidou 2014). Subsequently, part of this Corpus A was isolated to form Corpus B, i.e., these two corpora were not separately compiled, but they are separately 'examined' for the aims of our study. The analysis of Corpus A focuses on areas of research, while the analysis of Corpus B focuses on researchers and 'trends' influencing TS in Greece. The second corpus (Corpus B) is particularly important for the aims of our study, as it focuses exclusively on publications in Greek. More reasons for the separate examination of the initial corpus are given below. The data are presented and analyzed in the following sections of this paper.

---

8  "Καταγραφή της μεταφρασεολογικής έρευνας στον ελληνόφωνο χώρο και δημιουργία online διαδικτυακής Βιβλιογραφικής Βάσης Πληροφοριών" [Archiving of the translation studies research in the Greek-speaking world and creation of an online bibliographic database]. http://niobe.frl.auth.gr/hstbibliography/.

## 3.1 Data Presentation

As mentioned above, a large set of data was collected to form *Corpus A* and *Corpus B* as part of Corpus A to be separately examined:

a) Corpus A presents a large bibliographical set of data consisting of 664 publications by Greek scholars mainly between 1990 and 2011. The set of data was categorized into two sub-groups: Sub-group A1, containing publications in Greek (total: 406) and sub-group A2, containing publications in English, French, German, Spanish, Italian, or other languages (total: 258, of which approximately 87% concerns publications in the English language). This corpus was compiled by bringing together different types of texts, including doctoral dissertations, papers in collective volumes, papers in translation journals and conference proceedings, textbooks and monographs. This corpus was then analyzed according to areas of research addressed, following the classic categorization of translation studies provided by Holmes (1998[1972]). Since the main aim is to record overall tendencies, only the categorizations into 'pure' and 'applied' translation studies, as well as into 'descriptive' and 'theoretical' were taken into consideration.

b) Corpus B presents a smaller set of data. Since research on the profile of TS in Greece is still ongoing and no exhaustive data have yet been collected as regards scholars quoted and approaches adopted in the first corpus (Corpus A), such analysis will be conducted only on the basis of a smaller part of Corpus A, consisting of 111 papers (Corpus B) made exclusively in Greek during the period from 2007 to 2015, i.e., the period where the first five Meetings of Greek Translation Scholars[9] took place. More specifically, this smaller corpus consists of 35 papers from the 1st Meeting (all published online), 29 papers from the 2nd Meeting (17 published online and 12 published in a special thematic volume), 11 papers from the

---

9 This 'meeting' is a biannual conference which aims to bring together Greek-speaking scholars and to promote and advance the study of translation in all its facets in the Greek-speaking world. It also aims to provide a platform for young researchers and doctoral students to present and disseminate their work to a larger public. Finally, this conference also aspires to bridge the gap between academic research and translation industry in Greece, by providing an opportunity for practical issues and issues concerning the translation and interpreting professions and markets to be articulated and discussed.

3rd Meeting (all published in a special issue of *Syn-thèses*[10]), 17 papers from the 4th Meeting, and 19 papers from the 5th Meeting. The most recent meeting took place in May 2017 (6th Meeting), but the papers presented at this one have not been collected yet; therefore, we have not included them in the analysis of the present study. A noteworthy particularity of this corpus concerning the analysis of approaches adopted is that verbatim quotes are rather rare in the publications contained in it, since all of these publications are written in Greek and, probably, it was deemed more suitable and practical to cite scholars through other techniques such as summary or paraphrasing.

An overview of the two corpora is presented in Table 1:

TABLE 1    Overview of data: Corpus A and Corpus B

| | | Totals and subtotals | Language | |
|---|---|---|---|---|
| **Corpus A** | | 664 publications | | |
| | *Sub-group A1* | 406 | Greek | |
| | *Sub-group A2* | 258 | 87% | 13% other |
| | | | English | languages |
| **Corpus B** | | 111 publications | | |
| | *1st Meeting (2007)* | 35 | Greek | |
| | *2nd Meeting (2009)* | 29 | Greek | |
| | *3rd Meeting (2011)* | 11 | Greek | |
| | *4th Meeting (2013)* | 17 | Greek | |
| | *5th Meeting (2015)* | 19 | Greek | |

---

10    The journal is published by the Translation Section of the School of French Language and Literature at the Aristotle University of Thessaloniki. It is one of the very few journals of translation (studies) in the Greek-speaking area, along with Μετάφραση (*Metafrasi*), *MTM* (Ionian University of Corfu), and *Helios* (Rhodes International Center for Writers and Translators). The scarcity of specialized journals in the field of TS in Greece is—along with the small number of institutions (see Section 1) offering translation education—again indicative of the rather premature stage of TS in Greece.

## 3.2 *Methodology and Results*

The classic framework by Holmes (1998[1972]) for the categorization of translation studies as a discipline was the first tool to be used to analyze both corpora. Holmes' map, which was later taken up by Toury (1995) as well, provides a very clear categorization of the then newly born discipline, the main advantage being the classification of 'pure' translation studies into 'descriptive' and 'theoretical'. This is particularly important for the purposes of this study, given the rather strong tendency towards descriptive translation studies that was preliminarily observed before embarking on this study. The analysis according to areas of research was deemed a suitable tool to provide a first overall profile and "academic identity" of TS in Greece by highlighting some research 'preferences' shown by Greek-speaking scholars.

The analysis of the two sub-groups of Corpus A yielded the following results:

TABLE 2    Sub-group A1 (Corpus A) results

| Corpus A—Sub-group A1 Publications in Greek | | % |
| --- | --- | --- |
| *Pure / Descriptive* | 216 | 53,20 |
| *Pure / Theoretical* | 112 | 27,59 |
| *Applied* | 75 | 18,47 |
| *Various* | 3 | 0,74 |
| **Total** | 406 | (100%) |

TABLE 3    Sub-group A2 (Corpus A) results

| Corpus A—Sub-group A2 Publications in other languages | | % |
| --- | --- | --- |
| *Pure / Descriptive* | 133 | 51,55 |
| *Pure / Theoretical* | 77 | 29,84 |
| *Applied* | 35 | 13,57 |
| *Various* | 13 | 5,04 |
| **Total** | 258 | (100%) |

In each of the above tables, 'various' refers to different categories: In Table 2, 'various' includes publications which do not allow for a particular categorization into pure/applied or descriptive/theoretical, e.g., introductory notes, reviews etc. In Table 3, 'various' mainly includes publications in languages other than Western European, to which we have limited or no access at all. The two sub-groups were then taken together. The following table presents the overall results for Corpus A according to category:

TABLE 4    Corpus A overall results

| Corpus A—Overall | | % |
| --- | --- | --- |
| Pure / Descriptive | 349 | 52,56 |
| Pure / Theoretical | 189 | 28,46 |
| Applied | 110 | 16,57 |
| Various | 16 | 2,41 |
| Total | 664 | (100%) |

The second corpus (Corpus B) was analyzed on the basis of two different tools: Holmes' map was used again to classify the data into areas of research, so as to be able to compare Corpus B to the larger Corpus A in order to see if and how the overall tendencies identified for the whole period 1990–2015 are changing in the last nine years of that period (2007–2015). Corpus B was also analyzed according to the scientometric method presented by Gile (2000; 2006). This method consists of recording translation scholars quoted. In this way, according to Gile (2006, 26), it "[...] permet [...] de voir qui est cité par qui, quand et combien de fois, et ainsi mesurer l'importance de certains travaux et certains auteurs durant des périodes données" [enable[s] us to see who is cited by whom, when and how many times, and thus to measure the importance of certain works and authors in specific/different period(s)].[11] Therefore, it was decided to proceed with such analysis in order to gain an overview of the influence exerted by international research trends and theoretical models on the local academic production.[12]

---

11    Translated by G.F. and S.G.
12    See also Ekelund (2012) for a similar method applied for the investigation of literary scholarship on the basis of citations.

APPROPRIATION OF CENTRAL DISCOURSES VERSUS LOCAL TRADITION 193

The analysis of Corpus B according to Holmes' map yielded the following results:

TABLE 5    Corpus B overall results—classification based on Holmes (1998[1972])

**Corpus B**
**Publications between 2007–2015**

| | Meetings | | | | | Total | % |
|---|---|---|---|---|---|---|---|
| | 1st | 2nd | 3rd | 4th | 5th | | |
| *Pure/Descriptive* | 22 | 15 | 2 | 9 | 9 | 57 | 51,35 |
| *Pure / Theoretical* | 4 | 7 | 3 | 4 | 4 | 22 | 19,82 |
| *Applied* | 9 | 7 | 6 | 4 | 6 | 32 | 28,83 |
| Total | 35 | 29 | 11 | 17 | 19 | 111 | 100% |

The analysis of the same corpus according to authors cited revealed that 50 authors are cited more than once. The analysis then focused on those authors (out of the 50) who represent significant percentages, i.e., on those who are cited in more than 5% of the total of 111 articles. The following table presents authors with significant percentages:

TABLE 6    Corpus B overall results—authors cited

| Authors | Cited in | % |
|---|---|---|
| *M. Baker* | 13 articles | 11,71 |
| *C. Nord* | 13 articles | 11,71 |
| *G. Toury* | 13 articles | 11,71 |
| *S. Bassnett* | 11 articles | 9,91 |
| *A. Lefevere* | 11 articles | 9,91 |
| *P. Newmark* | 11 articles | 9,91 |
| *A. Pym* | 10 articles | 9,01 |
| *L. Venuti* | 10 articles | 9,01 |
| *C. Schäffner* | 9 articles | 8,12 |
| *M. Cronin* | 8 articles | 7,21 |
| *T. Hermans* | 7 articles | 6,31 |
| *E. Nida* | 7 articles | 6,31 |

### 3.3    *Analysis of Findings*

As regards Corpus A and based on the analysis according to the areas of research provided in Holmes' map, some important findings can be noted. Most publications by Greek-speaking scholars—both in Greek and in other languages—focus on issues pertaining to descriptive translation studies (52,56% in Corpus A and 51,35% in Corpus B). Research in the Greek-speaking world is thus mainly descriptively oriented. In other words, the majority of publications examines and analyzes translations in a specific language pair and direction (mainly English-Greek, French-Greek and German-Greek, but rarely in the opposite direction). In so doing, they attempt to define the function of these translations within the Greek-speaking sociocultural context. A less frequent endeavor is the attempt to define specific sub-processes carried out by translators during the overall translation process.

Another finding is that the next most significant area of research toward which Greek-speaking scholars are oriented is theoretical translation studies, but with a strongly decreasing tendency (28,46% in Corpus A, but 19,82% in Corpus B). Publications in this area attempt to describe or interpret a theoretical phenomenon, a set of notions, or basic parameters of the translation phenomenon, for example the medium, the register or the genre. Some other publications in the same sub-field attempt to study specific problems encountered in translation practice. Finally, publications which are oriented towards applied translation studies are also recorded, with a strongly increasing tendency (16,57% in Corpus A, but 28,83% in Corpus B). These focus mainly on the training and education of translators, on translation tools and on human-aided machine translation or machine-aided human translation.

It is worth noting that no significant differences in the orientation of research exist between publications in Greek and publications in other languages. The two sub-groups A1 and A2, i.e., the publications in Greek and the publications in other languages (mainly English), yielded very similar results regarding each category in Holmes' map. Another interesting finding is that more often than not, there are publications on the same or almost the same topic both in Greek and English (by the same author). This is probably an indication of the fact that Greek translation scholars usually seek to achieve a dual aim: on the one hand to advance the study of translation in the Greek-speaking world, on the other hand to address an international audience in order to achieve international recognition. The strong shifts noted between Corpus A and Corpus B, as regards 'theoretical' and 'applied' areas of research, reveal a very interesting 'sociological' shift in TS in Greece. The differences noted could be due to the fact that Corpus B publications come mainly from younger scholars who are active in research centers in Greece and abroad and are still in early stages of their careers. Applied translation studies are probably more appealing to them as younger scholars, since younger generations are much more conversant with technological advances and certainly more computer-literate than older generations of scholars. Such an investigation of demographic and/or other differentiations through data triangulation (e.g. interviews) would certainly be interesting and would offer a more solid explanation of findings. However, this goes well beyond the scope of this work, which, for the moment, focuses on outlining a general, overall profiling of TS in Greece (see Section 4).

Another interesting finding from a closer examination of the various publications is that descriptive works focus mainly on issues pertaining to (a) literary translation (novel, drama, poetry) and often use an empirical approach, and (b) style, with data coming again from literary texts. Very few descriptive publications are concerned with issues pertaining to terminology or interpreting. The strong presence of literary texts—be it as the object of study or as source of data—might be due to the facts that literary texts are more easily accessible than other text types and that translation research is conducted mainly in the context of university departments of foreign languages and literatures.

As regards the investigation of authors cited in Corpus B, one may note that the authors most cited publish almost exclusively in English. However, this does not entail that all of these authors represent the same tradition or school of thought. One may also note that the citations are rather similarly diffused, as the percentages do not reveal great differences, especially in eight out of twelve positions.

## 4    Discussion

The findings presented in the previous section allow us to attempt a 'profiling' of TS in Greece in relation to the international academic context. In other words, we will attempt to outline the kind of epistemological traffic the Greek academic production maintains with international trends. To this end, we will return to the initial research questions stipulated in the introduction of this article:

a)   What are the main research questions that concern Greek translation scholars and to what extent do these questions reflect contemporary concerns at international level? In other words, is translation research in the Greek-speaking world moving along the lines of international trends or is there any significant differentiation?

b) What are the (international) theoretical trends which have informed local contributions? Moreover, is translation research in the Greek-speaking world attempting any adjustments in order to adapt international trends to 'Greek' particularities?

c) Are we in a position to talk about the crystallization of a Greek research canon?

The first issue that needs to be noted here is that the increase in academic activity also signals a turn in the research interests of Greek translation scholars and in the way these interests are approached. Up until the '80s, thought on translation focused to a large extent on intralingual translation (translation from Ancient Greek or from *katharevousa*[13] into Standard Modern Greek, the so-called *demotic* language variety) mainly in order to stress the continuity of the Greek language (see Connolly and Bacopoulou-Halls 1998, 420). Beyond the particularities of intralingual translation, other important issues have also dominated translation thought over that period: the question of (un)translatability and the dichotomies concerning form vs. content and free vs. literal translation (see Koutsivitis 1994, 185). Our research confirms that Greek translation scholars have largely abandoned intralingual translation as well as more 'ontological' pursuits, which very often bring about false (and falsely urgent) dilemmas, such as that about translatability, for the sake of the *per se* study of various dimensions of the translation phenomenon. More specifically, Greek translation scholars are mainly concerned with problems arising from the translation of specific language phenomena (e.g., metaphors, proper names, proverbs, language varieties), specific text types and genres (e.g., literary texts, economic texts, news articles), or specific cultural elements. They also study translation as a vehicle of social and cultural change. Different types of transfer such as mediation, localization, audiovisual translation and multimedia translation also form the object of study in many works, while there is also some orientation towards the study of new technologies, translation tools, machine translation, and natural language processing, as well as towards issues pertaining to the translation profession itself, the training of translators, and the continuous education of translators.

Perhaps one of the most interesting aspects arising from the internationalization of local Greek academic production is the impact such opening-up seems to have on the way the very notion of translation is conceived in

---

13    This is an archaic form of the Modern Greek language, strongly resembling ancient Greek and thus considered to be 'pure', used as the official language variety in Greece and Cyprus until well into the '70s.

APPROPRIATION OF CENTRAL DISCOURSES VERSUS LOCAL TRADITION     197

the Greek-speaking world.[14] In earlier studies revolving either around intra-lingual translation or around the essence and ethics of translation practice, translation was understood as *re-interpretation* (see Kakridis 1948), while in the last twenty years, a rather western-theoretical concept of translation as transference is adopted. According to Maronitis (2008), the word μετάφρασις [metáphrasis, *translation*] in Dionysius of Halicarnassus (and later in Plutarch) refers to *interpretive transliteration*[15] and derives from the verb φράζω/φράζομαι [phrázo/phrázomai], which was recorded in Homer's work and is polyse-mic (meaning *to show the way, to explain, to consult, to propose, to reflect on, to perceive, to imagine, to observe*), preceded by the prefix μετά [meta], which denotes coupling in space and time. Thus Maronitis (ibid.) maintains that this term suggests that translation is indexical of and at the same time explains an original after reflective observation. Seen in this light, the text is not simply perceived as a numerical sum of words, but as an organic entity. Consequently, translation practice is seen as an act of re-enunciation. As a result, the deri-vation of the term μετάφραση [*translation*], the metaphors it allows emerging, and the semiotic connotations it creates can easily be paralleled to the etymol-ogy and meaning of, as well as the metaphors around, terms in non-Western languages and cultures such as Chinese and Hindi (see, for example, Tymoczko 2007; Chesterman 2006). These etymologies, metaphors and connotations refer to transformation and revival. In other words, they reveal that translation is considered to be rebirth and reconstruction into a different form, processes which imply *change* and *revitalization*. In any case, the discussion around pos-sible parallels to other discourses needs to be confined to the level of meta-phor. The idea of how narrow or wide the concept of translation is around the world has already been strongly contested, for example by Chang (2015) on the impact of western theories on China, where he stresses that the assumed narrowness of Western discourses as opposed to the assumed openness of the Chinese concept for translation is a misinterpretation.

It is not by coincidence that in the period immediately after the estab-lishment of the Modern Greek state (1830) translation, either from Ancient Greek or from foreign languages into Modern Greek, was considered to be one of the most important sources of education and renewal of the nation, as a means to form its identity and as an instrument par excellence for linguistic

---

14    This is particularly important if seen in the context of flourishing studies around the concept of translation in different cultural traditions, which prompt us to realize signifi-cant differentiations and possibilities for cross-fertilization, as, for example, in Tymoczko (2006) and Cheung (2006).

15    Our translation of the Greek ερμηνευτική μεταγλώττιση—G.F., S.G.

consciousness and the affirmation of the demotic variety. Translators were thought of as interpreting agents, creators and mediators between two worlds (see Kakridis 1948). Therefore, the Greek term for translation differentiated itself from other terms such as translation or traduction, which insist on the notions of transfer and passage and lead to such concepts as 'similarity', 'replacement' or 'equivalence'. In the last two decades, this is the understanding adopted by Greek translation research as well.

In a nutshell, there are strong indications that Greek translation research closely follows (Western) international trends, not only through the topics discussed, but also through gradually but overtly reconsidering traditional ways of understanding translation. In other words, the relatively recent systematic formation of TS in Greece leaves behind the traditional understandings of translation in favor of newly imported ones. This is not exactly re-contextualization or re-interpretation. As a matter of fact, this development points to a 'hiding' of the local tradition and, therefore, to a somewhat weird understanding of 'situatedness', since the 'imported' thought is not really negotiated against the local, but rather replaces it. This 'hiding' is very reminiscent of what happened to local traditions of ex-Soviet countries, e.g., Latvia, which were largely replaced by Western discourses after the fall of the communist regime (see particularly Sīlis 2009), and it offers an indication that the reasons for abandoning local traditions should also be sought beyond the local political developments and situation.

As far as the topics are concerned, the approaches adopted are varied and mainstream. Following Susam-Saraeva (2002, 194) regarding the problems inherent in a dichotomy between western and non-western approaches, a redefinition of research interests is recorded in the Greek-speaking world. Research interests seem to be moving away from traditionally followed, 'peripheral' domestic approaches towards more mainstream approaches imposed by the dominant center (Western conceptualizations), whatever this center may be formed of. In the last twenty years, references to early works of TS in Greece are extremely rare, while, at the same time, a wide variety of international traditions and approaches is referenced to. Such diversity is another interesting development. Contrary to what Gile (2006) observes regarding the citations by German scholars, there is a wider spectrum of bibliography used by Greek scholars, who do not favor one research tradition only, say the Anglophone one. Greek translation research tends to form a hub where different traditions and trends are combined. This is not very surprising, given the fact that the own tradition seems to be gradually abandoned, while Greek translation scholars, most of whom have been trained abroad, carry with them quite different educational backgrounds which meet on Greek academic grounds and, therefore,

APPROPRIATION OF CENTRAL DISCOURSES VERSUS LOCAL TRADITION    199

inevitably interact. Perhaps this is a good example of the advantages of being peripheral in terms of (a) lack of a longer tradition in translation studies; (b) language mostly used for academic activities, and, of course, (c) number of scholars and activities. Such peripherality may allow for more diversity and for avoiding encapsulation into the own tradition and production.

The question that arises in view of the above is whether we are in a position to talk about the crystallization of a Greek research canon. To attempt an answer to this question, we first need to briefly look into the notions of canon and tradition in translation studies. A 'canon' is a multi-dimensional term (see Kruger 2012 for the biblical canon) referring to a body of texts that are considered as most important and influential in shaping thought or research in a field of study. The general understanding of canon refers to a body of rules, principles or standards which are fundamental in a field of art/study. But apart from the concepts of standard and regulation, the canon is also interwoven with the concept of authority, since the question of who decides what is to be included in the final, closed list (see the 'exclusive' definition of canon in Kruger 2012, 3) inevitably arises when discussing the canon of any field. The notion of canon differs from the notion of tradition, since tradition "is based on organic connectivity and continuity, while the canon presupposes an eclectic reordering and hierarchization"[16] (Tziovas 1998, n.p.). Tradition seems to focus on natural continuity and is not ideologically loaded, while a canon is constructed and, therefore, amenable to reconsideration.[17] An important question arises with regard to the specific context of translation studies: how is the research canon formed in translation studies? Is it formed through lingual, national, or theoretical/methodological territories? A similar question arises when attempting to define center and periphery: How is a dominant academic center formed? The issue at stake here is whether academic dominance is a matter of geopolitical (economic, national), lingual (language of publication), or epistemological criteria (theoretical models followed), especially since the language of publication does not necessarily imply a specific approach. Susam-Saraeva (2002, 194) notes that "[t]he center and the periphery of translation studies do not exactly correspond to those of the world's geopolitical situation today. As a consequence of the subject matter of the discipline, they are rather language-bound".

---

16    The original in Greek: "[...] βασίζεται στην οργανική συνεκτικότητα και την αδιάσπαστη συνέχεια, ενώ ο κανόνας προϋποθέτει την επιλεκτική ανασύνταξη και ιεράρχηση"—Translated by G.F. and S.G.

17    According to Searle (1990, n.p.): "[...] there never was, in fact, a fixed 'canon'; there was rather a certain set of tentative judgments about what had importance and quality. Such judgments are always subject to revision, and in fact they were constantly being revised".

The Corpus B data analyzed above on the basis of citations do not allow us to consider language or nation as satisfactory criteria for the formation of a Greek research canon. On the contrary, theoretical/methodological (conceptual) criteria could prove more suitable for this purpose. The fact that most citations come from works written in English—and given the Anglocentrism in the academic publishing industry—does not allow concluding that a certain tradition plays a dominant role in TS in Greece, since the traditions represented by the scholars cited, albeit in English, represent different theoretical approaches to translation. The use of English is indicative of the power relations on the geopolitical level, not the academic one. It is also indexical of a patronage play by non-academic groups (e.g., the publishing industry), which strive to impose a single language of academic communication for purely cost-effective reasons and thus favor the use of English. Therefore, a canon in terms of an influential body of texts or an influential body of principles that guide Greek academic production in translation has not yet emerged. TS in Greece maintain a peripheral character and are more regarded as a site of bringing together different approaches rather than as having reached a certain research canon. To answer question (c) in the introduction, international discourses have been adopted rather overwhelmingly (against the local tradition) and concurrently.

## 5    Conclusions

Some of the preliminary conclusions of this paper may be summarized in (a) the identification of strongly descriptive-oriented research trend; (b) the concurrent adoption of different international 'centers' within TS in Greece and, at the same time, (c) the abandoning of the local—to a large extent pre-theoretical and rather hidden—conceptualizations of translation, which, in the light of current rediscoveries and historiographical discussions of translation, open up a discussion very similar to the already ongoing one about eastern approaches to translation. In a nutshell, the most prominent conclusion of this paper is that—contrary to what could be expected—what was reinterpreted in the Greek-speaking world was not so much the concepts and methodologies which were 'imported' from international trends and 'centers', but the very own tradition in terms of both research focus and conceptualization of the translation phenomenon itself.

The analysis of Greek academic production of the last two decades revealed that important turns are recorded both in the choice of topics to be investigated and in the models and trends chosen to discuss them. The ethnocentric focus on intralingual translation is abandoned in favor of contemporary international

# APPROPRIATION OF CENTRAL DISCOURSES VERSUS LOCAL TRADITION 201

topics and trends, which are approached by a diverse apparatus of mainstream theoretical models. This turn has also marked a significant change in the way the very notion of translation is understood in the Greek-speaking world. TS in Greece remain a mainly descriptively oriented discipline still in the making and we might suspect that this is probably the case in most 'peripheries' that share common traits with the Greek-speaking world in terms of size and development. The main disadvantage is that potentially refreshing stances towards translation, such as those prevalent in earlier—and to a certain extent pretheoretical—approaches and at earlier stages of TS in Greece, have become weaker. But the undeniable advantage is that TS in Greece gain from crossfertilization due to the felicitous meeting of various different approaches and trends on the same territory.

### References

Ammann, Margret. 2014. *Βασικές αρχές της μεταφρασεολογίας: Ένα εγχειρίδιο για επίδοξους μεταφραστές και διερμηνείς* [*Grundlagen der Modernen Translationstheorie*]. Translated by Anthi Wiedenmayer and Despoina Lambrou. Athens: Diavlos.

Benjamin, Walter. 2014. *Η αποστολή του μεταφραστή: Και άλλα κείμενα για τη γλώσσα* [*Die Aufgabe des Übersetzers*], translated and edited by Giorgos Sagriotis. Athens: Diavlos.

Chang, Nam Fung. 2015. "Does 'translation' reflect a narrower concept than 'fanyi'? On the impact of Western theories on China and the concern about Eurocentrism." *Translation and Interpreting Studies* 10 (2): 223–242.

Chesterman, Andrew. 2006. "Interpreting the meaning of translation." In *A man of measure. Festschrift in honour of Fred Karlsson on his 60th birthday, A special supplement to SKY Journal of Linguistics*, edited by Michael Suominen et al., 3–11. Helsinki: The Linguistic Association of Finland.

Cheung, Martha, ed. 2006. *An Anthology of Chinese discourse on translation. Volume 1: From earliest times to the Buddhist project*. Manchester: St. Jerome.

Connolly, David, and Aliki Bacopoulou-Halls. 1998. "Greek tradition." In *Routledge encyclopedia of translation studies*, edited by Mona Baker, 428–438. London: Routledge.

Cronin, Michael. *Μετάφραση και παγκοσμιοποίηση* [*Translation and Globalization*]. Translated by Panagiotis Kelandrias. Athens: Diavlos, 2007.

Ekelund, Bo G. 2012. "The citational universe of Swedish literary scholarship" In *Rethinking cultural transfer and transmission: Reflections and new perspectives*, edited by Petra Broomans, Sandra van Voorst, and Karina Smits, 15–32. Groeningen: Barkhuis.

Filippidou, Aikaterini. 2014. "Εξερευνώντας το ελληνόφωνο μεταφρασεολογικό τοπίο με οδηγό τον χάρτη του Holmes: Μια βιβλιογραφική βάση δεδομένων." [Researching the Greek-speaking translation studies landscape on the basis of Holmes' map: A bibliographic database]. Unpublished MA thesis, Aristotle University of Thessaloniki.

Gile, Daniel. 2000. "The history of research into conference interpreting. A scientometric approach." *Target* 12 (2): 299–323.

Gile, Daniel. 2006. "L'interdisciplinarité en traductologie: une optique scientométrique." In *Interdisciplinarité en traduction. Actes du ne Colloque International sur la Traduction organisé par l'Université Technique de Yildiz*, edited by Öztürk Kasar, 23–37. Istanbul: Isis.

Gouadec, Daniel. 2008. *Επάγγελμα μεταφραστής [Profession: traducteur]*. Translated by Eleni Kalogianni. Athens: Texto.

Holmes, James R. 1998[1972]. "The Name and Nature of Translation Studies." In *Translated!*, edited by Raymond van den Broeck, 67–80. Amsterdam: Rodopi.

Kakridis, Ioannis. 1948. *Το μεταφραστικό πρόβλημα [The Translation Problem]*. Athens: Ikaros.

Kassapi, Eleni. 2009. "Η μεταφρασεολογία ως αυτόνομη επιστήμη και τα γνωστικά αντικείμενα στα Φ.Ε.Κ. διορισμού μελών Δ.Ε.Π. στα ελληνικά Α.Ε.Ι." [Translation studies as an autonomous discipline and the specialties of members of faculty at Greek universities]. In *Proceedings of the 7th conference of ELETO, Athens 22–24October2009*. http://www.eleto.gr/download/Conferences/7th%20Conference/7th_35-19-KassapiEleni_Paper2_V03.pdf

Koutsivitis, Vassilis. 1994. *Θεωρία της Μετάφρασης [Theory of Translation]*. Athens: Hellenic University Publications.

Kruger, Michael. 2012. "The definition of the term 'canon': Exclusive or multidimensional?" *Tyndale Bulletin* 63: 1–20.

Ladmiral, Jean-René. 2007. *Θεωρήματα για τη μετάφραση [Traduire: Théorèmes pour la traduction]*. Translated by Katerina Kollet and Marie-Christine Anastassiadi. Athens: Metaichmio.

Maronitis, Dimitris. 2008. "Intralingual translation: Genuine and false Dilemmas." In *Translation and the classic*, edited by Alexandra Lianeri and Vanda Zajko, 367–86. Oxford: OUP.

Mounin, Georges. 2002. *Τα θεωρητικά προβλήματα της μετάφρασης [Les problèmes théoriques de la traduction]*. Translated by Ioanna Papaspyridou. Athens: Travlos.

Munday, Jeremy. 2004. *Μεταφραστικές σπουδές: Θεωρίες και εφαρμογές [Introducing Translation Studies: Theories and Applications]*. Translated by Aggelos Philipatos. Athens: Metaichmio.

Nord, Christiane. 2014. *Η μετάφραση ως στοχευμένη δραστηριότητα: Εισαγωγή στις λειτουργικές προσεγγίσεις [Translation as a Purposeful Activity: An Introduction to*

APPROPRIATION OF CENTRAL DISCOURSES VERSUS LOCAL TRADITION 203

*Functional Approaches*]. Translated by Simos Grammenidis and Despoina Lambrou. Athens: Diavlos.

Schleiermacher, Friedrich. 2014. *Περί των διαφόρων μεθόδων του μεταφράζειν* [*Über die verschiedenen Methoden des Übersetzens*]. Translated by Konstantinos Kotsiaros. Athens: Gutenberg.

Searle, John. 1990. "The storm over the university." *The New York Review of Books* 37, no. 19 (December 6, 1990).

Sīlis, Jānis. 2009. *Tulkojumzinātnes jautājumi: teorija un prakse* [*Issues of Translation Studies: Theory and Practice*]. Ventspils: Ventspils Augstskola.

Susam-Saraeva, Şebnem. 2002. "A 'multilingual' and 'international' translation studies?" In *Crosscultural transgressions. Research models in translation studies II. Historical and ideological issues*, edited by Theo Hermans, 193–205. Manchester: St. Jerome.

Toury, Gideon. 1995. *Descriptive translation studies—and beyond*. Amsterdam and Philadelphia: Benjamins.

Tymoczko, Maria. 2006. "Reconceptualizing translation theory: Integrating non-Western thought about translation." In *Translating others: Volume 1*, edited by Theo Hermans, 13–32. Manchester: St. Jerome.

Tymoczko, Maria. 2007. *Enlarging translation, empowering translators*. Manchester: St. Jerome.

Tziovas, Dimitris. 1998. "Παράδοση ή κανόνας" [Tradition or Canon]. *Vima*, July 12.

Williams, Jenny, and Andrew Chesterman. 2010. *Ο χάρτης. Η έρευνα στις μεταφραστικές σπουδές: Οδηγός για νέους ερευνητές* [*The Map: A Beginner's Guide to Doing Research in Translation Studies*]. Translated by Andromachi Vassalaki, Irini Diamantara, Dimitris Kassis, Efrosyni Manta-Kolovou, and Aikaterini Feka. Athens: Ypsilon.

CHAPTER 10

# Total Translation: From Catford to Torop

*Anne Lange*

### Abstract

The article focuses on Peeter Torop's concept of total translation as it stems out of the Tartu-Moscow semiotic school of thought and comes within an interdisciplinary dialogue with other branches of the humanities studying culture. Torop has developed a cultural and semiotic interpretation of one of Catford's types of translations and conceptualizes translation in terms of communication and auto-communication. Acknowledging translation as a metaphor for the universal mechanism of producing meaning, Torop finds the concept is of relevance beyond translation studies. The article, however, attempts to position his theory within TS, comparing it to post-colonial approaches to translation that were significant at the time when Torop finalized his monograph in 1995, and to Tymoczko's cultural translation, which is similar in its content. As my teaching experience with students of translation has convinced me that the natural language with its cultural connotations is also of explanatory value for the rationale of a theory, the academic and institutional contexts of Torop's theory are complemented by an etymological analysis of the Estonian word for translation that supports Torop's conceptualization of translation.

To define the object of translation studies (TS) with any precision, it is first necessary to answer the question of what translation is. As the myriad pages written on the concept within and beyond translation studies aptly demonstrate, translation can be seen as a problem rather than a technical solution for resolving linguistic differences. This is perhaps inevitable given the wide variation in the practice of translation, as a translation is an utterance by and for someone, dependent on the various circumstances of translation. As the everdifferent practice of translation is the only rationale for studying it, the concept of translation is borne by the cultural experience of its practitioners, which is always embedded in social history with its temporal and regional specifics. The multiple conceptualizations of translation and its multiple theories are partly a result of meaningful communication within and for a cultural community with its idiosyncratic conceptual traditions. Put like this, any global and disciplinary unification of translation studies looks like a thin hope. Unification of

© KONINKLIJKE BRILL NV, LEIDEN, 2021 | DOI:10.1163/9789004437807_011

metalanguage in translation research would even be questionable: a common conceptual framework in all the branches of TS would rather harm than advance our knowledge. It is only the diversity and variety of aspects of translation that can foster a multidimensional and reflexive approach to it. But a homogeneity of the discipline can still be achieved, once we translate mutually the various traditions of translation research pursued in various natural milieus.

Translation studies as an academic institution is by and large an English language discourse. In introducing it to students who have a mother tongue other than English—in my case this language is mostly Estonian except for the Erasmus students—I have observed that the course of translation theory can be made more meaningful by discussing not only the disciplinary contexts of translation studies but also the cognitive presumptions that my students have and that stem from their mother tongue; by the time anyone comes to translation research, they have had some experience of translation both in practice and in reflecting on it. Theories and concepts have to come to terms with the presuppositions of the translator that have been shaped by the cultural media of their native language.

Reading translation studies in Estonia equally cannot be done without awareness that there is not much dialogue between Estonian-language and English-language TS discourse. Although this may be observed, it need not be complained about as long as the international discourse can be complemented by the regional one in that place, showing where traditions overlap or are separate. The reading list for a course of translation theory and practice in Estonia can differ from those suggested by the English language readers of translation studies and include authors and texts that are not in those lists. The local need not be parochial, but neither need the canon of international translation studies be parochial with its limited set of texts available in English.

Including authors who have been shaped by various systemic developments outside the mainstream discourse of modern TS highlights the problem of translation as a significantly social and political issue. Pointing out the overlapping aspects of theorization in different parts of the world may make newcomers to the canon seem redundant because they may not contribute major new insights into translation, and their suggestions may be only the historical products of different linguistic and institutional circumstances. Noting the divergence, however, may show a less known conceptualization to be a national maverick that stands apart from international developments. The labels of "a newcomer" or "a canon" can be problematic, as their use tends to affect dialogues between different traditions. These traditions have to be mutually translated to each other so that their uniqueness and their intellectual value may be appreciated.

## 1    Translation Studies in Estonia

Translation first became a field of academic research in Estonia in the 1930s (Palm 1932; Annist and Saar 1936), and then, after a break and more extensively, in the 1960s when Estonia had become a part of the Soviet Union. The thematization of translation at this time was largely related to the work done in the Department of Slavic Philology of the University of Tartu, where attempts were made to develop conceptual tools that would subject translation to verified analysis. The research was pursued in the two frameworks of semiotics and the reception of Russian literature in Estonia, two possible approaches to translation that complement each other by bringing empirical evidence together with theorization. In the background of these academic developments was Estonian translation culture with its history.

Translations have dominated Estonian book production over the centuries (Antik 1936; Samma 1962), and so a lot had been written in Estonia by that time about the significance of translation in shaping the receiving culture (Annist 1939; Vinkel 1958, 1965; Nirk 1966). Originals and translations have been reviewed on equal terms in literary periodicals that have commissioned annual reviews of translations into Estonian (see the most influential ones by Ott Ojamaa (1926–1996) as reprinted in Ojamaa 2010, and an analysis of reviews by Enn Soosaar (1937–2010, the major critic of the next generation, in Lange 2012) because it was realized that the role of translations in the dynamics of culture is of equal significance to that of originals. In the Estonian language discourse on translation there has always been cultural criticism in parallel to the quantitative observation of the abundant presence of translations (Oras 1931; Soosaar 1980), which is also to be expected given the perspective of a small nation endangered not only by political and economic challenges but also by cultural colonization. Translation has been seen as a means of modernizing Estonian culture, while at the same time it has not been able to undermine the importance of native authors and discourses. The aspiration to change without cultural identity being lost has resulted in a cultural policy that favors a diversity in cultural contacts (Karjahärm and Sirk 2001, 346–352; Lange 2017) that can prevent subordination to a single hegemonic influence.

The scholar who spelt out clearly that translation studies was an emancipated academic discipline and was necessary for Estonia was Peeter Torop, who was a student of the Department of Slavic Philology at the University of Tartu in 1969–1974. It seems obvious that his ideas were influenced by the Tartu-Moscow semiotic school of thought and by Juri Lotman, his academic mentor, as Torop conceptualizes translation in terms of communication and

TOTAL TRANSLATION: FROM CATFORD TO TOROP

auto-communication and acknowledges this as the universal mechanism for producing meaning. The conceptual tradition within translation studies that Torop himself delineates (2011, 96–111) goes back to Roman Jakobson, who had participated in a summer school of semioticians in Tartu in 1966. Combining semiotics with translation, Torop is primarily known today as "one of the few persistent explicit spokespeople for translation semiotics" (Sütiste 2012, 271). The present article analyzes Torop's conceptualization of translation within the discourse of translation studies. The focus will be on his umbrella concept of total translation, which brings together translation and culture as interdependent and complementary, as translation is always a cultural phenomenon, and culture is always translational.

Although translation studies in Estonia cannot be limited to the work done by Torop, other scholars and their contribution to research into translation will be omitted from what follows for lack of space. A justification of the choice is that the duration of Torop's impact on translation studies in Estonia spans more than thirty years.

## 2    Translation and Culture

The first co-occurrence of the words 'culture' and 'translation' in Torop's work dates back to 1979 (Sütiste 2012, 270). A more thorough discussion of the relationship between them comes from 1984, when Torop wrote a critical review of the translations of Soviet literature into Estonian that had been published a year before. The article combines the academic traditions available to him and the traditional Estonian language discourse on translation. In a way the review continues that discourse, with its emphasis on the target circumstances as the primary context for translation. In 1969 Ott Ojamaa, an Estonian translator of French and Spanish literature, had written:

> ...[tõlke] väärtus tekib alles pärast tema ilmumist sõltuvalt meie kirjanduse juba varem väljakujunenud struktuurist või süsteemist (midagi niisugust on kirjanduses kindlasti olemas, ja ilmselt mitte üks, vaid palju). See väärtus ja koht, mis teosel on algkeeles, on peaaegu tähtsusetu. Tõlkimine paneb ta nagunii hoopis teise kohta.

> [... [a translation] acquires its value only after it has been published, and it depends on the already existent literary structure or system (any literature is a system, or more probably a set of systems). The value and the

208 LANGE

place a work has in the original language are of almost no significance. Translation situates the work in an entirely different location.][1]

OJAMAA 2010[1969], 76

Not only is the review situated in the local circumstances of official Soviet culture counterbalanced by the individual cultural interests of people living in Estonia, it also has a theoretical part that is much larger than the descriptive part. Torop writes on the various aspects of a translation culture, using a taxonomy of the features that characterize it: (1) its orientation through the languages and cultures that are preferred; (2) its statistical-sociological profile from numeric data on print runs, the share of translations in book production, and the prestige of translation; (3) the availability of paratexts; and (4) the translators and whether they are professional and specialize in specific text types or authors or not.

The review opens by pointing out that a literary culture, and translation culture as part of it, is a communicative system that regulates the perception and reception of reading, which is a conventional practice, and as such it rests on the cultural experience of the reader: *Niisiis algab tõlke lugemine mitte teksti jõudmisega lugeja kätte, vaid palju varem.* [So, our reading of a translation starts long before we actually get hold of it.] (Torop 1999, 67[2]). Torop describes the prevalent translation culture [of Estonia?] as dominated by habitual practices (ibid., 69): reading conventions are seldom circumvented and tend instead to become more ingrained, comments on translation rather than on the original are rare, and translation need not be recognized as a text type of its own at all. Emphasizing that any translation is just one of the possible versions of the original, he writes: *tuleb lausa imperatiivses vormis väita, et* tõlge peab lugeja jaoks tõlkeks jääma, mitte aga olema originaali asendaja. [it has to be an imperative *to read a translation as a translation that cannot efface the original* (ibid.)—Emphasis in original—A.L.]

In the article the statement appears next to the 1983 catalogue of translations of Soviet literature into Estonian. That year 33 different titles were translated in the category, 23 of which from Russian, the primus inter pares of all the languages of the Soviet Union. Having first read the more general observation by Torop that a book is a commodity but it is also a policy (ibid., 74), a reader of

---

1 All Estonian sources in the article are quoted in the author's translation.

2 While referring to the 1984 article, its (unchanged) republication in Torop's 1999 collection of essays *Kultuurimärgid* [Signs of Culture] in the series *Eesti mõttelugu* [Estonian History of Ideas] has been used. The latter includes bibliographical references to the original publication.

TOTAL TRANSLATION: FROM CATFORD TO TOROP    209

the article could easily see that the representation of any culture in its translation into Estonian had to be viewed with a certain skepticism, as a translation could have been commissioned with its possible readership firmly in mind, or it could have been launched to follow the party line for its ideological value.[3] A reference to a publication from 1983 also highlights this point, as a translation of Fyodor Gladkov's *Cement* was issued in that year, it being arguably the best novel of Soviet Socialist Realism though it was written in 1925 and had long since lost its topicality (ibid., 75), while there were still no Estonian translations of Russian symbolist prose. Listing translations that could primarily be treated as articles of commerce as they were popular and sold out quickly having been preceded by a popular TV series or a film, the review also testifies that the consumption of books is a social practice, and the majority of readers are not independent as their choices are conditioned by social rather than individual psychological factors.

An annual profile of a translation culture for what has been translated and what not reflects the whole of the literary culture around it. That culture, mediating the actual texts we are reading, unites an author, his work and its reader, and regulates the communicative processes; the literary culture and the possible significance of a text precedes and follows the act of reading and functions as a mechanism that controls, instructs, and directs cognition. This general premise of the 1984 article by Torop contains in a nutshell his concept of total translation, which we will soon come to. As this early but theoretically consistent review addresses not the academy but the reader of *Looming* [Creation], the literary monthly of the Estonian Writers' Union, it contains explanations that are helpful for those unfamiliar with the academic history of translation studies. What does it actually mean to say that our reading of a translation starts long before we actually get hold of it? A culture, whether a literary or translation or reading culture, is a means for decoding and recoding a text so that it is related to other texts and contexts. The ability to recognize a text as such at all—or to 'meet' a text as Torop puts it—depends on the reader's

---

3  Years later Torop (2011, 143) recalled a case that illustrates well the intricacies of translation policy in Soviet Estonia: in the mid-1970s Estonian literary scholars planned a series of translations of theoretical texts in order to advance literary studies. The initial plan was to begin with translations of Juri Lotman, but given that he was officially a *persona non grata*, the first volume in the series was to be a collection of articles by Mikhail Bakhtin, who was more acceptable for Glavlit, the all-Union censorship office, as he was not living in Estonia. But even Bakhtin's collection could only be published after two books by ideologically orthodox Soviet literary scholars had been translated into Estonian. Although the intellectual value of these two books was considered to be low, the translations were published and sold as compulsory attachments to books that people were inclined to buy.

210 LANGE

cognitive expectations (ibid., 67), and these may not be compatible with those the original author had in mind. This is mostly the case with translations, and therefore the dominant adaptive processes of reception tend to wash away the author and the cultural context of the source. The conventionality of reading can be assuaged by a second reading of a text that draws on its metatexts such as research, criticism and reviews to inform about the discourses of the original.

The concept of culture is not thematized in the article and has been used without a definition. Torop's articles for a wider audience in general typically use concepts conventionally[4] as he puts his trust in the natural language when writing, while remaining conscious that in another context many of its references are terminologically loaded (a typical example here is Torop 1999, 13). He clarified his point of view in his later monograph:

> *Tõlke ja kultuuri analüüs algab mõlema mõiste määratlemisest. Need mõisted on enamikule selle raamatu lugejatest ilmselt intuitiivselt arusaadavad. Samas on nende ühetähenduslik defineerimine peaaegu võimatu. /---/ Teaduste metodoloogias on see tegelikult üldisem nähtus. Keel, mille abil teadus oma tulemusi vahendab, kirjeldus- ehk metakeel, areneb koos teaduse enda ja tema uurimismeetoditega. Metakeele ühetähenduslikkusest saab rääkida vaid operatsionaalselt, seda konkreetse uurimuse puhul määratledes.*

> [An analysis of translation and culture starts from the definition of the two concepts. These are concepts that most of the readers of the book probably understand intuitively. At the same time a univocal definition of them is almost impossible. /---/ This is actually a more general phenomenon in the methodology of science. The language that a science uses to mediate its results—the descriptive or metalanguage—develops together with the science and its research methods. Metalanguage can be univocal only operationally when it has been defined for a specific piece of research.]

> TOROP 2011, 13

---

4  The definitions of culture in the 1979 *Võõrsõnade leksikon* [Dictionary of Foreign Words] that are relevant here are that culture is (1) an aggregate of material and mental values created by mankind, the fruits of the physical and mental work of human beings as opposed to natural phenomena; in a narrow sense, the aggregate of various forms of the mental life of a society reflected in education and upbringing, science, philosophy, the arts, moral and social conventions and related institutions; (2) a level achieved in a specific field such as work culture or communication culture.

TOTAL TRANSLATION: FROM CATFORD TO TOROP                     211

So, he relies on culturally shared meanings as much as on conceptual accuracy. As a result, we cannot find concise or prescriptive definitions of culture, just as we cannot find any concise definition of translation like "the replacement of textual material in one language (SL) by equivalent textual material in another language (TL)" (Catford 1965, 20). Rather, we are taken to the problem of culture, and the problem of translation, and are shown various complementary aspects of them. The very title of the 1984 review—*Tõlkekultuur ja tõlkeaasta* [Translation Culture and Translation Year]—coins translation and culture into a compound noun *tõlkekultuur* [translation(al) culture] that refers to both the culture of translation, or how we translate, and culture as translation, which is culture as a broader mechanism of translation where a translated book stands next to its original, a cinematic or theatrical production, a newspaper editorial, and a text-book (Torop 1999, 79). The systemic nature of culture is stressed throughout the review, showing that every translation has its function either as a commodity, a policy, a piece of memory or a piece of art, transferring new subjects and means of expression into the translating culture (ibid., 71).

References at the end of the article show that Torop draws from material in English, French and German (Roman Jakobson, John Robinson Pierce, Georges Mounin, and Ralph-Rainer Wuthenow) as well as in Slavic languages, and he was following developments in various other disciplines for the study of culture alongside translation studies.


3      **Culture as Text**

Indeed when he recently explained to his Estonian readers the Tartu-Moscow school's manifesto on the semiotic nature of culture, which proposed a systematic approach to cultural research in 1973, Torop (2011, 31) observed that in the same year Clifford Geertz had published his "Thick Description: Toward an Interpretive Theory of Culture" (in Geertz 1973), which has some analogies with the manifesto. In both approaches culture is interpreted as a 'text' functioning in different sign systems that are not isolated but are mutually dependent in order to be of communicative significance. A text is thus not only an individual material but more significantly an abstract mental unit in the memory of a group or an individual. It is not only an end but also a beginning of human activities, either constraining or enabling communication and translation. The parallel development in anthropology and semiotics can be taken as a sign that there is common ground between separate disciplines and traditions that study culture.

212 LANGE

Despite what has been quoted above, that there are concepts that most of us intuitively understand, Torop has also observed throughout his academic career that the different conceptual uses of culture, translation or text in various disciplines from anthropology to literary studies can be a source of confusion. In 1981 he wrote a lengthy article on the theory of metatexts with a dedication to Anton Popovič, an article that he has also included in his 1999 collection of essays. This is a survey written in Estonian of the work done by the school of Nitra, and it points out that the theory of metatexts was also 'born' (Torop 1999, 31) in 1973 when Popovič published his article "Text a metatext" [Text and Metatext] in *Slavica Slovaca*. After discussing the work of Popovič in comparison with work by Mikhail Bakhtin, Tzvetan Todorov, Julia Kristeva and others, Torop arrives at the conclusion that the various conceptualizations cannot easily be brought together into a general theory of text as different researchers work with different conceptualizations, and have subdivided the concept into various narrower ones, all of which refer to different systemic relations that structure a text differently: micro- and macrotext, geno- and phenotext, architext, prototext, intertext, intext, and metatext. In consequence the theoretical premises have to be resolved before the object of the research can be defined.

In a footnote (ibid., 433) Torop even agrees with János S. Petöfi who had supposed in his article "Meaning, Text Interpretation, Pragmatic-Semantic Text Classes" that text is perhaps too general a term for designating the object of research of various different fields. The theoretical ideal for Torop was a terminology that would be unambiguous, and his ideal asked for a systematic methodology that could advance both theoretical and empirical research. To reach that goal interdisciplinarity, not disciplinary isolation was needed.

Years later Torop, as already noted, acknowledges the operational value of a concept of text that both uses and creates languages. The acknowledgement stems from the realization that in a semiotic sense culture is a multi-language system, consisting of both primary modelling systems, or natural languages, and secondary modelling systems such as mythology, ideology and ethics. Secondary modelling systems are either based on natural languages, like literature, poetry and law are, or employ natural languages in their description or explanation, like music and ballet do, or use language analogization, such as in the language of theatre or the language of movies (Torop 2011, 199[5]).

Thus, text only symbolizes the definition of the object of study but does not define it; the object is an operational concept that depends on the needs of the research (ibid.). At the same time the text allows the object to be dissected into

---

5   The Estonian language monograph has an English language summary and whenever possible this has been used as an authorized translation.

structural levels or units, and a system to be constructed for these. The conceptualization of culture in terms of textuality is a methodological device that depicts objects of research as artefacts with clearly delineated borders so they can be analyzed better. As abstract mental units such as love are also subjected to textualization, the methodology lets cognitive aspects of culture be treated in a similar way to those of material texts; this is an analysis of the concrete and the abstract, of the static and the dynamic, of communication within and beyond a text. And the methodology allows more than just the verbal aspect to be included in textual analyses, as processing a text relies not only on the linguistic, but also on the visual or tactile or auditive cognition of the reader.

Juri Lotman, in his attempt to clarify and expand the notion of text within the framework of semiotics, came up with the concept of the semiosphere (Torop 2011, 52). The two concepts, the text and the semiosphere, are conspicuously similar as both of them are structured and coherent phenomena constituted by their borders. The dividing line in semiosphere between what is inside and outside is not as clear-cut as it is with text. Like the generative nature of text, which both uses and creates language, the semiosphere is also a "space outside of which semiosis [and language] cannot exist" and "functionally [the semiosphere] precedes the singular isolated language and becomes a condition for the existence of the latter" (Lotman 2005[1984], 205). Including the totality of languages available to a mind that is translating between them, the semiosphere is a dynamic site of dialogue where the partial and the whole as well as the objective and the subjective meet.

Writing within translation studies, Torop seldom refers to the semiosphere but concentrates on clarifying the concept of 'text', the earlier vocabulary of semiotics, that is more compatible with the history of translation studies, and as such also with the daily practice of interlingual translation.

Drawing on various disciplines that study culture and translation, Torop has shown us that knowledge is cumulative as various metalanguages from different disciplines contribute to the sort of understanding that is interdisciplinary on the cognitive level. Could it be that the cumulative nature of knowledge can also be established within translation studies by bringing together its early texts and later developments?

## 4     Total Translation

Integrating the vocabulary of late 20th century translation studies seems to have been one of Torop's inquiries in his 1995 Russian-language dissertation Тотальный перевод [Total Translation], which was his second PhD taken at

Helsinki University, and which presents a comprehensive treatment of translation. Torop develops a cultural and semiotic interpretation of Catford's notion. Total translation for him is not a type of translation, as Catford has it, but is antecedent and subsequent to any strategy. It is a self-reflexive process, the cultural production of meaning that we all are subjected to. This means the concept of translation has been widened to include cognitive perception from the perspective of a culture. Total translation is a cultural process:

> Translating as an activity and translation as the result of this activity are inseparable from the concept of culture. The translational capacity of culture is an important criterion of a culture's specificity. Culture operates largely through translational activity, since only by the inclusion of new texts into a culture can the culture undergo innovation as well as perceive its specificity.
>
> TOROP 2002, 593

This is the totality of a culture, interpreted as a text that either constrains or enables communication, that affects translation; and culture itself as a text with its beginning and its end is total translation. Although Catford's *A Linguistic Theory of Translation* included references to the translation of cultural elements, it is Jakobson's "On Linguistic Aspects of Translation" that states clearly that translation—"to be more precise and less narrow" (Jakobson 1959, 232)—is a semiotic fact rather than a linguistic one.

The Jakobsonian element in Torop's work is significant but there is an important difference in the emphasis between the 1959 Jakobson essay and Torop's contribution of 1995: unlike Jakobson's "[a]ll cognitive experience and its classification is conveyable in any existing language" (ibid., 234), Torop's dissertation dedicated many a page to the limits of translation. He discusses translatability within the framework of a typology of parameters that can be applied to interlingual translation as well as to intralingual translation within a national culture and between various sign systems. The parameters of language, time, space, text (here in the narrow sense referring to the specifics of the genre or the authorial lexicon and syntax), work (as a discursive whole in the reader's response), and socio-political manipulation all contribute to translation that aims for a cognitive coherence that is achieved by interpreting all the parameters simultaneously, with some of them preserved and others not. Treating translation ontologically as a secondary text, Torop's ideal whatever the real-life circumstances may be is to relate translation to its source by using the abundant possibilities for additional metatexts that can complement interlingual translation.

# TOTAL TRANSLATION: FROM CATFORD TO TOROP

*Одну из миссий переводческой деятельности (в идеале) мы видим в противостоянии культурной нейтрализации, нивелирующему равенству, приводящему в разных обществах, с одной стороны к безразличию к культурным "приметам" человека или текста (особенно в многонациональных государствах), с другой же стороны к поискам национального идентитета и культурных корней. Даже в случае развитых демократических стран можно говорить не столько о тотальном сколько о тоталитарном переводе, т.е. о переидеологизирующем (в самом широком смысле слова) "переписывании" перевода.*

[Ideally, one of the missions of translation is to stand against the cultural neutralization and levelling override that stems, on the one hand, from the indifference of many (mostly multinational) societies towards the cultural 'specifics' of a person or a text, and on the other hand from the attempt to determine one's national identity and cultural roots. Even in democratic countries we can speak about totalitarian rather than total translation, i.e. about translations that have re-ideologized (in the broadest sense of the word) and 'rewritten' their source.]

TOROP 1995, 68

Translatability has been widely discussed in translation studies, with topics ranging from possible strategies for bridging linguistic and cultural lacunae on the surface level to the realization that culture as a set of lasting dispositions is the domain where human differences are most manifest (Tymoczko 2007, 221). When we problematize culture sufficiently and realize that its values are encoded so deeply in the psyches and bodies of the members of that culture that they function "at every moment as a *matrix of perception, appreciation, and actions*" (Bourdieu 1977, 82, original emphasis), we recognize that "difficulties in perceiving cultural difference are always entailed in the positionality of a translator" (Tymoczko 2007, 236), and so translation must involve self-reflexivity from the part of the translator. Like in Maria Tymoczko's understanding of cultural translation, Torop combines interlingual translation with internal cognition:

What does the translation process mean from the methodological viewpoint? It is a process that takes place within a translator's mind, but also within language, culture, and society. A cognitive, linguistic, cultural or social process can take place between minds, languages, cultures and societies, but it can also take place within a single mind, language, culture or society.

TOROP 2011, 202

When he brings together communicative and auto-communicative aspects of translation, Torop does not underline the socio-political contingency of translation in the way it is done in the culturally oriented research that was an important paradigm of translation studies in the 1990s when Torop finalized his dissertation. Instead, he is cautious of the practice of giving power relations and political history an all-explanatory nature. In one of his articles Torop has asked:

> *Harjutud on mõttega, et tõlkimine ühest keelest teise on ühtlasi tõlkimine ühest kultuurist teise. Kas aga tõlkimine ühest keelest teise ja ühest kultuurist teise on ühtlasi ühe keele ja kultuuri tõlkimine teiseks keeleks ja kultuuriks? Või tõlgitakse siiski autoreid ja tekste?*

> [We are used to the idea that translation from one language into another is also translation from one culture into another. But is translation from a language and a culture into another also a translation of them into [= their becoming] another language and culture? Or do we translate authors and texts instead?]

TOROP 1999, 13

The postcolonial perspective, like the suggestion of translating "the differences [between history] into a kind of solidarity" (Bhabha 1994, 170), was at odds with the immediate socio-political circumstances of translation that had informed Torop in the years of Soviet censorial control over cultural mediation. Although translation can become a culture and is a way that newness enters the world, it is not there to level out cultural differences. Instead, it is there to cherish the plurality of cultures, and of authors and texts. It not only guarantees cultural innovation but also enables the culture to perceive its own specificity. Translation, if total, has its beginning and its end, and reflects the receiving culture's ability to respect differences, including its own; it is about becoming but it is also about staying; it is not only newness, it is also consistency.

Total translation with the semantic ramifications of the adjectival part of the concept is both an indication of the interdisciplinary nature of translation studies and the processual nature of translation. As such it conforms well to the axiomatic identity of translation studies as formulated by Gideon Toury (1995, 174):

TOTAL TRANSLATION: FROM CATFORD TO TOROP

> ... the locus of study [in translation research] is never the text as an entity in itself, whether a mere target-language utterance or even a replacement and/or representation in the target language of another text, pertaining to another language, literature, culture. The locus is rather what the texts can reveal as concerns the *process* which gave rise to them: the options at the translators' disposal, the choices made by them and the constraints under which those choices were affected, on the way to extracting such shared factors as are reflected by larger bodies of texts which have been brought together on the basis of one organizing principle or another; especially if and when those shared factors can be tied up with the organizing principle. [Emphasis in original—A.L.]

Torop's counterpart to Toury's "organizing principle" of the translation process is its 'dominant', another concept he borrowed from Roman Jakobson (Torop 1999, 145). This is the element of a text that has been viewed as most important while all the other components are subject to it and determined and transformed by it. Although the dominant in itself is an objective factor of any translation, detecting it retrospectively requires an intellectual effort (ibid.).

The processual character of translation studies within total translation has been further accentuated by the concept taking in not only the plurality of processes but also different types of translation that complement each other:

> The types are textual translation or ordinary translation; metatextual translation or description via criticism, advertising and other texts; in-textual and intertextual translation or transmitting or introducing a foreign word into a text, and extratextual translation or translating out of text, using other semiotic material.
>
> TOROP 2002, 596–597

So Torop, like Popovič, treats quoting, or in-textual and intertextual translation, on equal terms with ordinary translation, and he acknowledges, like Jakobson, the relevance of all the five senses in translation through extratextual translation, as they all contribute to the production of meaning.

As Toury's classic quote above (Toury 1995, 174) testifies, this is the processual invariant in various traditions of translation research that serves as a basis for a unified identity of translation studies internationally; translation studies is concerned not so much with the product of translation, as contrastive linguistics or comparative literature are when they study translations, but with the invisible process that can be fragmentarily observed under laboratory conditions or inferred from the traces it leaves as changes in language, culture, and society. Observing that "present-day translation studies do not form a methodologically unified discipline", Torop notes that "a movement in this direction takes place" (Sütiste and Torop 2007, 190). Given the processual 'imperative' in translation research, the dynamic nature of the discipline that trusts in dialogue is but expected. Torop characterizes modern translation studies by a growing tendency

> (1) to bring closer translation practice and theory; (2) to increase the capacity of different concepts for dialogue within translation studies; and (3) to arrive at the creation of comprehensive systemic translation studies. (ibid., 191)

His own conceptualization definitely serves these aims as the concept of total translation symbolizes an attempt to transform the heritage of various translation scholars—and of various disciplines at that—into a methodologically coherent interdisciplinary approach. What has previously been said about the concept of text could be repeated here: total translation only symbolizes the definition of the object of study but does not define it; it is an operational concept dependent on the needs of the research.

A contemporary of Torop's 2007 attempt to reconsider the nature of translation studies (Sütiste and Torop 2007) is Maria Tymoczko's *Enlarging Translation, Empowering Translators*, which came out the same year. The monograph gives an overall picture of ongoing translation research with an emphasis on the cultural turn and the clear commonalities between translation and cultural studies. Suggesting a holistic approach to translating culture—an approach that would see beyond the surface elements of cultural difference like realia— Maria Tymoczko states the need to "address the mainsprings of cultural difference [---] in [a] systematic way" (Tymoczko 2007, 233). Having explained that culture is not only a collective but also an individual phenomenon stemming from the *habitus* of the cultural subject understood in Bourdieu's terms, Tymoczko writes:

> ... I am arguing for attention to a broader field of cultural phenomena, as well as additional specific facets of culture, than has been the practice in translation studies thus far. I take the view that a holistic approach to cultural translation rather than a selective focus on a limited range of cultural elements enables greater cultural interchange and more effective cultural assertion in translation, allowing more newness to enter the world. (ibid.)

# TOTAL TRANSLATION: FROM CATFORD TO TOROP

As the title of her monograph already indicates, the concept of translation, and the concept of culture, have to be enlarged in order to empower translators. Tymoczko is trying to narrow the gap between translation practice and theory, and that can be achieved by extensive dialogue within and beyond translation studies, which can result in a comprehensive concept of translation as practiced in different cultures.

But of course, the developments are not uniform, even if they happen at the same time. Tymoczko's methodology for cultural translation has an *ad hoc* character: she proposes to research translation using the signature concepts of a culture—i.e., the key elements in its social organization, practices and dispositions—that have to be composed separately for each culture (ibid., 238–241). Torop, in comparison, proposes a universal model of translation with the aim of moving towards disciplinary unity at the backdrop of the numerous translational processes, all of which can be described in very different meta-languages. In order to overcome the resulting metalinguistic Babel, he brings the processes closer to their cause and effect as the beginning and end, thereby fixing the pulsating reality in the concept of text as functioning in mutually dependent different sign systems. The beginning and the end are not solid products but systemic processes that can be studied in isolation only in theory.

## 5    The Model of the Translation Process

In the same way that the umbrella concept of total translation has its history in translation studies, Torop's processual model begins with the dichotomies that are all too familiar from translation research. Just like James Stratton Holmes (1988) he refers to the expression and content planes, describing translation as a simultaneous recoding of the expression plane and transposition of the content plane. Both processes include analysis of the source text and synthesis of the target text, with one of them attributed greater importance in each given case. Different translations are characterized by different relations between the two planes as both the content plane and the expression plane can be translated autonomously (A), or one of them may dominate the other (D). Thus, the model (Torop 1995, 27; 1999, 147; 2011, 177) looks like this:

(adequate) translation

| | recoding | | | | transposition | | |
|---|---|---|---|---|---|---|---|
| analytic | | synthetic | | analytic | | synthetic | |
| A | D | A | D | A | D | A | D |
| (1) | (2) | (3) | (4) | (5) | (6) | (7) | (8) |

A translation that focuses on the expression plane is either (1) an autonomous analytic recoding, or, to use the traditional vocabulary of translation studies, an interlinear gloss; (2) a dominant analytic recoding, which is a formal translation that subjects other text elements to a chosen element of the expression plane; in poetry translation, for example, it may mean imitation of the meter or rhyme scheme; (3) an autonomous synthetic recoding, which is a word-for-word translation, but quotable, unlike an interlinear gloss; or (4) a dominant synthetic recoding, which is microstylistic translation usually described in translation studies as an exoticizing translation. When the translational solutions are drawn from the content plane, the choices are (5) autonomous analytic transposition, which is descriptive translation like poetry into prose; (6) dominant analytic transposition, which is thematic translation, or content transposed in familiar forms; (7) autonomous synthetic transposition, or free translation; or (8) dominant synthetic transposition, which is like Nida's dynamic equivalence. By minimizing his conceptual tools as recoding/transposition, analytic/synthetic, and autonomous/dominant, Torop aims to make translation processes more comparable within and beyond translation studies. As the model applies to translation not only of verbal texts but also of cognitive or social texts through the translation of either historical or cultural time, or of social and psychological space, or of a genre, or of the presuppositions of the author, or of the norms of the source text, or of other such features, the 1995 dissertation repeats the scheme several times in different chapters on different types of translation (textual translation, p. 108; metatextual translation, p. 133; in- and intertextual translation, p. 159, and extratextual translation, p. 182), highlighting that a text is a process with its beginning and end in the human mind.

Within the scope of translation studies, the model—like that of Steiner's hermeneutic motion—allows the process of translation to be described on various levels, whether at the level of a single translation or of a translator, or equally at the level of different historical periods in a translation culture.

> If we want to understand translation, we need to look at all its aspects from the psychological to the ideological. And we need to see the process of translation both as a complex of linguistic, intralinguistic, and intersemiotic translation, and as a complex of linguistic, cultural, economic, and ideological activities.
>
> TOROP 2011, 204

The advanced systematicity is a strength of the model that can easily be turned into a weakness. When the vocabulary is applied to all the processes

TOTAL TRANSLATION: FROM CATFORD TO TOROP 221

of translation, letting the metalanguage of textual analysis structure all of them, it could easily come across as overemphasizing the verbal and product-centered aspects of translation despite the intention of describing multiple dynamic processes. But the unified approach can also be maintained without a unified vocabulary being maintained. In his 2011 *Tõlge ja kultuur* [Translation and Culture] Torop discussed various texts of cultural significance in Estonia, including a cult film and a politically controversial sculpture, keeping his methodological tools of recoding/transposition, analysis/synthesis, and dominant/autonomous covert but discernible from an interrogation of the methodology of the monograph. As the monograph also includes purely theoretical chapters, the totality of the approach has been emphasized.

Similarly, the model can be combined with others in order to communicate better the specifics of interlingual translation—that is a 3-in-1 process (Jakobson 1959)—as a system of its own that is still compatible with other social systems. This has been my experience (Lange 2015) in writing my *Tõlkimine omas ajas* [Towards a Pragmatic Understanding of Translation in History], which combined Torop's taxonomy for different types of translation on the micro-level of translation with the social systems theory of Niklas Luhmann as used in translation studies by Theo Hermans and Sergey Tyulenev. The latter theory differs from the probably more widely used systemic approach to translation, the polysystem theory, in its reliance on temporal rather than spatial metaphors: "Where polysystem theory sees sets of interconnected points coalescing into spider's webs, social systems theory sees chains forming over time as elements propagate by interlinking" (Hermans 2011, 16). Thus, the approach is suitable for a historical perspective.

Translation as a system of its own in Estonia originates from the late 19th century when a clear difference was established between an original and a translation, and since then willful adaptations have been reviewed as scandalous violations of copyright. In describing the dynamics of translation at its micro-level in the years 1895–1985, as it moved from the free translations of the late 19th century through the microstylistic translations of the 1930s, to the thematic translation of content transposed in familiar forms in the 1960s, I was able to observe, using the vocabulary of Torop's model, that translation has oscillated from transposition to recoding back to transposition, while the transpositions of the late 19th century were oriented towards their target (synthetic), and those of the late 20th century towards their source (analytic). As different types of translation—translations of different *skopoi*—cannot be compared in terms of good and bad since qualitative estimations can be done within one translation type only, it was easy for me to state that the adaptations of the 19th century were as effective as means of communication and auto-communication as the exotizations of the source of the 1930s.

## 6 On Linguistic Contingencies

Within the framework of translation studies, "total translation" stems from a Catfordian type of translation; in sign systems studies it stems from the Jakobsonian statement that the meaning of any linguistic sign is its fuller development in translation. But as observed earlier in this chapter, a theory can be made more meaningful when it also refers to the cognitive presumptions that stem from an etymological interpretation of its key concepts. So "total translation" can be related to the semantics of the Estonian language that must inevitably be relevant for Torop: the Estonian word for translation *tõlge* is a loan from the Russian толк, which has been glossed as "gist, kernel, essence; understanding; sense, point". The same Russian толк has also given Estonian the word *tolk* [here the 'o' has no tilde on it], which is defined in dictionaries as 'point, reason'. There are Estonian idiomatic expressions like *sest ei ole tolku* [there in no point in it], or *ei saa tolku* [it makes no sense to me]. So, in the Estonian *tõlge* it is evident that translation, from the face value of the word, is an attempt to make sense and to have an opinion. If we conceptualize translation etymologically, translation in Estonian is inevitably a cognitive interpretation and a decision-making process that determines the dominant of the utterance. The Estonian etymology of *tõlge* does not relate to carrying over/transferring something intact at all as the English "to trans-late" or German *über-setzen* or Russian пере-водить are interpreted (Tymoczko 2007, 56); rather, the Estonian *tõlge* refers to the understanding and production of meaning, and that is what total translation amounts to according to Torop.

Not every Estonian translator or reader of translation is necessarily aware of this etymological connection, as the /o/ and /õ/ in *tolk* and *tõlk* are different phonemes, and the /l/ in *tolk* is unpalatalized whereas the /l/ in *tõlk* is palatalized. So *tolk* need not be associated with *tõlk*, and anyway not everyone speaks Russian. But the same etymological innocence applies for translators and readers of translations working with Indo-European languages, not all of whom necessarily know that 'translation' is *trans + fero, tuli, latum, ferre*, making it a word containing the most irregular and highly polysemic Latin verb. The *nomen* could also be treated as an *omen* in English, for the products and the processes of translation are irregular indeed.

A deconstructionist approach highlights that a language does not use only one tongue, but uses several (Derrida 1985), and once the linguistic diachrony enters its synchrony, there are various ways a concept can be interpreted. The etymological ramifications exist in all natural languages but are different for different ones. While we may recognize that etymological deconstruction makes sense, we should also recognize that neither students nor practitioners

# TOTAL TRANSLATION: FROM CATFORD TO TOROP

of translation are necessarily etymologists, so the linguistic contingencies and choices have to be identified during their studies. To complicate the situation further, there are two separate concepts in Estonian contemporary usage: *tõlge* for 'translation' and *tõlgendus* for 'interpretation', just as in Russian (*толковать* = "to interpret", and *переводить* = "to translate") or in English where these are two separate practices of written translation. At some point in the language's history there must have been a need for a word that would differentiate a willful interpretation from an adequate translation that respects the copyright of the original.

From courses of translation studies in Estonia, in both Estonian and English, the situatedness of theorization not only in different academic traditions but also in different languages becomes inescapably apparent. But with due consideration to different histories and linguistic differences, a common identity of translation studies becomes equally undeniable. It also needs to be stressed to students that multilingual lists of partial synonyms have to be compiled in order not to confuse or ridicule research, as they simply allow communication and cherish the plurality of histories and of languages.

The very name of the discipline for Estonian students—*tõlketeadus*—is worthy of comment. Both parts of the compound are problematical: *tõlke-*, the genitive of *tõlge* [translation], and *-teadus*, which is equated in dictionaries with 'science'. Writing above on the Estonian concept of *tõlge*, I did not distinguish between the practice and the product, and used the logic of the English language where 'translation' refers to both. But the Estonian *tõlge*, a noun, is most immediately understood as the product of translation, and the verbal noun *tõlkimine* [translating] is used to refer to the process. Writing in Estonian about the nature of translation studies Torop (2011, 172) said: *tõlketeadus on tõlke ja tõlkimisega tegelev teadus* [translation studies is the study of translation and translating]. In Estonian it is the only way to highlight the nature and identity of translation studies, which is centered on "what the texts can reveal as concerns the *process* which gave rise to them" (Toury 1995, 174, emphasis in original). With Torop the identity of translation studies is no different, and only the way it is stated is different:

> *Kui tõlketeadus on tõlke ja tõlkimisega tegelev teadus, siis on loomulik, et oma identiteeti saab ta kujundada tõlke ja tõlkimise kokkupuutealal. Selleks alaks on tõlkeprotsess.*

> [If translation studies are concerned with translation and translating, it is natural that it can shape its identity in the area where these two meet. The area is the process of translation.] (2011, 172)

224                                                                    LANGE

The second part of the name of the discipline in Estonian, -teadus, categorizes translation studies as a science, as if James S. Holmes had never presented his paper in Copenhagen. The primary reason for using *teadus* rather than *uuringud* [studies] lies in the conventions and present taxonomy of the Estonian humanities. *Tõlketeadus* stands next to *kirjandusteadus* [the science of literature] and *keeleteadus* [the science of language] in the German academic tradition, where research into the humanities is *Wissenschaft*. The presence of either sciences or arts, of empirical evidence or of their interpretation, is not determined by a lexical label even so, but by the affiliation of a researcher to a particular method.

## 7    Conclusion

Coming back to the suggestion earlier in the article that including scholars from outside the mainstream in modern translation studies may not result in any fundamental innovation, it should be recognized that this is the case. Translation as it has been practiced and theorized in Estonia is not essentially different from what has been practiced and theorized elsewhere. Perhaps Estonia has been spared the phase of purely linguistic translation research divorced from its context that preceded the birth of modern translation studies in the 1970s–1980s. In cultural criticism of translation, Estonian translators have always underlined how translation depends on communication, even in the crudest model:

> *Situatsiooni ja kogemusi arvestades T kas võimendab või summutab, jätab vahele või lisab juurde, seletab või ajab selged asjad segi, peab seda tahes-tahtmata tegema, sest informatsiooni kasutegur, tema mõistmine ja mittemõistmine sõltub suurelt osalt objektiivsetest põhjustest. Ja nii paradoksaalne kui see ka on – kõik ülalloetletud 'tõlkevead' pole mitte ainult paratamatud, vaid enamasti normaalseks kommunikatsiooniks vajalikud.*

> [Considering the situation and previous experience, T [the transformer, equaling here the translator] either amplifies or turns down, skips or adds, explains or makes simple things complicated, and willy-nilly has to do it because the efficiency of information, its significance or insignificance depends largely on objective reasons. And as paradoxical as it is—all those 'mistakes of translation' are not just inevitable but usually necessary for normal communication.]

> OJAMAA 2010[1969], 57

# TOTAL TRANSLATION: FROM CATFORD TO TOROP

Under the circumstances, Estonian translation scholars have also emphasized the communicative aspects of translation that have been seen as a means for modernizing as well as preserving Estonian culture. Given the limited number of possible colleagues available at home, the reading list of Estonian translation scholars has usually been international and researchers have attempted to bring together the local and the global. Torop has been in dialogue with classical texts of both Eastern and Western European translation research, as pursued independently or within semiotics. Therefore, his concept of total translation addresses different traditions of translation research in his felicitous attempt to reach both disciplinary homogeneity and interdisciplinarity in translation studies. He does so mainly by expanding Catford's 1965 concept of total translation into a concept that would better suit the present global realization that translation is a cultural rather than a linguistic operation.

While reading the classical texts of translation studies with my students, I have experienced that untranslatability is not confined within the limits of poetry as Roman Jakobson once suggested. The constituents of the verbal code are as important in theoretical texts. The diverse implications at either the etymological or the disciplinary level have to be highlighted in order to show the significance of translation within translation studies too. Any translation culture has its theoreticians that have attempted to create a system of their own—a system that would match both international and local knowledge and be meaningful theoretically while also helping in the daily practice of translation under specific social and political circumstances.

Catford has described total translation—one of the eight types of translation he differentiated—as "what is most usually meant by translation" (Catford 1965, 22). The same can be said about Torop's total translation: most usually translation is about the production of meaning, it is a plurality of processes, most of which usually complement each other in order to make sense of the ever-changing cultural environment of the translator.

### References

Annist, August, and Gustav Saar. 1936. *Jean Paul ja Witschel. Akadeemilise Kirjandusühingu toimetised. Publikationen der Akademischen Literarischen Vereinigung zu Tartu XI. Acta et Commentationes Universitatis Tartuensis (Dorpatensis)* B XXXIX₃. Tartu: Akadeemilise Kirjandusühingu Kirjastus.

Annist, August. 1939. "Meie iseseisvusaegne tõlkeklassika ja Eesti Kirjanduse Selts." [Classical translations from our years of independence and the Estonian Literary Society]. *Eesti Kirjandus* 5: 198–221.

Antik, Richard. 1936. *Eesti raamat. Das estnische Buch 1535–1935.* Tartu: Eesti Raamatu-koguhoidjate Ühingu Toimetis.

Bhabha, Homi K. 1994. *The location of culture.* London and New York: Routledge.

Bourdieu, Pierre. 1977. *Outline of a theory of practice,* translated by Richard Nice. Cambridge: Cambridge University Press.

Catford, John Cunnison. 1965. *A linguistic theory of translation: An essay in applied linguistics.* London: Oxford University Press.

Derrida, Jacques. 1985. "Des tours de Babel.", translated by Joseph F. Graham. In *Difference in translation,* edited by Joseph F. Graham, 165–207. Ithaka and London: Cornell University.

Geertz, Clifford. 1973. *The interpretation of cultures: Selected essays.* New York: Basic Books.

Hermans, Theo. 2011. "Introduction. How is translation possible?" In *Between cultures and texts. Itineraries in translation history // Entre les cultures et les textes. Itinéraires en histoire de la traduction,* edited by Antoine Chalvin, Anne Lange, and Daniele Monticelli, 11–18. Frankfurt am Main: Peter Lang.

Holmes, James Stratton. 1988. "Translation theory, translation theories, translation studies and the translator." In *Translated! Papers on Literary Translation and Translation Studies,* 92–98. Amsterdam: Rodopi.

Jakobson, Roman. 1959. "On linguistic aspects of translation." In *On translation,* edited by Reuben Arthur Brower, 232–239. Cambridge: Harvard University Press.

Karjahärm, Toomas and Väino Sirk. 2001. *Vaim ja võim. Eesti haritlaskond 1917–1940.* [*The mentality and the power: The Estonian intelligentsia in 1917–1940*]. Tallinn: Argo.

Lange, Anne. 2012. "Performative translation options under the Soviet regime." *Journal of Baltic Studies* 43 (3): 410–420.

Lange, Anne. 2015. *Tõlkimine omas ajas: kolm juhtumiuuringut Eesti tõlkeloost.* [*Towards a pragmatic understanding of translation in history: Three case studies from the Estonian history of translation*]. Tallinn: TLÜ Kirjastus.

Lange, Anne. 2017. "Editing in the conditions of state control in Estonia: The case of Loomingu Raamatukogu in 1957–1972." *Acta Slavico Estonia IX:* 155–173.

Lotman, Juri. 2005 [1984]. "On the semiosphere", translated by Wilma Clark. *Sign System Studies* 3 (1): 205–229.

Nirk, Endel, ed. 1966. *Eesti kirjanduse ajalugu. II köide. XIX sajandi teine pool.* [*History of Estonian literature. Volume 2. The second half of the 19th century*]. Tallinn: Eesti Raamat.

Ojamaa, Ott. 2010. *Armastus seaduslikus abielus. Eesti mõttelugu 92* [*Estonian history of ideas. Love in legal marriage*], edited by Jüri Ojamaa and Jaak Rähesoo. Tartu: Ilmamaa.

# TOTAL TRANSLATION: FROM CATFORD TO TOROP

Oras, Ants. 1931. "Mõtteid tõlkekirjanduse puhul." [On translated fiction]. *Eesti Kirjandus* 12: 609–617.

Palm, August. 1932. "Kuidas tõlgitakse meil ja kuidas peaks tõlkima." [How we are translating and how we should translate]. *Looming* 1: 20–28; 3: 123–131.

Samma, Otto. 1962. "Üht-teist tõlkimiset ja tõlkijatest." [A few remarks on translation and translators]. *Keel ja Kirjandus* 7: 385–392.

Soosaar, Enn. 1980. "Tõlkeilukirjandus 1979 (vaatlusi ja tähekepanekuid)." [Translated fiction in 1979: Observations and comments]. *Looming* 4: 564–575.

Sütiste, Elin and Peeter Torop. 2007. "Processual boundaries of translation: Semiotics and translation studies." *Semiotica* 163, (1/4): 187–207.

Sütiste, Elin. 2012. "On the paths of translation semiotics with Peeter Torop." *Sign System Studies* 40, (3/4): 269–278.

Torop, Peeter. 1995. *Тороп, Пээтер. Тотальный перевод.* [*Total translation*]. Tartu: Tartu Ülikooli Kirjastus.

Torop, Peeter. 1999. *Kultuurimärgid.* [*Signs of culture*]. Eesti mõttelugu 30. [*Estonian history of ideas*]. Tartu: Ilmamaa.

Torop, Peeter. 2002. "Translation as translating as culture." *Sign System Studies* 30 (2): 539–605.

Torop, Peeter. 2010. "Translation as communication and auto-communication." *Applied Semiotics. Semiotique appliquée* 9 (24): 3–10. http://french.chass.utoronto.ca/as-sa/ ASSA-No24/Article1en.html.

Torop, Peeter. 2011. *Tõlge ja kultuur.* [*Translation and culture*] Heuremata. Humanitaarteadulikke monograafiaid. [*Monographs on the humanities*]. Tallinn and Tartu: Tartu Ülikooli Kirjastus.

Toury, Gideon. 1995. *Descriptive translation studies and beyond.* Amsterdam and Philadelphia: John Benjamins.

Tymoczko, Maria. 2007. *Enlarging translation, empowering translators.* Manchester and Kinderhook: St. Jerome.

Tyulenev, Sergey. 2012. *Applying Luhmann to translation studies: Translation in society.* London and New York: Routledge.

Vinkel, Aarne. 1958. "J.J. Rousseau teoste tõlkest ja tundelisest kirjandusest XVIII sajandi Eestimaal." [On the translation of J.J. Rousseau and sentimental literature in the 18th century Estonia]. *Keel ja Kirjandus* 1: 21–24.

Vinkel, Arrne, ed. 1965. *Eesti kirjanduse ajalugu. I köide. Esimestest algetest XIX sajandi 40ndate aastateni.* [*History of Estonian literature. Volume I. From first texts to mid-19th century*]. Tallinn: Eesti Raamat.

# Index of Personal Names

Amyot, Jacques   26
Aragon, Louis   111–115

Barkhudarov, Leonid   149
Baudelaire, Charles   117–123, 126–128
Brang, Peter   157, 162, 172–176

Catford, John Cunnison   11, 149, 172, 204, 211,
   214, 222, 225
Chesterman, Andrew   4, 19, 21–22, 37–39
Chukovskii, Kornei   138–139, 144–145, 149,
   159, 161n
Cicero, Marcus Tullius   24–25, 27
Comte, August   20
Cronin, Michael   4, 187

Dante Alighieri   28, 45, 144
Derzhavyn, Volodymyr   43, 48–50

Éluard, Paul   111–115
Etkind, Efim   38, 148
Even-Zohar, Itamar   9, 47, 82, 87–101, 124,
   129–130

Fedorov, Andrei   10, 48, 135, 139–140,
   145–149, 155–162, 165–178
Finkel, Oleksandr   36, 43, 47–50
Franko, Ivan   34, 36, 44–48, 54

Geertz, Clifford   211
Gentzler, Edwin   108, 117, 130
Gile, Daniel   182, 192, 198
Gor'kii, Maksim   138, 141, 143
Gumilev, Nikolai   138–140, 159

Hermans, Theo   36, 124–125, 129, 221
Holmes, James Stratton   6, 35, 38, 182, 189,
   191–194, 219, 224
Holton, Gerald   34, 36, 40–42, 55
Humboldt, Wilhelm von   47, 172

Ivanov, Vyacheslav   60, 63–71, 82

Jakobson, Roman   63, 66–76, 81–82, 87–94,
   97–99, 137, 140, 171–172, 207, 214, 217,
   221–222, 225

Jingrong, Chen   117, 120
Joyce, James   23, 141

Kakridis, Ioannis   197–198
Kashkin, Ivan   143–144, 148, 160
Kochur, Hryhoriy   36, 43, 50–51
Koptilov, Viktor   36, 38, 43, 50–52
Kuhn, Thomas   39, 167

Ladmiral, René   20, 22
Lefevere, André   107, 119, 124–125, 161–163,
   170
Levik, Wilhelm   117–118, 121–128
Lotman, Juri   8–11, 60–65, 74–83, 206, 209n,
   213
Luther, Martin   23

Maronitis, Dimitris   197
Min'iar–Beloruchev, Riurik   149–150
Morin, Edgar   18–19

Newmark, Peter   22, 175
Nida, Eugen   22, 149, 172, 175, 220
Novykova, Maryna   36, 43, 52–53

Piotrowski, Rajmund   150
Polivanov, Evgenii   137, 140, 142
Popovič, Anton   6, 38, 72, 212, 217
Potebnia, Aleksandr   47, 137, 139

Retsker, Iakov   148–149, 157–158
Revzin, Isaak   60, 63–72, 81–82, 171

Said, Edward   10, 160–161, 165
Sartre, Jean-Paul   113–115
Shveitser, Aleksandr   149
Stalin, Joseph   10, 64n, 157–159, 166–171, 176
Strikha, Maksym   34, 36, 53–54
Susam-Sarajeva, Şebnem   2, 161, 163, 198–199

Toporov, Vladimir   60–65, 73–74,
Torop, Peeter   11, 36, 61, 72, 204–225
Toury, Gideon   9, 82, 94, 191, 216–217
Tymoczko, Maria   3, 11, 108, 126, 135, 197, 204,
   215, 218–219
Tynianov, Iurii   139–140

# Index of Subjects

adaptation   18, 25–26, 88–91, 97, 101, 161, 165, 171, 221
anthropology   177, 211
appropriation   182–201

Bible   23, 28, 53

categorical meaning   70, 81
causality   88, 95
censorship   10, 136, 209n
circulation of ideas/knowledge   2, 23, 156, 162, 169
codex/codices   23, 25–26
communication   8–9, 11, 19, 21, 54, 78–80, 159, 204–207, 211, 213–214, 221, 224
compartmentalization   8, 17
continuity/discontinuity   9, 22, 41, 63, 87, 95, 101, 199
copying   25, 47, 51, 101
corpus-based approach   21, 182, 188
cybernetics   8, 64, 66, 70, 74, 81

descriptive approach   11, 20, 140, 175, 189, 191–195, 200, 220
  *see also* descriptive translation studies
digital culture   23–27
discontinuity   *see* continuity
diversity   4, 7, 19–20, 25, 198–199, 205–206

East(ern) and/or West(ern)   3–6, 10, 22n, 23, 35, 52, 92, 108, 147, 150, 155, 157–169, 172–178, 192, 197–198, 225
empiricism   19, 21
epistemology   17, 19–20, 29, 96
equivalence   6, 21, 26, 76, 79, 149, 198, 220
Eurocentrism   1–4, 22

Formalism   *see* Russian Formalism

historiography *see* translation historiography
  *see* historiography of translation studies
historiosophy   8, 34–42

ideologization   164–165
ideology   9, 107–112, 115–130, 135, 155, 162–170, 173

institutionalization   6, 17, 26, 34–37, 46
intercultural exchange/process   2, 28, 91–93, 96–98, 161
interdisciplinarity   7, 8, 17, 19, 99, 212, 225
interpretive system/theory   29, 97, 100, 197, 211

language
  management   22n, 28
  national   26, 29, 168
  native   54, 205
  natural   69, 76, 78, 196, 204, 210, 212, 222
  poetic   68, 137
  vernacular   26, 28
lingua franca   22, 28, 177
linguistic approach (to translation)   10, 145–150, 155, 166–167, 171
linguistics   *see* structural linguistics
localization   8, 18, 23, 28, 196

manipulation   9, 107, 113, 125, 129, 161, 170, 214
map/mapping   89, 100, 191–194
Marxism   10, 46, 166, 169
media history (of translation)   17–18, 23–24
mediator   28, 94, 156, 163–165, 198
meme   17, 21
methodology   37, 93, 135, 138, 144–145, 212–213, 219, 221

oral/orality   18, 24–27, 70

patronage   25, 107, 119–122, 125, 130, 162–163, 200
periphery/peripheral   82, 101, 182–183, 198–200
periphrastic   70, 81
poetic model   67–70, 81
poetics   9, 48, 51, 64–65, 74–77, 81, 107, 117–119, 126–130, 161–163
poly-discipline   8, 18–19, 21–22
polysystem (theory)   29, 82, 101, 107, 117–118, 125, 130–131, 221
power   5, 19, 46, 92, 108–112, 125, 161, 200, 216
print/printing   23–28

# INDEX OF SUBJECTS

readership   168–172, 209
realistic interpretation   122–124, 127
realistic translation (theory)   143, 148
recoding   66, 71, 75–76, 209, 219–221
recontextualization   87, 101
rediscovery   10, 19, 156, 177
regular correspondences   148
re-interpretation   182–183, 187n, 197–198
rewriting   107, 116–120, 125, 156, 161, 164–165, 177
roll   23–26
Russian Formalism   47, 63–64, 72–73, 81–82, 140–141

scientificity   6, 10, 156, 162–166, 169, 177
scientometric   7, 22, 182, 192
semiosphere   79–83, 213
semiotics   2, 8, 60–66, 69–73, 79, 82, 149, 206–207, 213, 225
semiotics of culture   62, 82
situatedness   1–4, 183, 198, 223
Socialist realism   10, 110, 113, 117–119, 123, 135, 142–143, 209
structural linguistics   8, 64, 69, 81, 149
structuralism   2, 51, 72–73, 82
supermeme   *see* meme
system   *see* polysystem

Tartu-Moscow School   8–9, 11, 60, 64, 82, 204, 206, 211
   *see also* semiotics
temporality   9, 87, 101
themata   34, 40–42, 55
transfer
   analysis   95–97
   theory   4, 9, 87–94, 97–98, 102
transformation   67, 79, 90, 95, 97, 161
translatability/untranslatability   21, 47, 66, 79–81, 146, 148, 168, 172–174, 177, 196, 214–215, 225
translateme   51–52
translation
   adequate   75–81, 219, 223
   art of   42, 46, 72, 72n, 139, 145
   as a cultural force   8, 36, 44
   as a linguoaesthetic phenomenon
      8, 36, 47–48, 55
   as an identity-forming act   53–55

as a social capital   8, 36, 44–45, 55
as a stylistic parallel   8, 36, 50–52
as communication and auto-
   communication   11, 204, 207, 221
as cultural interpretation and
   re-creation   8, 36, 52–53
as stylization   36, 48–50, 55
collaborative   23–25
conceptualization (of )   1–4, 37, 39, 45–46, 51, 53, 61, 87–88, 94, 97–102, 200, 204–207
concept(ualization)   2, 34–39, 42–45, 48, 51, 55, 157
criticism   108, 135
cultural   11, 19, 204, 215, 218–219
exact   75–78
historiography   34–35, 39–43, 47
history   18, 43, 74n, 94, 109, 145–146
interlingual   18, 26, 66, 70, 76, 89, 92–93, 213–215, 221
intersemiotic   66, 70, 89, 97, 220
intralingual   18, 66, 70, 76, 89, 91, 97, 184, 184n, 196–197, 200, 214
knowledge   3, 7, 139, 182–183
literary   36, 49, 71–72, 81, 109, 125, 129, 135–150, 159–160, 195
machine   8, 24, 64–71, 81, 150, 171, 194, 196
practice   2, 9, 43, 135–136, 140–142, 145–150, 194, 197, 218–219
reflection   2–3, 7
strategy   10, 25–26, 101, 169, 173
theory   9–10, 35–38, 42–43, 67, 70, 72, 87–91, 98, 135, 142–150, 166, 169, 171, 184, 205
total   6, 11, 61n, 62n, 204–225
universals   1, 4
translation studies
   applied   19, 175, 189–195
   descriptive   70, 82, 191, 194
   development of   157, 184, 186
   historiography of   17, 20, 24, 29
   history of   17n, 37, 44, 209, 213
   identity of   216–217, 223
   modern   155, 174, 218, 224
   nature of   216, 218, 223
   turns of   17, 20–22, 35, 39, 92, 108–109, 124, 218

transposition 48, 66–67, 219–221
travelling theory 7, 10, 155–156, 160–164, 169, 177

untranslatability *see* translatability

West(ern) *see* East(ern)

Printed in the United States
by Baker & Taylor Publisher Services